MW01627076

Wildfowl
Art

Wildfowl Art

Carvings from the Ward World Championship

Photographs by Ernie Sparks
Text by Laurel Aziz

FIREFLY BOOKS

Cataloguing-in-Publication Data

Aziz, Laurel, 1956-
Wildfowl art : carvings from the Ward World Championship

Includes index.
ISBN 1-55209-043-4

1. Wood-carving – United States – Competitions. 2. Wood-carving – Canada – Competitions. 3. Game and game-birds in art – Competitions. 4. Waterfowl in art – Competitions. 5. Decoys (Hunting) – United States – Competitions. 6. Decoys (Hunting) – Canada – Competitions. 7. Ward Foundation World Championship Carving Competition. I. Sparks, Ernie. II. Title.

NK9712.A85 1996 730'.973 C96-930948-1

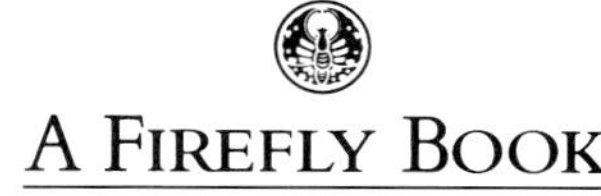

Published by
Firefly Books Ltd.
3680 Victoria Park Avenue
Willowdale, Ontario
Canada M2H 3K1

Published in the U.S. by
Firefly Books (U.S.) Inc.
P.O. Box 1338, Ellicott Station
Buffalo, New York 14205

Produced by
Bookmakers Press Inc.
12 Pine Street
Kingston, Ontario K7K 1W1

Design by
Linda J. Menyes
Q Kumquat Designs

Color separations by
Friesens
Altona, Manitoba

Printed and bound in Canada by
Friesens
Altona, Manitoba

Printed on acid-free paper

Front Cover: *Florida Red-Shouldered Hawk*, 1995, Philip Galatas.
Back Cover: *In the Tide*, 1996, Michael Arthurs.

Fine art prints of these and other wildfowl sculptures are available from:
Sparks Galleries
1656 Grousewood Lane
Kingston, Ontario K7L 5H6
and
Sparks Galleries
P.O. Box 85
Alexandria Bay, New York 13607
Telephone: (613) 531-8200
Fax: (613) 542-9994
E-mail: sparks@limestone.kosone.com
Web Site: www.kosone.com/sparks/

The Ward Museum of Wildfowl Art
909 South Schumaker Drive, Salisbury, Maryland 21801

For my wife Jackie and my children,
Tanya and John

Contents

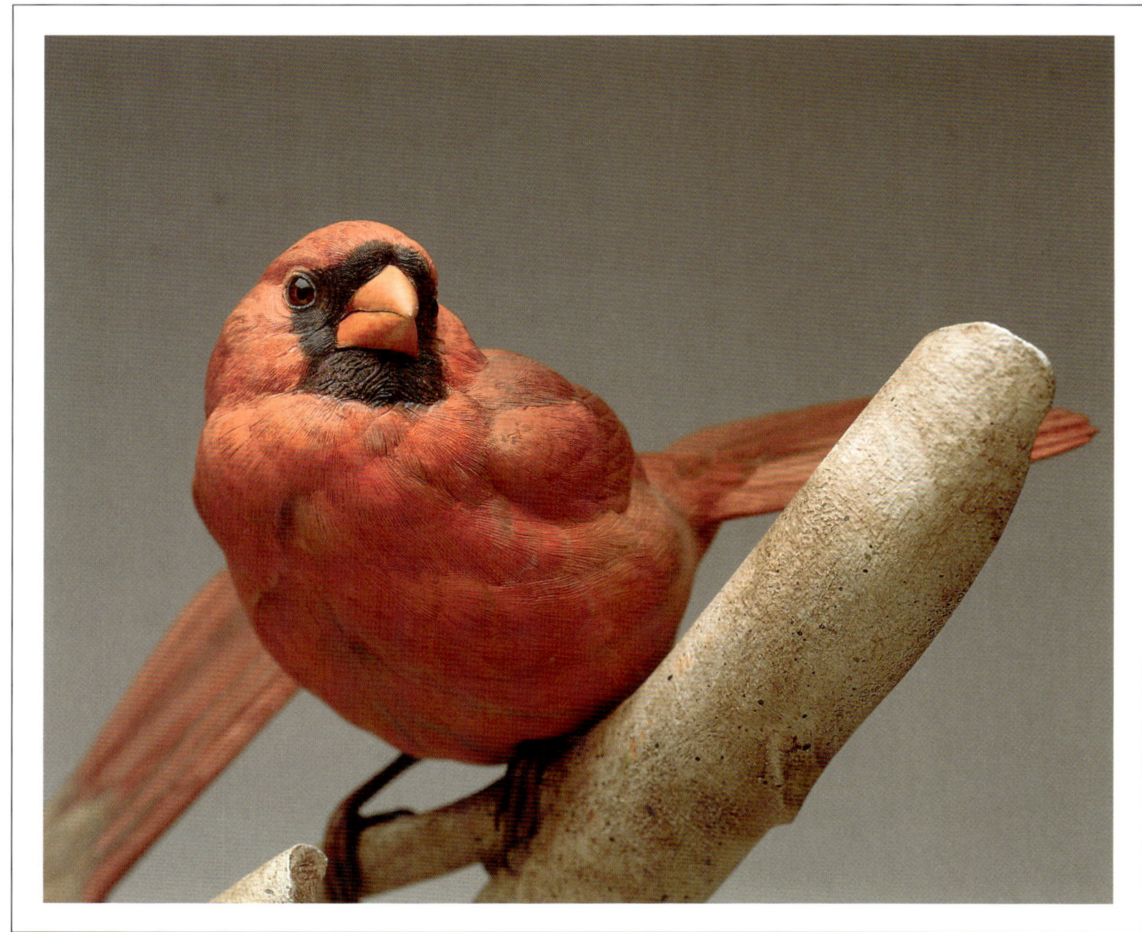

Gordon Hare
Cardinal Pair, 1994 (detail)

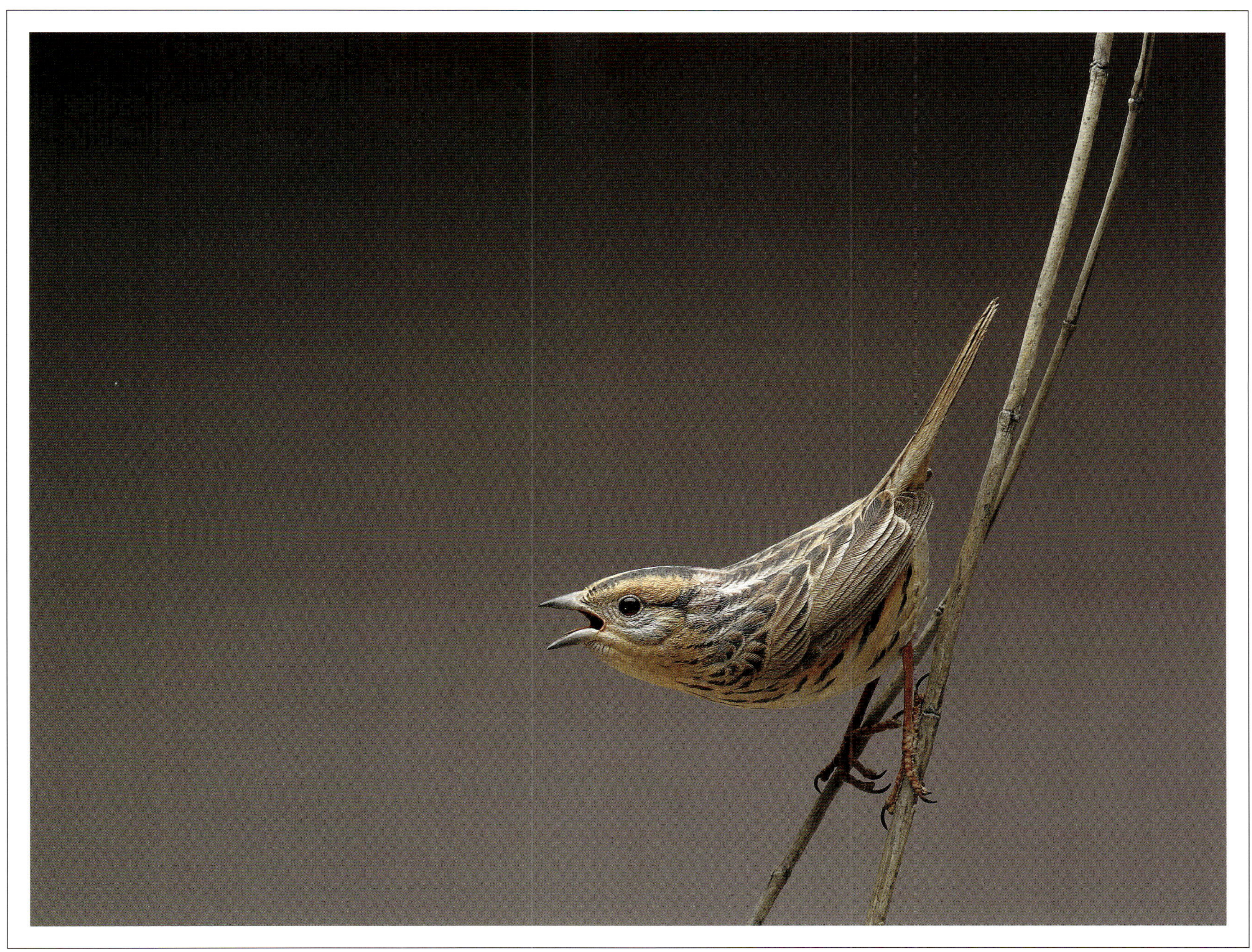

Keeping the reed shape simple, Guge exploits its form to reflect the elegant contours of the Le Conte's sparrow, whose muted striped pattern is shown to advantage in its headfirst posture. The golden feathers around the bird's head and neck appear in subtle shades.

Bob Guge
Le Conte's Sparrow, 1992

Introduction

Resplendent in their plumage, agile on air, often melodious but occasionally haunting of voice, birds embody an accomplished elegance that has captivated the imaginations of artists through the ages. Bird sculpture itself is a traditional art form that has both a functional and a decorative history dating back thousands of years. Today, in studios scattered across North America, a core of little-known wildfowl sculptors continues to bring avian fauna to animated three-dimensional life.

To understand the brief history of contemporary wildfowl sculpture in North America, however, one need travel no further back in time than to 1918, when two young brothers from Crisfield, Maryland—Lemuel and Stephen Ward—started carving decoys. By the late 1940s, the Wards were the first and best-known carvers to break with convention by eventually creating handcrafted wooden birds for purely artistic reasons. Their birds were carved in gracefully artistic poses and featured colorful feathers painted in realistic detail.

Nearly 20 years after the Ward brothers first presented their ornamental decoys to the world, a group of art and wildlife lovers from the Salisbury, Maryland, region set up a foundation in their honor. Established in 1968, the Ward Foundation is dedicated to the promotion of "wildlife, wildlife carvings, wildlife art and wildlife conservation." Since 1971, it has also sponsored an annual competition, the Ward World Championship, which has become the premier exhibition and competitive venue for wildfowl artists.

Celebrating its 25th anniversary in 1996, the Ward World Championship, which is held each April in Ocean City, Maryland, has served as a meeting place for wildfowl artists who produce all manner of works in wood. Some 2,000 hunting rigs, floating decorative waterfowl, interpretive sculptures and decorative life-size and miniature works compete for recognition each year. By definition, the latter two decorative events, which are featured in this collection, marry the anatomical accuracy of realistic carving with artistic design. While the sculptures that comprise one or more birds must be fashioned in wood, other materials may be used for habitat and structural purposes. With the exception of the birds' eyes, which can be stock or custom-made for the sculpture, all elements must be hand-formed. The sculptures are judged on craftsmanship, accuracy, essence of species and artistry. In the miniature category, there is an additional constraint: the birds must be one-half life size or less; the maximum length, regardless of the species, is eight inches.

The one thousand artists who attend the exhibition participate in novice, intermediate, open and world-class levels of competition. The rank of "world" designates those select events, including decorative miniature and life-size categories, in which artists receive purchase awards—$5,000 and $20,000, respectively—in exchange for their winning sculptures' becoming part of the permanent collection of the Ward Museum of Wildfowl Art in Salisbury, Maryland.

The creative ambitions of wildfowl sculptors have changed dramatically since the early days of this art form, as a chronological tour of wildfowl sculpture and its rich legacy of styles and techniques will quickly disclose. Despite the perpetually changing emphasis in carving technique and composition, however, each artist continues to bring to his sculpture the same essential talents: all are informed naturalists, skilled craftsmen and gifted painters and designers.

A comprehensive knowledge of bird anatomy—how a species looks, the grouping and colors of its feathers and the basic mechanics of movement—and an understanding of bird behavior are both fundamental to the creation of these works. “The accuracy of the birds is a given,” says Floyd Scholz of Hancock, Vermont. The carvers spend countless hours in the wild, observing, studying and sketching their subjects. Some belong to avian conservation, research and rescue groups and can take advantage of rare close encounters with a species to discern the essence of the live bird. Several are also licensed falconers who fly birds of prey daily as part of their firsthand research.

Translating that knowledge into wood demands a skill and an artistry which nearly all accomplished carvers have acquired through thousands of solitary hours of trial and error. While many have had basic instruction in carving or whittling during childhood, under the guidance of a father, a grandfather or an uncle, most of these skills are self-taught once the artist has decided to pursue a career in carving.

Louisiana tupelo, an astonishingly lightweight swamp wood, is the medium of choice for a significant number of carvers. Available in large chunks, tupelo is grainless and therefore behaves predictably when carved. Once it dries, it does not change shape or crack like other hardwoods. Some carvers, however, also use basswood. Todd Wohlt, for example,

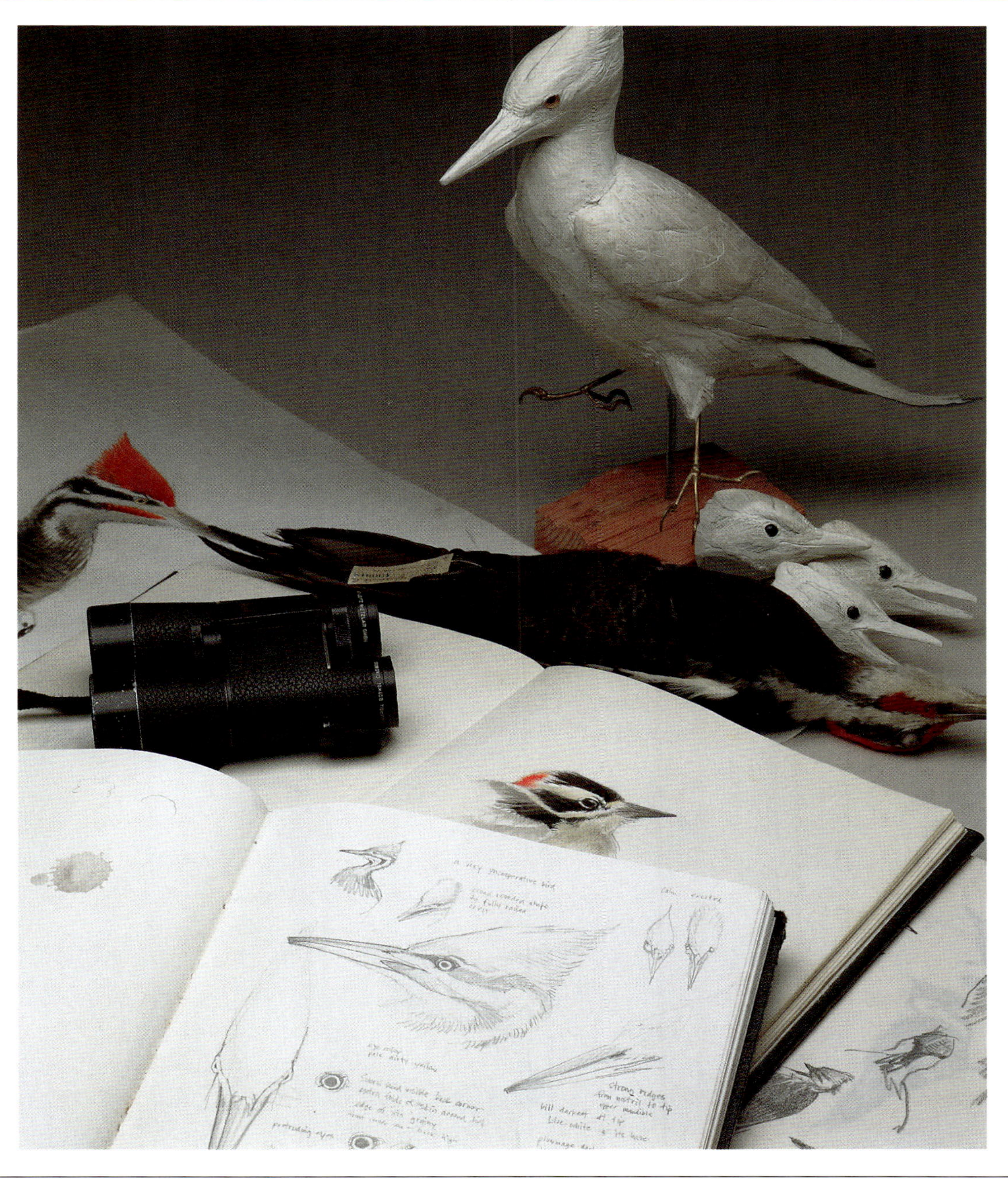

Equipment and drawings on Barth's workbench show the two stages of creating wildfowl sculpture. Step one begins with detailed illustrations of birds, their expressions and shapes from in-the-field research. Step two is the in-hand observation that takes place at a banding station with a live bird or with a study skin from a museum. With this specimen, Barth begins to experiment with proportion, color and feather groupings.

Larry Barth's Studio

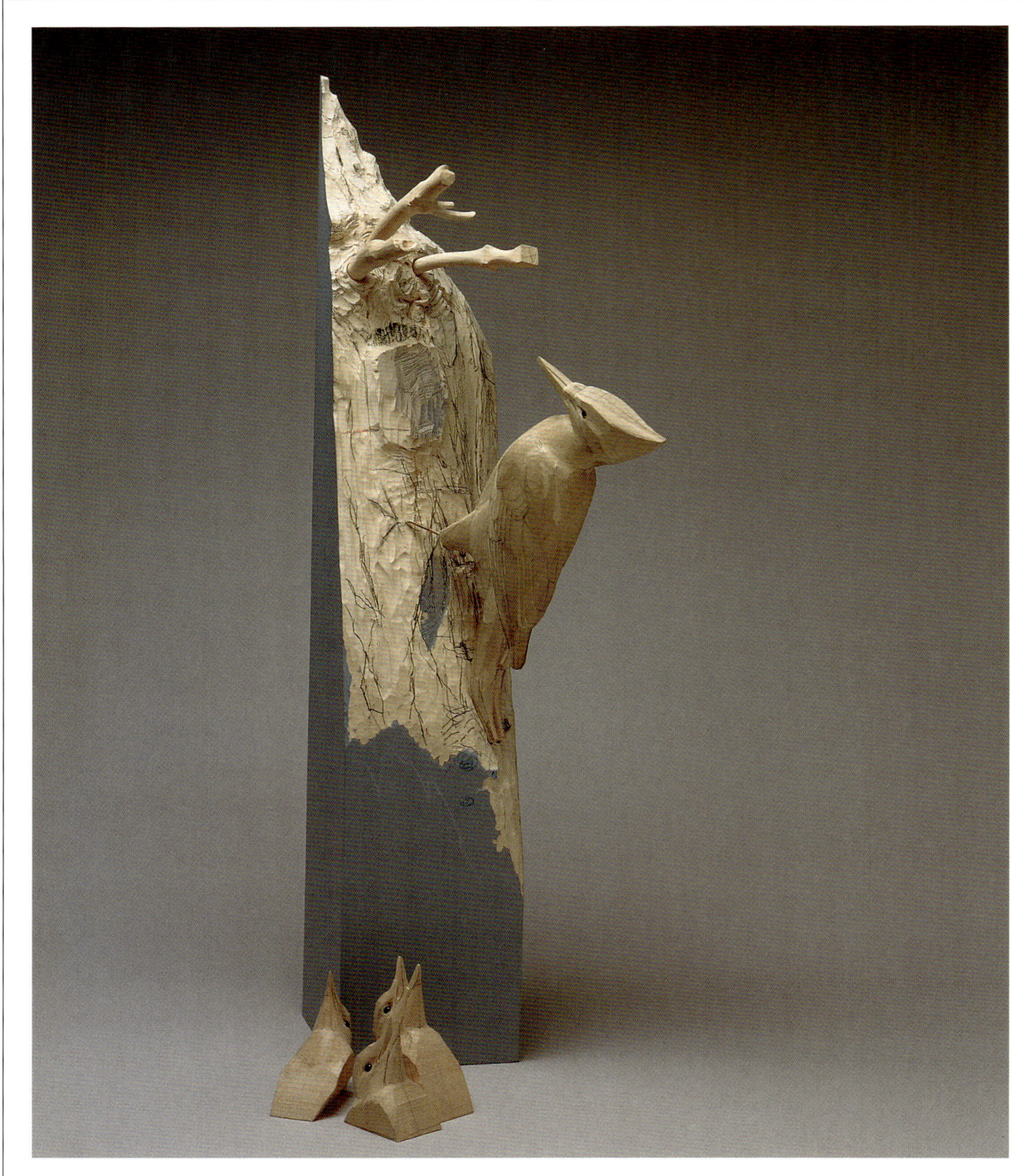

Larry Barth
Pileated Woodpecker and Nestlings, 1996
(in progress)

Barth's woodpecker-family-in-progress is a 3½-foot-tall embodiment of family harmony. Once the sculpture is complete, the artist will anchor the king of the northern woodpeckers to a tree trunk and fully etch the bark with ridges and grooves. The chicks will be naturally positioned within the nesting hole.

finds that this light-colored furniture wood is superior for holding fine feather detail and texturing.

Today's wildfowl artists rely on a variety of traditional hand tools and sophisticated power tools. Jett Brunet of Galliano, Louisiana, carves large decorative birds using the same method he has used all his life as a decoy maker. Except for roughing out a bird on a band saw or with a chain saw, he relies almost exclusively on knives and other manual tools. In part, Brunet chooses this style because he carves from his imagination, and knives allow him to sculpt the bird gradually with his hands.

Several artists consider themselves to be "power carvers," using power tools and fine grinders to create even the most exacting detail. Ernie Muehlmatt of Springfield, Pennsylvania, has developed an unprecedented technique: Using *only* power tools, Muehlmatt renders his birds from head to foot, working on each stage in painstaking detail.

While these artists all use wood-burning pens to create dark vermiculations and barring in the feather patterns, their painting techniques differ dramatically. Jim Sprankle, Patrick Godin and Floyd Scholz use acrylics, which are quick-drying and can be thinned and applied in washes to suggest color depth in the plumage and provide smoother transitions between feather groups. Others, however, prefer oils. Jett Brunet has perfected a meticulous technique for painting rich, velvety plumage, while Greg Woodard likes oils for the freedom they allow when applying bold and easy colors. Philip Galatas, who had painted with acrylics for many years, returned to traditional oils for his *Florida Red-Shouldered Hawk*, a sculpture that has inspired a passionate outpouring of emotion from observers. "All I can say is that I went back to my old style of painting," explains Galatas. "I took my time and used small brushes, and the look is a bit softer and more mellow."

It is the arresting realism of the sculpture's finely detailed feathers and rich plumage that initially catches an observer's eye, but these artists consider their impeccable craftsmanship simply one aspect of their work and *not* its message. "From a carving point of view, there isn't anything that I worry about being able to do," admits Larry Barth, expressing a common sentiment. "But we aren't trying to succeed on subject matter and craftsmanship alone."

Design and composition are the elements that separate bird carving from sculpture. Patrick Godin, himself a two-time world champion and a carver who came to wildfowl sculpture through the

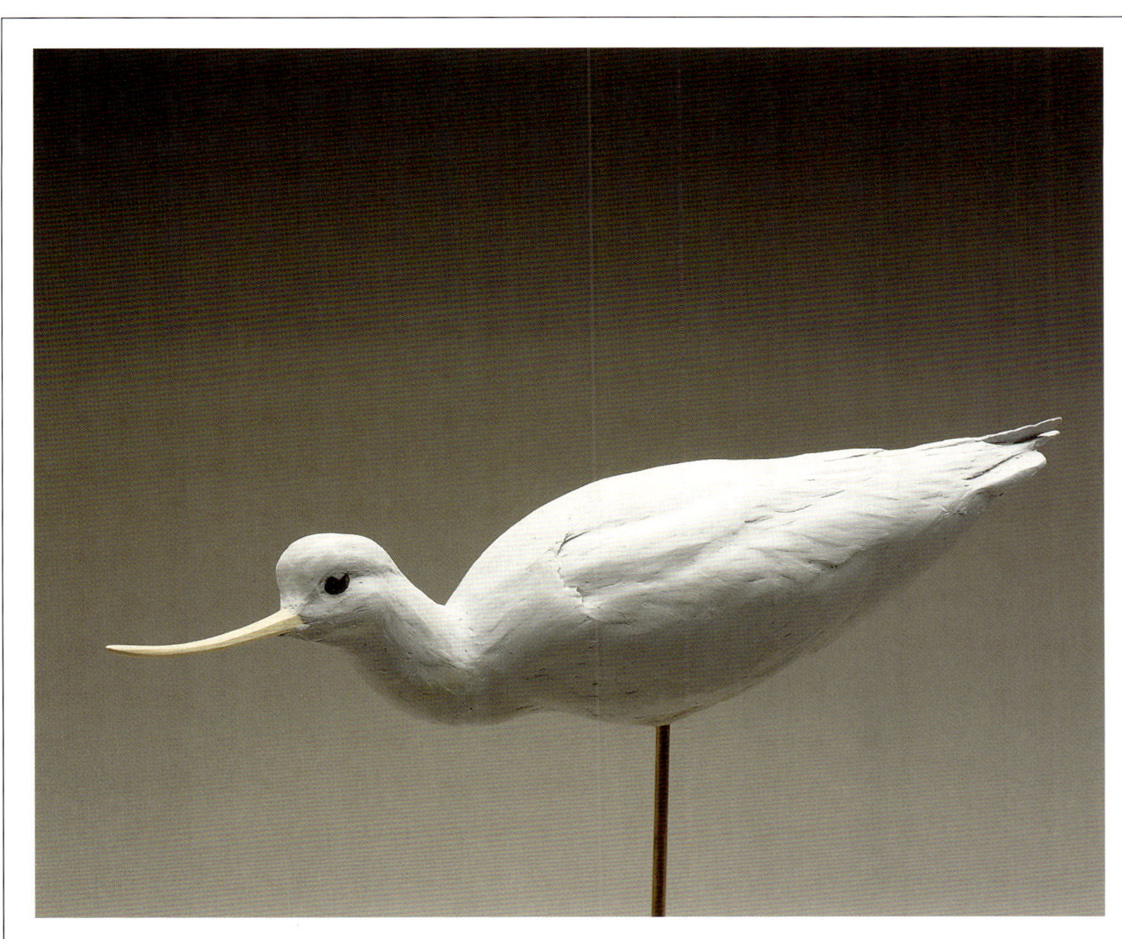

With this spontaneous clay sculpture, Arthurs established the basic composition of his animated American avocet. From the initial clay sculpture to the final carving, he refined the body posture of the bird, increasing its lifelike attitude by turning its head and tail slightly to suggest movement.

Michael Arthurs
American Avocet
Clay Model, 1996

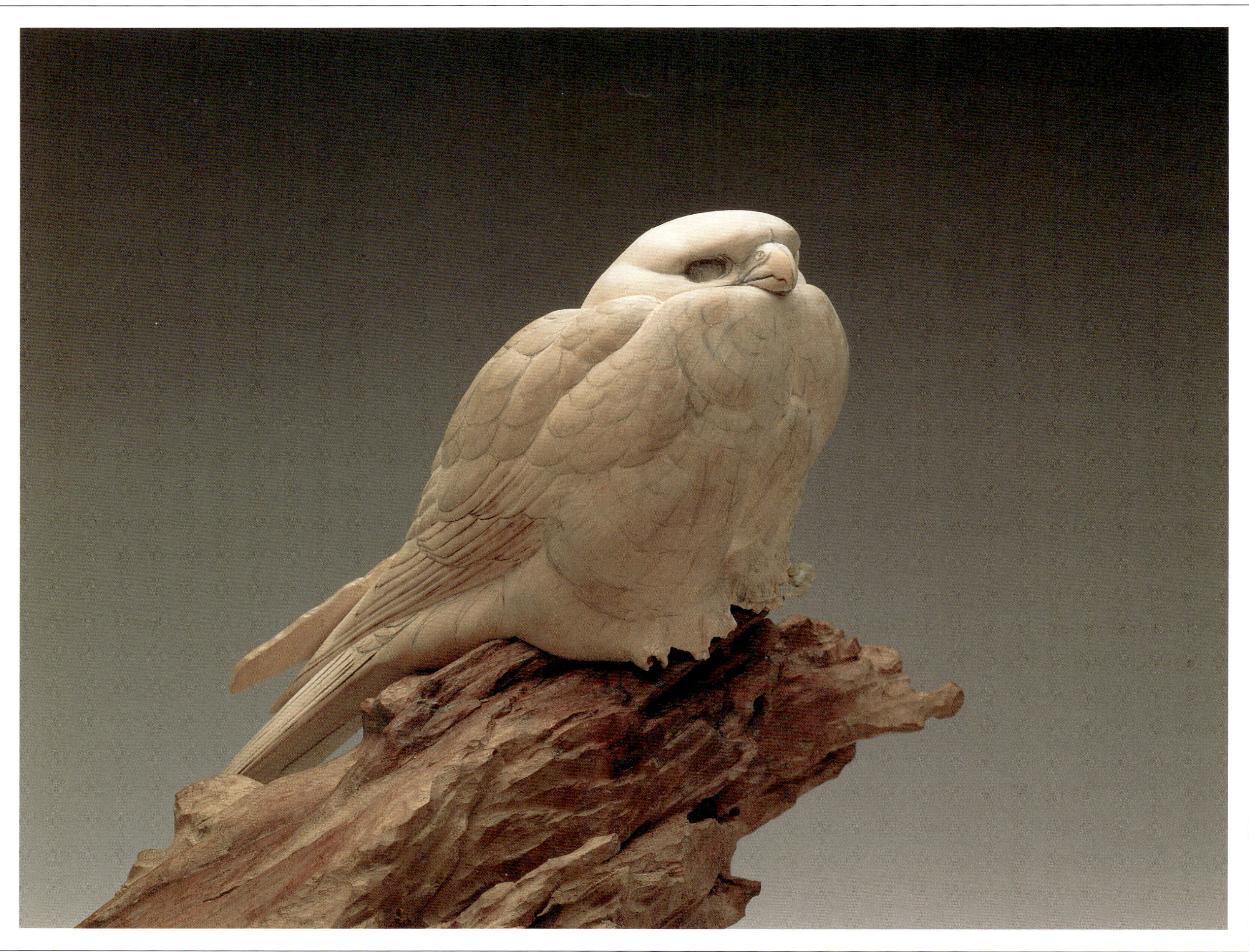

Pete Zaluzec
Merlin, 1996 (in progress)

Zaluzec's merlin-in-progress highlights the detail in wood that infuses the 12-inch-long life-size bird with its dramatic air. Perching the hunter on a worm-eaten walnut base, Zaluzec has given the bird oval eyes, a shape that he will repeat in the head and body of the piece.

floating decoy tradition, is both a skilled carver and one of the form's leading artists. "After a certain point, there are no more technical leaps to make," he says. "It becomes a matter of pushing yourself with ideas and design." At that stage, too, observers are no longer fixated on *how* the work is made but, rather, with what it has to say, says Barth: "I don't want people puzzling over how I did something. I want them to feel it first and respond to it as a piece of art."

The inspiration to deliver wildfowl carving to the realm of fine art originated in the 1970s with the late John Scheeler, the unofficial leader of the contemporary wildfowl sculpture. Scheeler took up carving in his early forties, after seeing an exhibition at the Ward Foundation. Within three years, he was a world-champion artist and was sufficiently inspired to give up his career as an industrial painter to become a full-time sculptor. Technique was the backbone of Scheeler's style, but his vision spawned a generation of wildfowl carvers. "A life force runs through his work that very few carvers have yet achieved," wrote one observer. Scheeler's name appears on the $20,000 purchase award that accompanies the decorative life-size world championship each year, a fitting tribute to the man who influenced the best of today's wildfowl artists. "There is a lot more to a bird than the final finish," Scheeler once said. "You have to create an illusion."

Scheeler's words resound among present-day wildfowl sculptors. Evidence that the movement continues to evolve is apparent in the individual style of every carver who stays true to the basic parameters of the medium but breaks fresh artistic ground with each new work. Carvers, for example, are divided in their preference for single-piece versus mixed-media sculptures. Artists such as Ernie Muehlmatt and Jett Brunet, who use a subtractive-sculpture technique, see an added integrity to the piece when it is shaped, without inserts, from a single piece of wood. Similarly, Todd Wohlt and Greg Woodard prefer their wood sculptures to be unadorned by other elements, a look that communicates a simple message and a feeling of permanence which are integral to their art.

Patrick Godin, Bob Guge, Larry Barth and Jeffrey Whiting, on the other hand, are all advocates of a mixed-media presentation and make a strong case for the argument that as sculpture, a work can include whatever materials are necessary to convey the message. "These are the most complete pieces of wildfowl sculpture, because you have other elements to create a design with, in addition to the birds," explains Godin, an innovator in sculptural techniques. Unusual materials used by such artists include metal for leaves, seedpods and pine needles; treated plastics for moss and habitat; carved stone for water; and even epoxied dental floss for milkweed down.

Contemporary carvers also continue to push the boundaries of the art form by broadening the concept of realism. In its infant stage of development, wildfowl sculpture strove to perfect the "real" birds in a completely literal sense by emphasizing upturned and textured feathers and increasingly lifelike painting. As the art form has matured, however, many of the artists, hungry for new modes of expression, are shifting their focus away from detail by broadening their understanding of realism and experimenting with perspective. Some are exploring more interpretive renderings of habitat and, occasionally, attempting impressionistic details on the birds themselves. By simplifying and downplaying certain carving calisthenics, carvers are stepping back from technique and strengthening the overall artistic impact of each piece.

One of the first such breakaway works was Larry Barth's *Vantage Point*, a 1991 world-championship

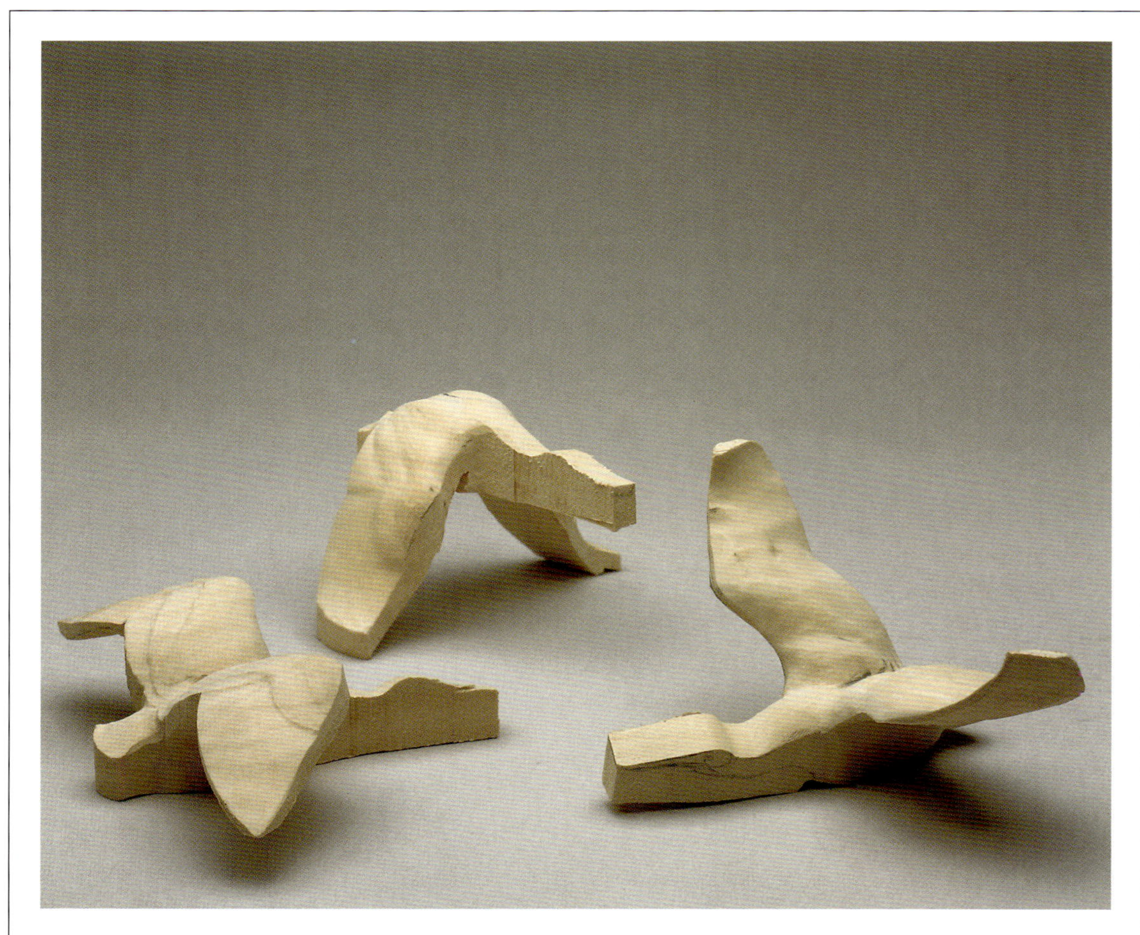

Michael Arthurs
Roseate Spoonbills
Evening Flight, 1996 (in progress)

These miniature birds in the rough show the range of concave and convex shapes necessary for the artist to create the varying wing thicknesses in the final carving.

carving. Barth made an unorthodox decision to leave the bird's hawthorn-stem perch unpainted, burnishing it instead in dark brassy tones and polishing the thorns themselves to a high luster. "If you were looking at the shrike through binoculars," says Barth, "the detail of the hawthorn branch would fall away." By simply tweaking the perspective, Barth remains true to the highly rendered sculpture while giving it a twist that intensifies the presence of the colorful bird and reinforces the sculpture's dramatic predatory theme. A similar ground-breaking piece by Chris Bonner, entitled *On Silent Wings*, depicts a barn owl pursuing a red bat. The impressionistic mood of Bonner's painting style combined with his decision to make the bird slightly oversized (despite competition rules) gives the sculpture the skewed reality of a speedy chase on a hazy summer night, and the piece thereby catches the "illusion" that John Scheeler talked about.

As that illusion continues to shift with aesthetic styles and trends, wildfowl artists will dig deeper, tapping into the imagination that allows them to interpret avian life in wood. Employing texture, color and form, they throw open a window to the natural world, thereby communicating the beauty, grace and mystery inherent in living birds.

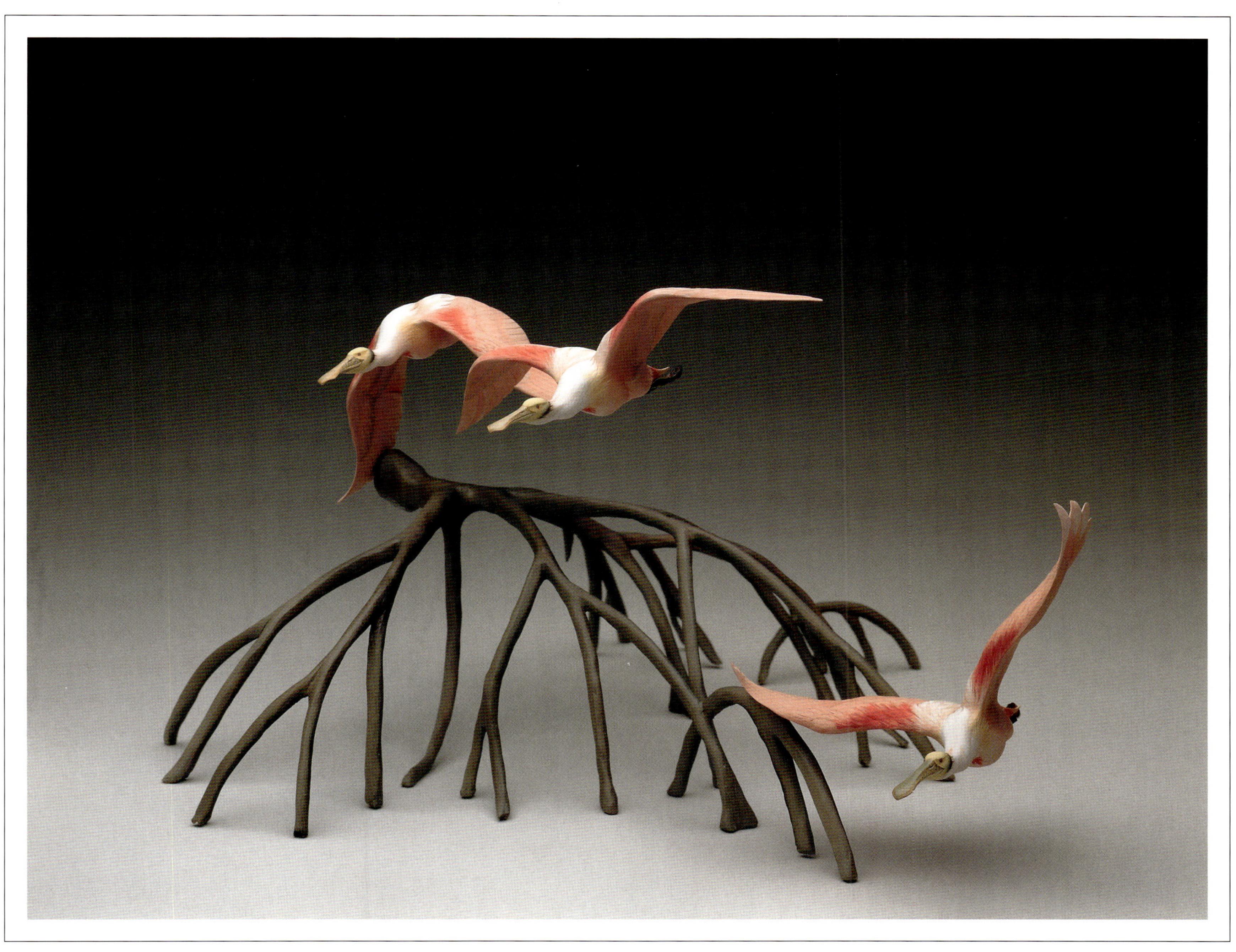

Taking flight late in the day, Arthurs' breeding roseate spoonbills, cloaked in colorful plumage, strike a dramatic contrast to the shadowy roots of a stylized mangrove swamp. By selecting the miniature format for his world-championship sculpture, Arthurs conveys the elegance and beauty inherent in the clownish birds.

Michael Arthurs
Roseate Spoonbills
Evening Flight, 1996

Michael Arthurs

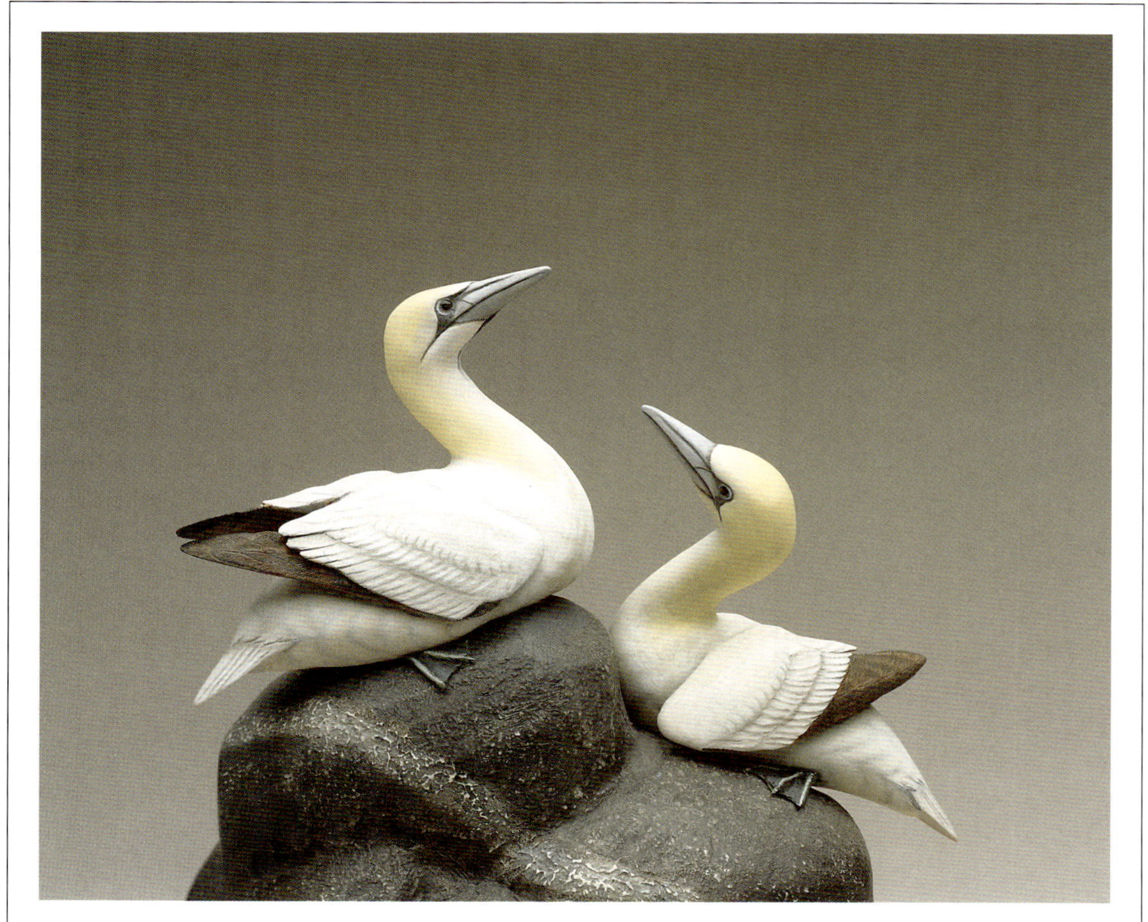

Michael Arthurs
Northern Gannets
Springtime Rivalry, 1992

The near-porcelain finish of the plumage of Arthurs' miniature northern gannets mimics the unruffled look of live birds in their rocky coastal breeding colonies. To underscore the smooth, integrated look of the birds and their basalt habitat, Arthurs created his carving from a single piece of wood, at the same time incorporating the familiar bill-banging behavior characteristic of these highly territorial breeders.

"All my work has an edge," explains Michael Arthurs. "The design is artistic and the composition is balanced, but there is something just a little bit uncomfortable about it. It always leaves an unanswered question for the observer."

An avid birder who started his carving career in 1981 making decoys, the North Bay, Ontario, artist draws his inspiration from two sources: While a bird, by virtue of its pose or the striking pattern of its plumage, might catch Arthurs' eye, it is just as likely that he will respond to an inanimate form, such as the downward curve of a mangrove root. The result: a carving of a trio of spoonbills in flight above their favorite breeding habitat.

Arthurs relies on field sketches and photographs as his key references, which he roughs out first in clay. The methodical carving process stands in sharp contrast to the unpredictable pace of his life as an emergency-room physician. "Art elevates me and helps me escape from the chaos of my work," he says. Free from the demands of producing sculpture for sale, 42-year-old Arthurs is able to stay passionate about his art, responding freely to the inspiration around him. "If I spend time on the sculpture that I want to do," he says, "people have a strong emotional response to it."

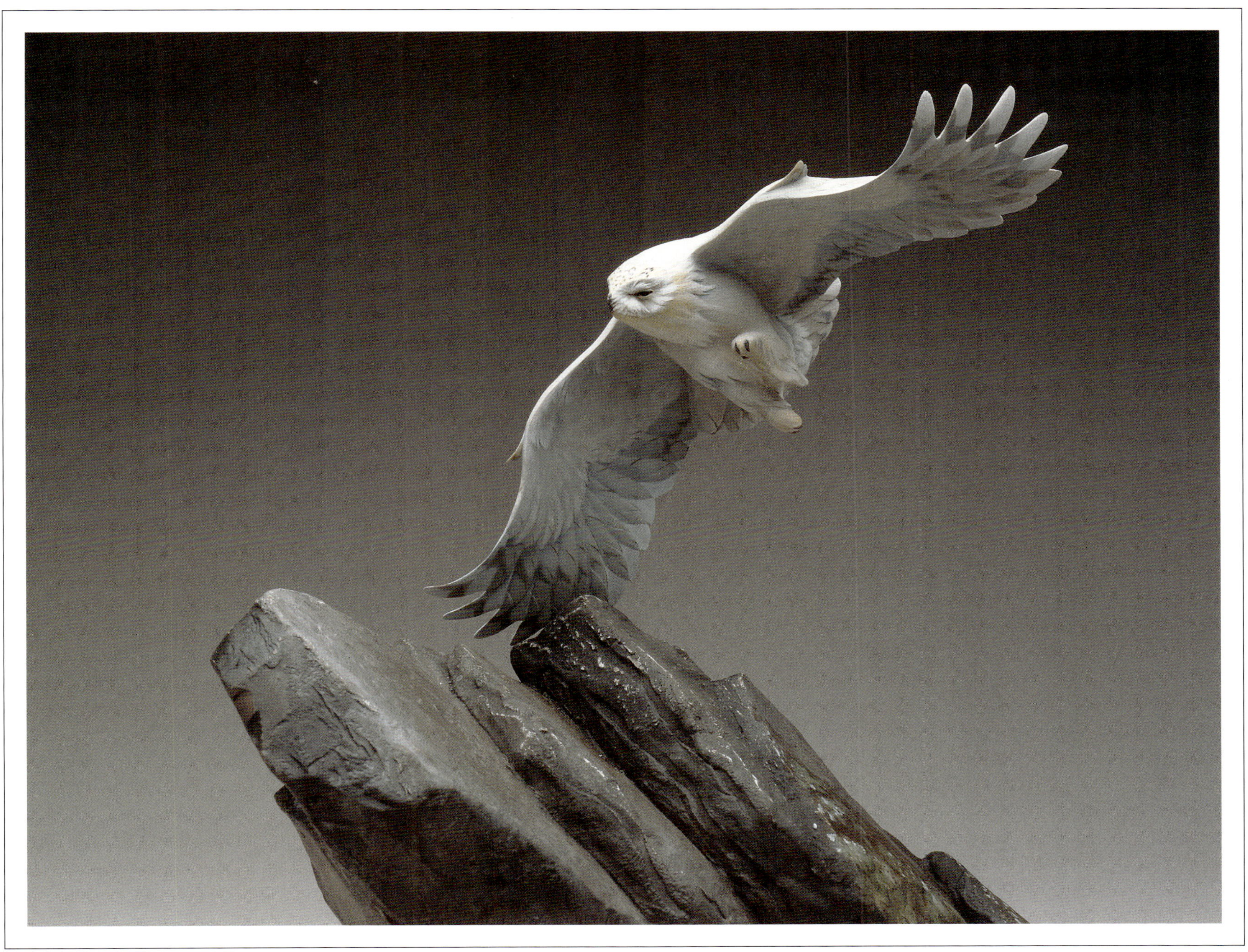

Arthurs' miniature snowy owl floats on enormous wings that suggest its graceful power. Set against the stark lichen-covered rock in day's waning sunlight, Arthurs' owl—painted with acrylics—reflects the sunset shades of blue, gray, pink and yellow on the underside of its typically plush white plumage. Part of a birds-in-flight series, *Detected!* captures the agility of an airborne raptor through such animated details as the fanned tail and wrist feathers and a leg swinging into strike position.

Michael Arthurs
Snowy Owl
Detected! 1995

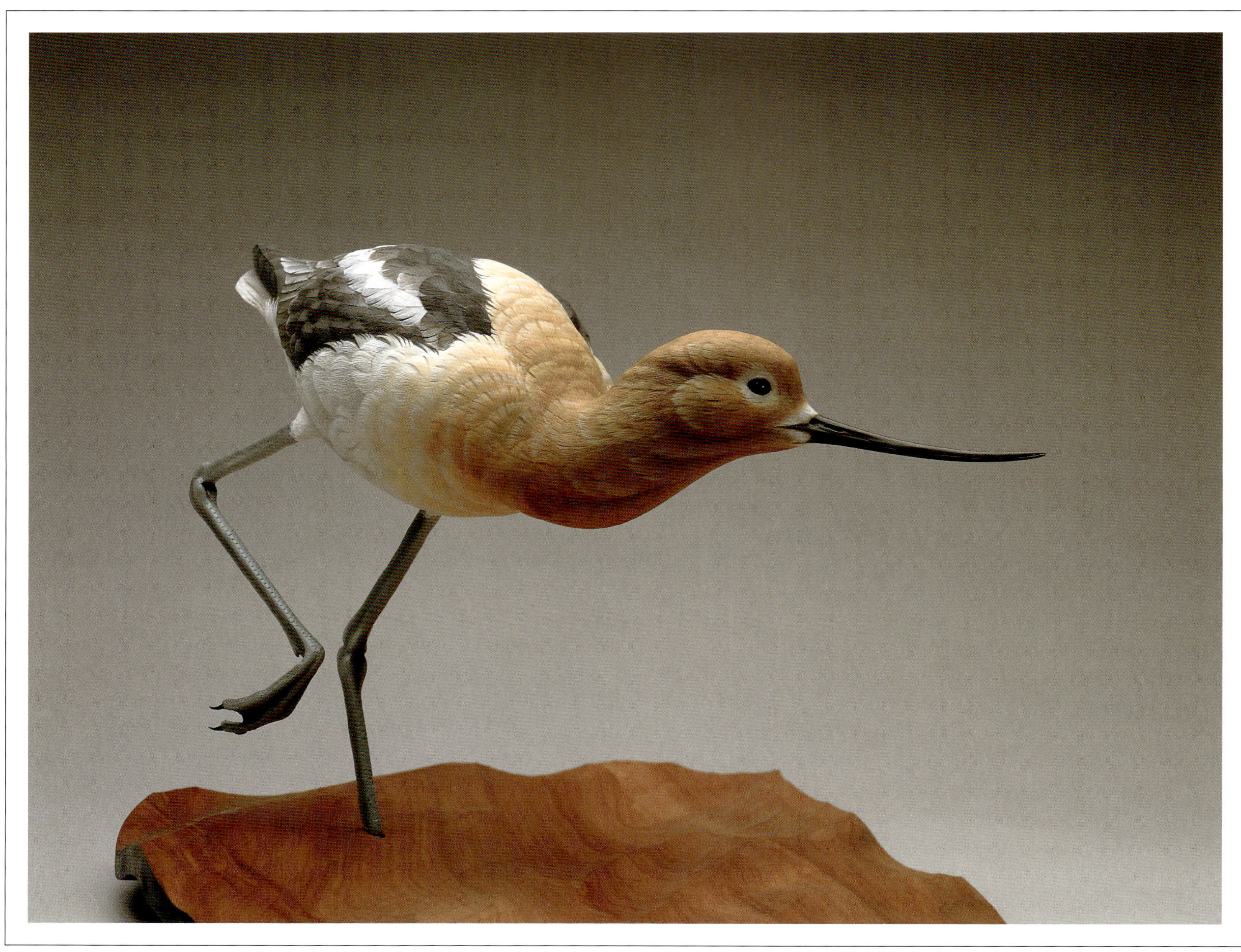

Michael Arthurs
American Avocet
In the Tide, 1996

Arthurs' use of negative space—accentuated by the life-size American avocet gazing across a boundless tidal pool—subtly animates his carving with the sense that the bird, standing ankle-deep in water, is about to step forward. The unpainted natural colors of the base, carved from red gum, provide a warm complement to the muted acrylic palette of the bird.

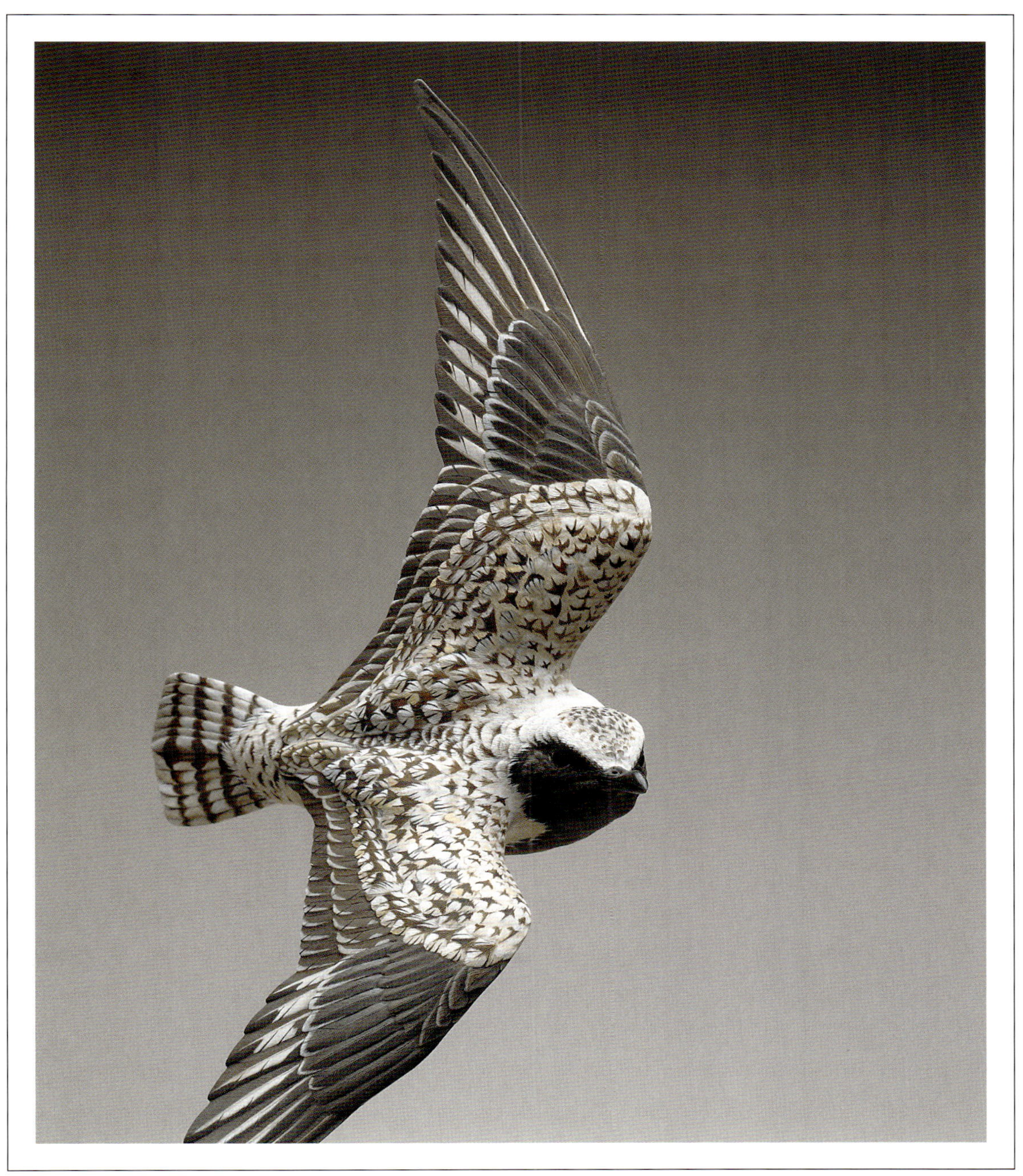

Arthurs chose a full-flight formation to present the tweedy textures of the black-bellied plover's plumage. Using knives, grinders and chisels to carve the tupelo bird in this sharp banking composition, the artist employed a bronze feather to anchor his bird at the base. Arthurs' dramatic transcontinental transient earned a best-in-show ribbon at the world championship in the open decorative life-size category.

Michael Arthurs
Black-Bellied Plover
Tundra Spring, 1994

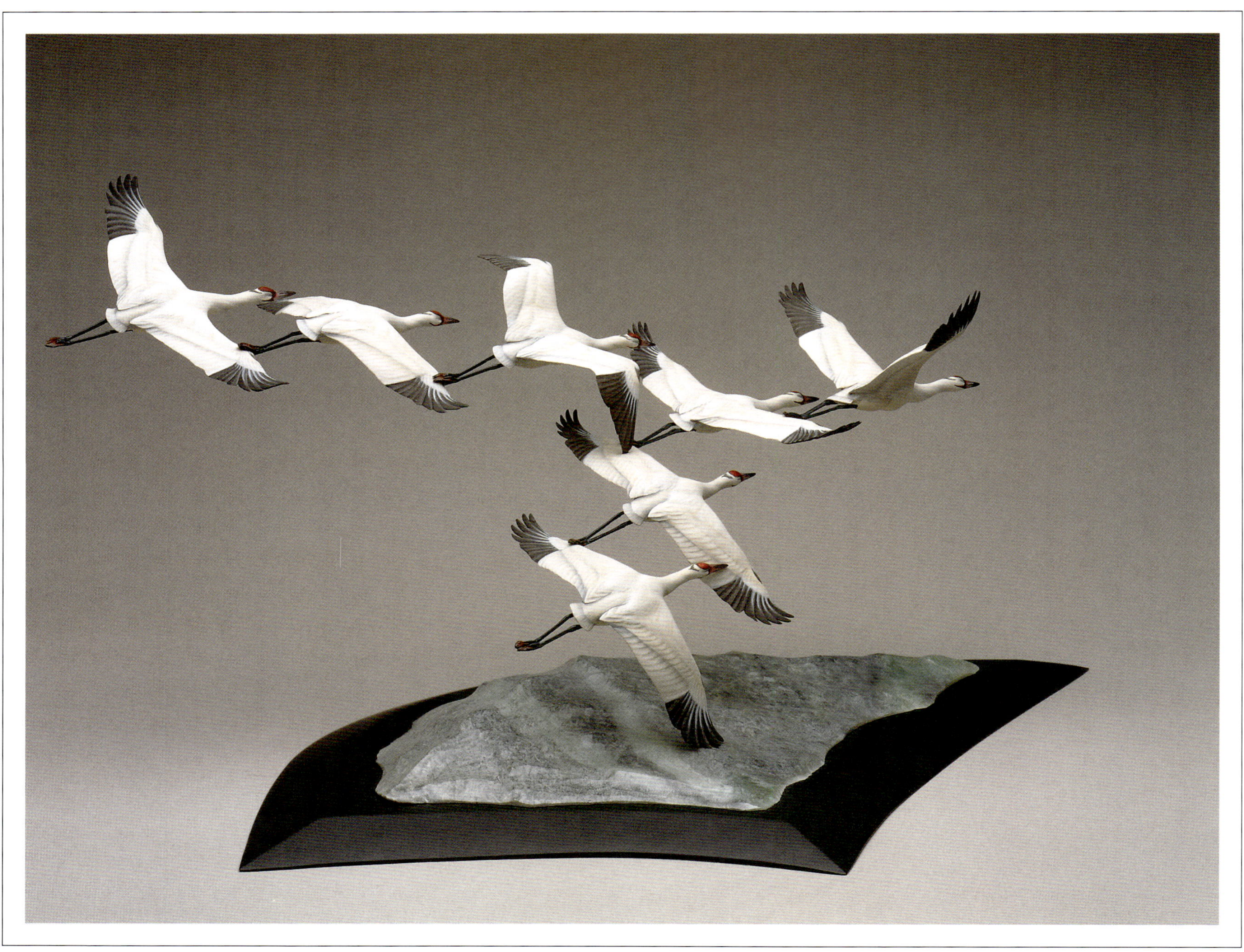

Michael Arthurs
Whooping Cranes
North to the Breeding Grounds, 1993

Arthurs' long-necked, long-legged whooping cranes—his first carving with multiple birds in flight—are a striking subject for his "design in white." The artist infuses the miniature piece with its airy feeling by connecting each bird at a single wing tip. The sculpture telescopes down to one delicate feather anchored to the base. A bronze infrastructure supports the seven-bird flock.

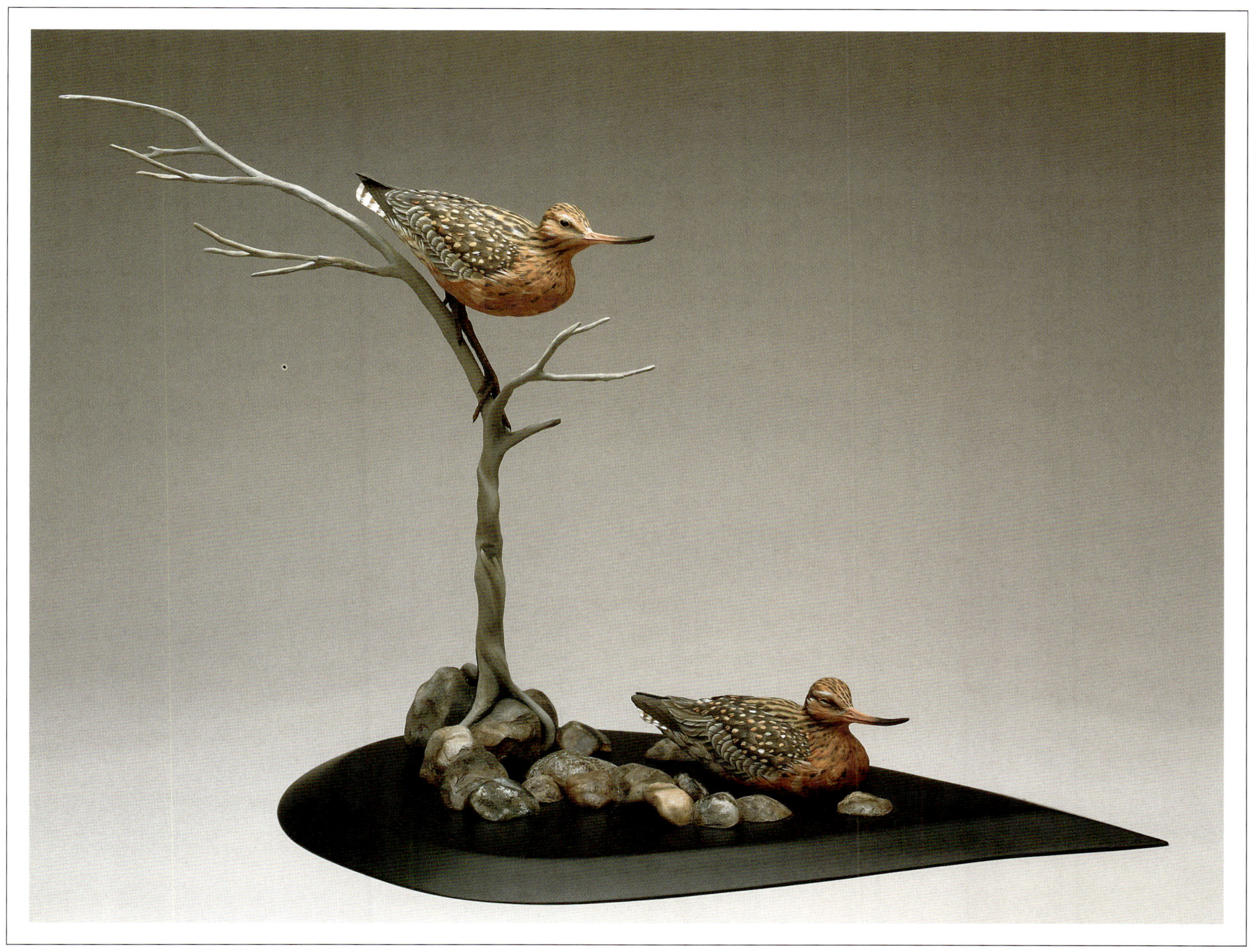

Something is about to happen in this miniature carving of bar-tailed godwits. Embodying the "edge" that is characteristic of the carver's work, Arthurs' godwits assume antithetical poses: the defending male perches precariously in the fork of the tree branch, while the female rests on barren ground. Balancing the asymmetry of the sculpture's composition is the parallel attitude of the birds, which are linked by the position of their heads and bills.

Michael Arthurs
Bar-Tailed Godwits
The Sentinel, 1995

Larry Barth

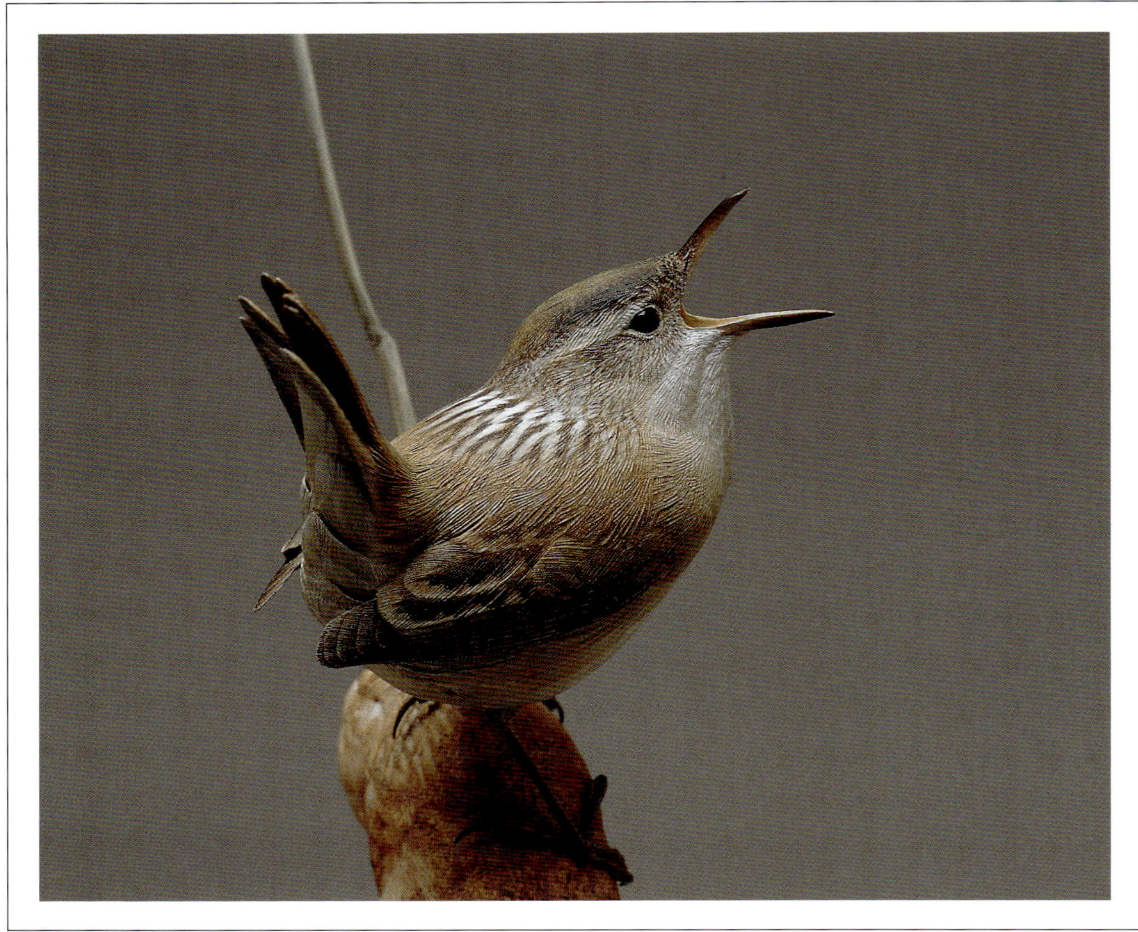

Larry Barth
Marsh Wren
In the Cattails, 1993 (detail)

"I've been interested in birds and art for as long as I can remember," admits Larry Barth. At the age of 14, the artistically inclined Barth picked up a cast-off picnic-table leg and began carving, only learning years later that a forum for his hobby existed. On a vacation during his freshman year in design at Carnegie-Mellon University, Barth happened upon an exhibition of the Ward Foundation in the fall of 1975. "I had such a rush of emotion when I walked into that room," he remembers. "From that moment on, I knew what I wanted to do."

When Barth returned to school, he shifted the focus of his program, devising a self-directed curriculum in fine art that would prepare him for his destiny as a professional wildfowl sculptor. Within three years, Barth made his world-class premiere at Ocean City, rocking the show with his college-thesis project—a wall-mounted great horned owl and two downy nestlings. His sculpture claimed second best-in-world honors.

That was 1979, and the Stahlstown, Pennsylvania, artist is now a four-time world champion. "Something more than the birds themselves keeps me growing," says Barth, 39. "I want each piece to succeed in design, shape and form. If it happens on those levels, then it works as sculpture."

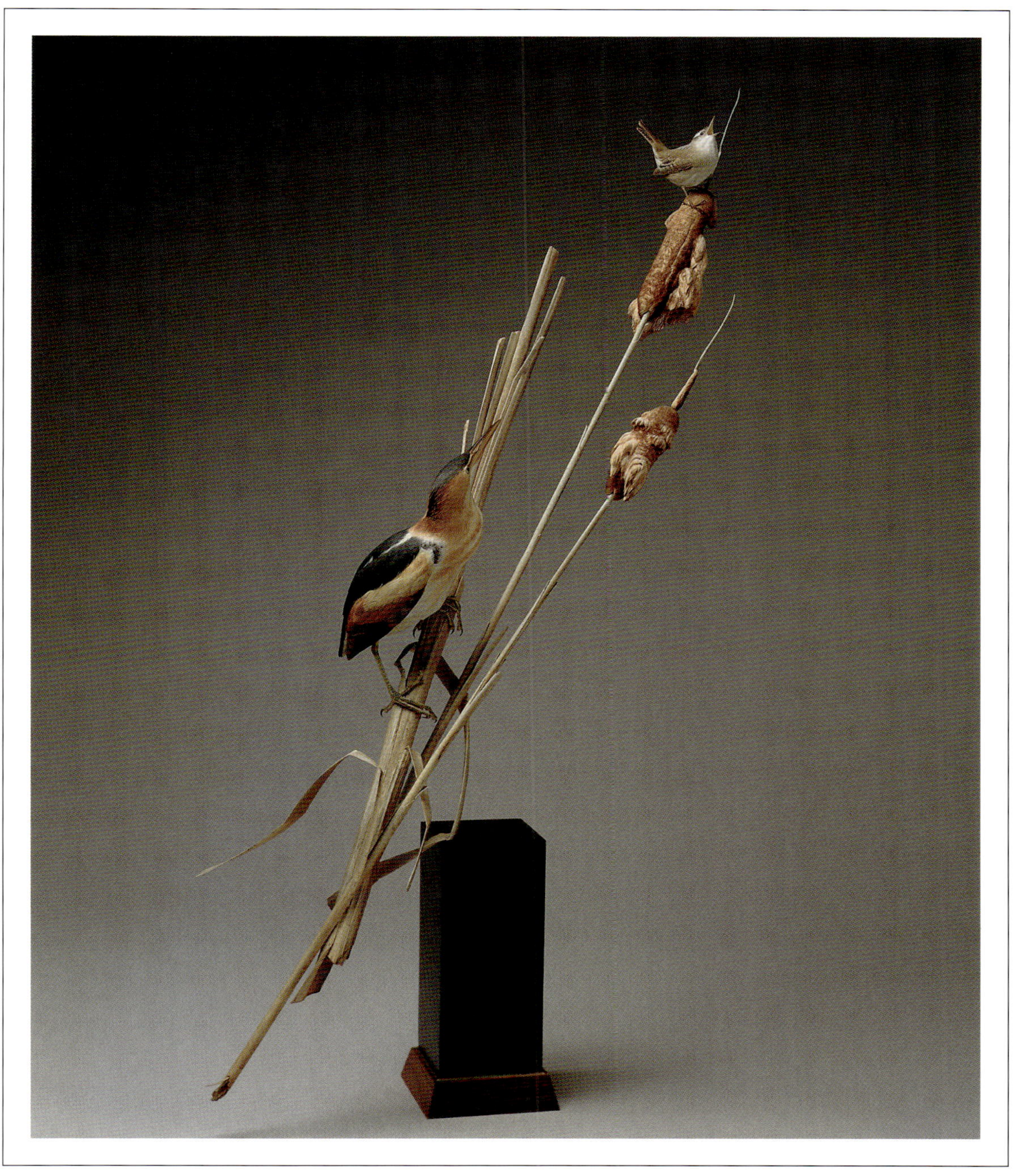

The chaos of a cattail marsh is distilled in this playful life-size sculpture of a discreet least bittern casting a perplexed gaze at an extravagantly vocal marsh wren. Barth uses a clay model to finalize all his design and composition ideas—which he calls "the hard part"—before carving, which for Barth then becomes "the long part."

Larry Barth
Least Bittern and Marsh Wren
In the Cattails, 1993

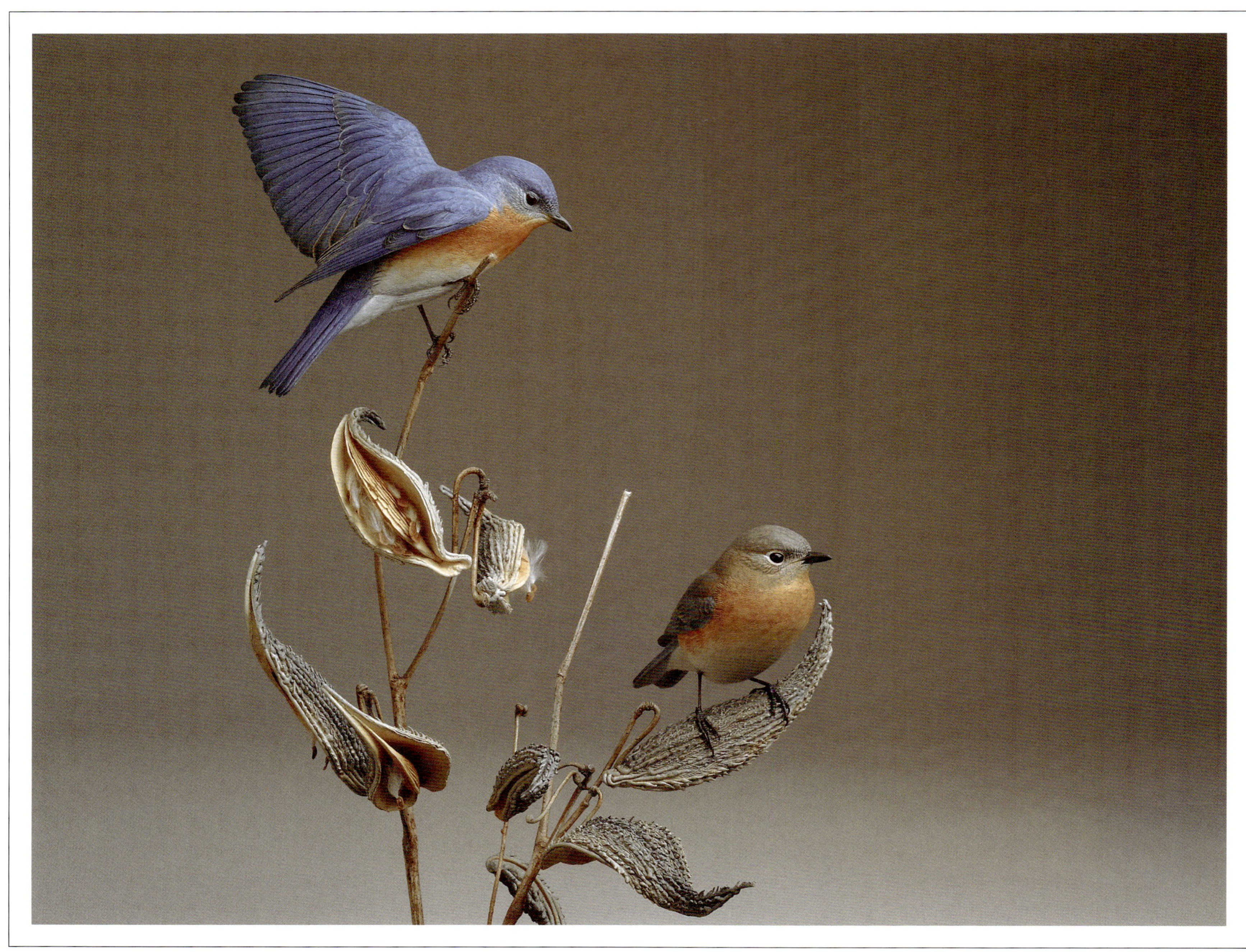

Larry Barth
Bluebirds and Milkweed, 1995

A self-described bluebird fan, Barth captures the spirit of a mating pair returning to its rural nesting ground in early spring. Remnants of weather-beaten milkweed provide a perch for the warm-toned life-size female and the colorful male, whose wing-waving pose suggests that he has just alighted. Barth's lifelong carving experience has made him fluent with all sculpture media and technologies, which here included torching bronze to fashion the pods and branches.

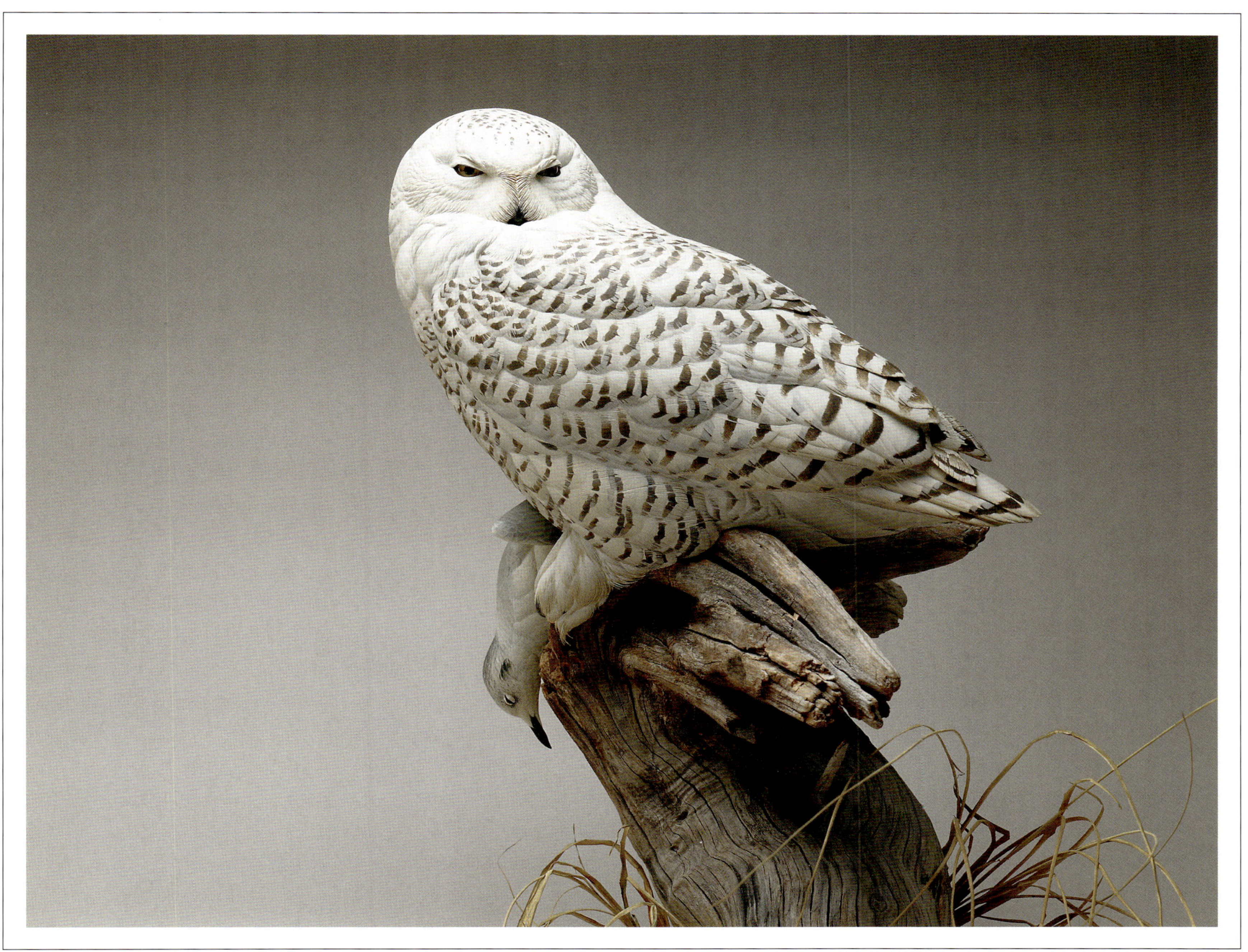

Barth's snowy owl and Bonaparte's gull communicate a timelessness that has earned the artist well-deserved accolades. With its flawless craftsmanship and artistic storytelling, *Winter Lakeshore* projects a strong contrast in moods and color, and the 1985 life-size sculpture broke the mold of traditional wildfowl sculpture. More artist than technician, Barth relies largely on field observations rather than photographs for his research. "I find that I see better with a sketch pad," he says.

Larry Barth
Snowy Owl and Bonaparte's Gull
Winter Lakeshore, 1985

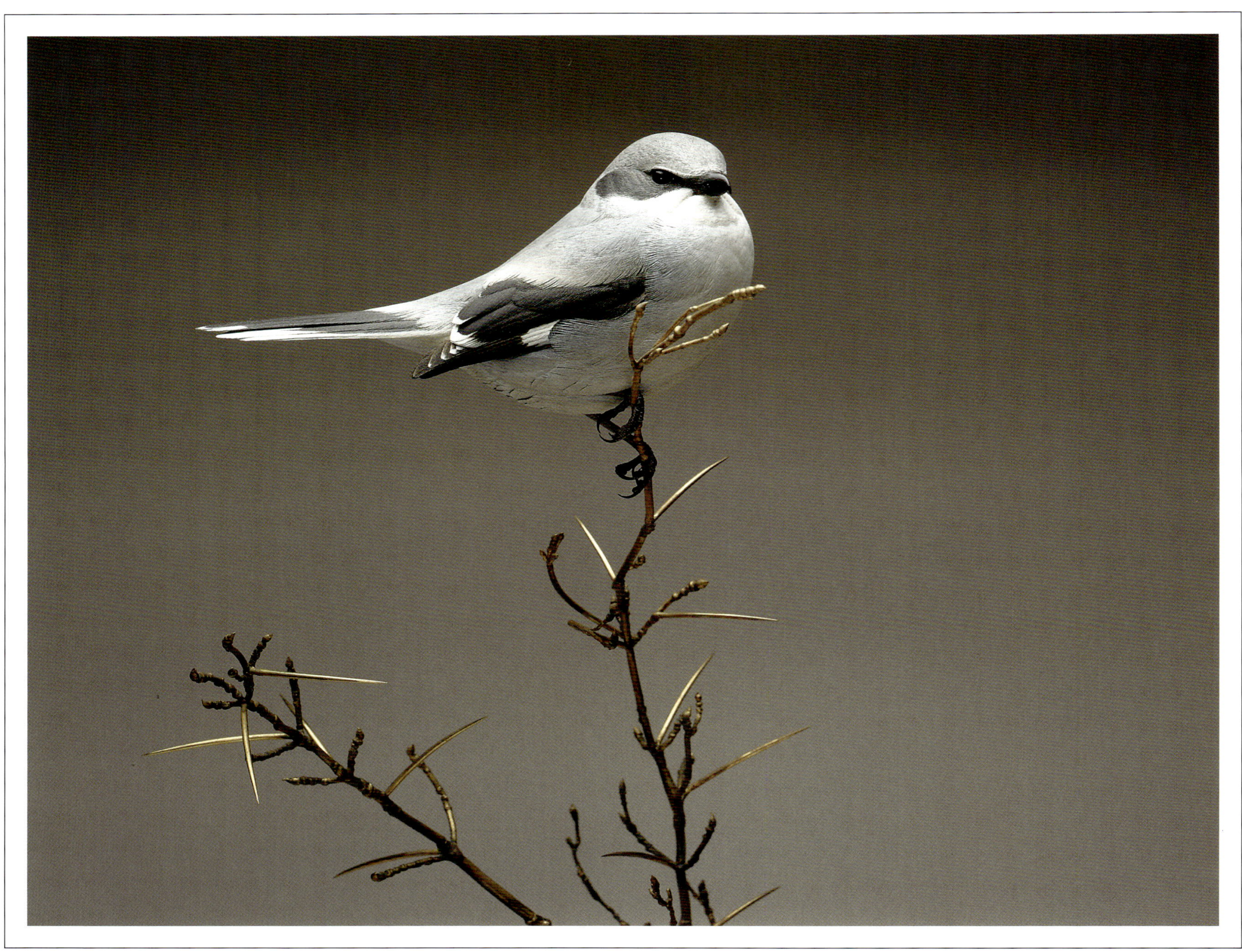

Larry Barth
Loggerhead Shrike
Vantage Point, 1991

A cold-blooded killer elegantly perched on a cold-blooded tree is the life-size subject of *Vantage Point*. Barth's predatory loggerhead shrike and hawthorn branch depart from the convention of realistically painting the habitat. To dramatize the lethal dynamic between bird and branch, Barth burnished the tones of the bark and polished the thorns. "Over top of the abstract foundation," he explains, "you build a literal facade."

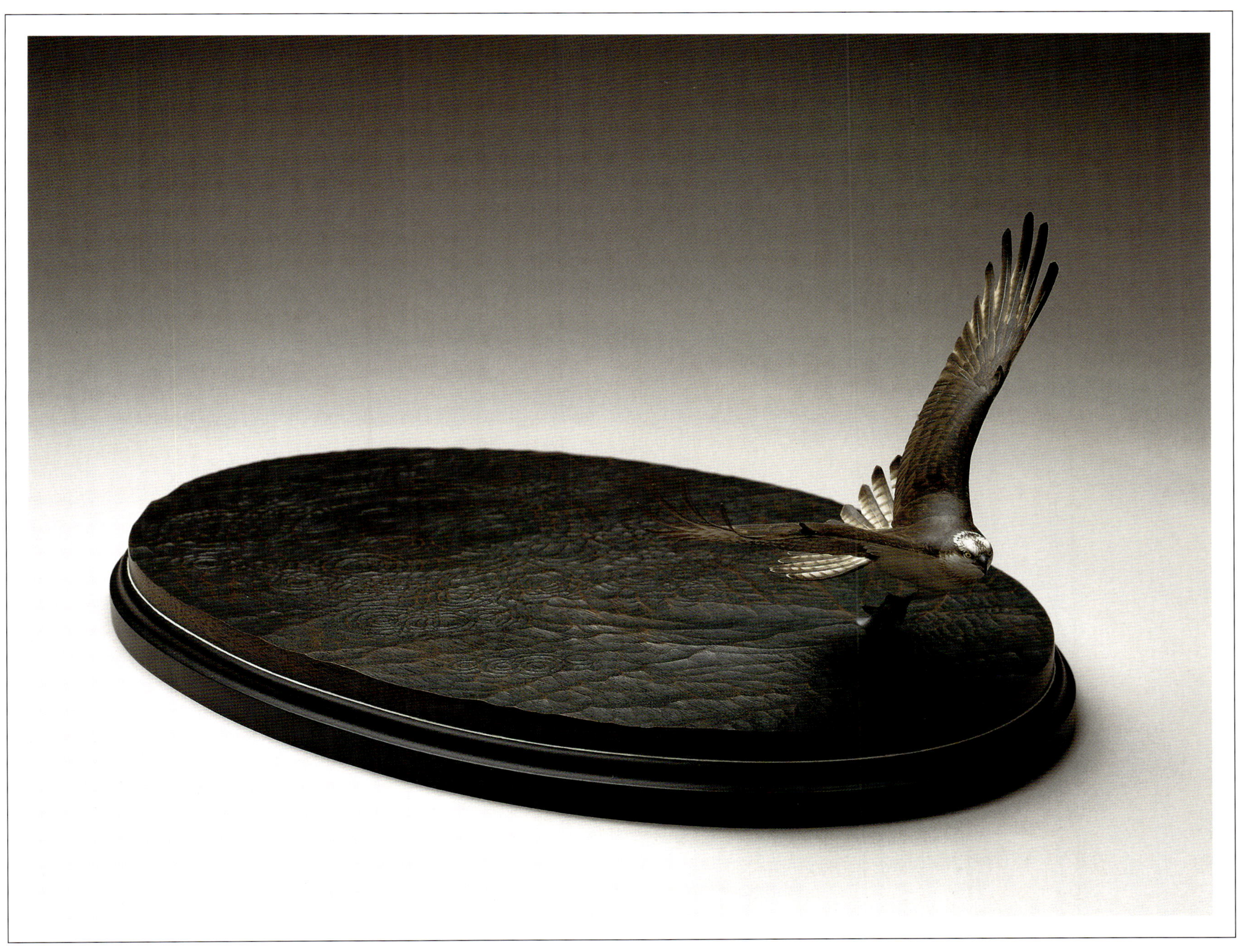

Larry Barth
Osprey and Atlantic Salmon, 1995

Part of a series of works on water that are each designed to fit an oval, this osprey is Barth's attempt to capitalize on the miniature format by tackling a piece that, at full size, would fill a room. Presenting a temporal sequence, Barth portrays the fish-hunting bird making a catch, which it then drags and shakes across the surface of the lake. To create the darkly iridescent water, Barth carved it in walnut and used stain rather than paint.

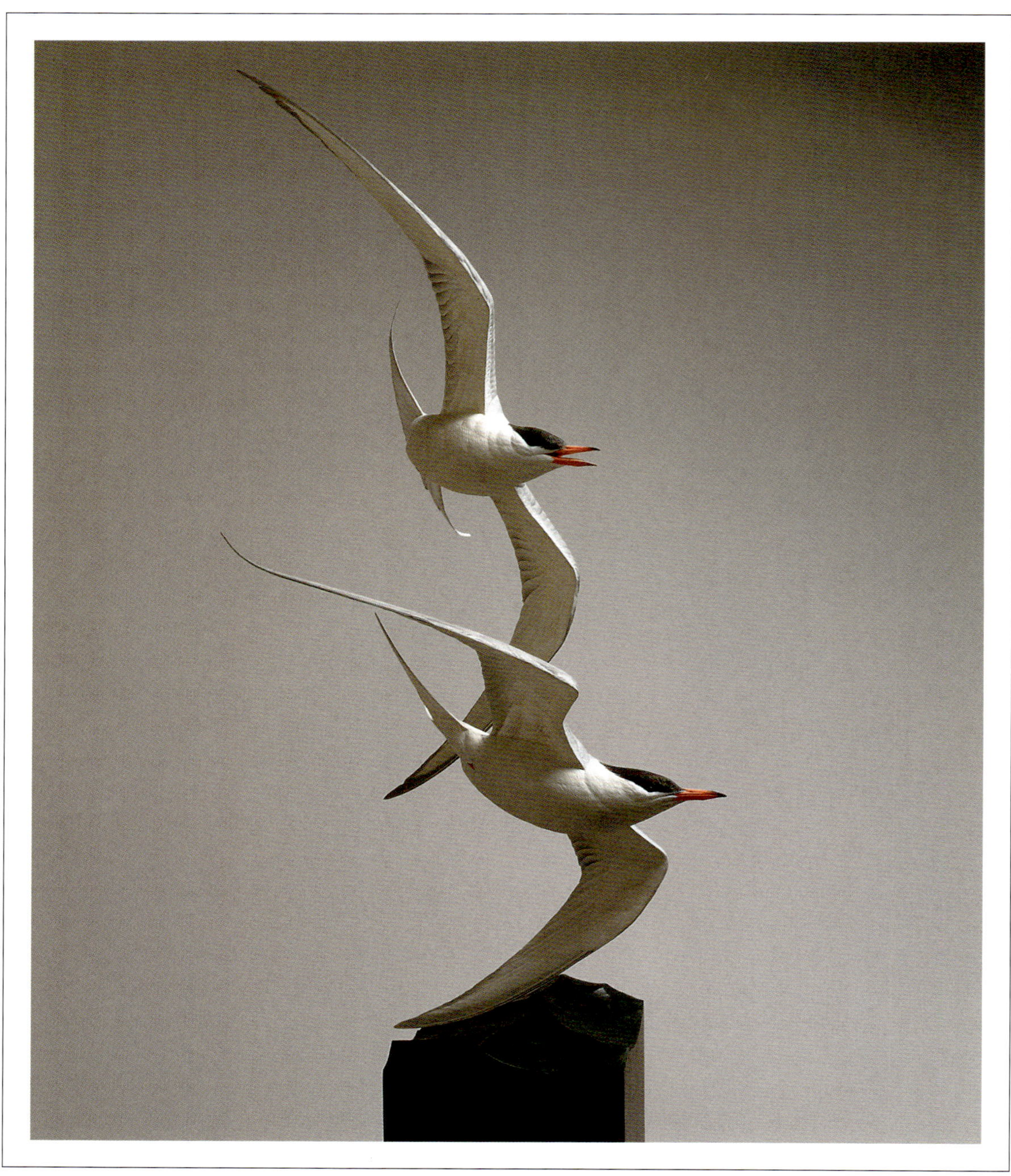

Larry Barth
Terns in Flight, 1986

The very model of effortless flight, these common terns belie the complex engineering and joinery of airborne subjects as they lightly brush wing against tail. Stripped clean of all but a hint of their abstractly rendered habitat, which is sculpted into stained walnut, Barth's life-size transcontinental travelers are painted with light and shadow as they rocket past in full sun.

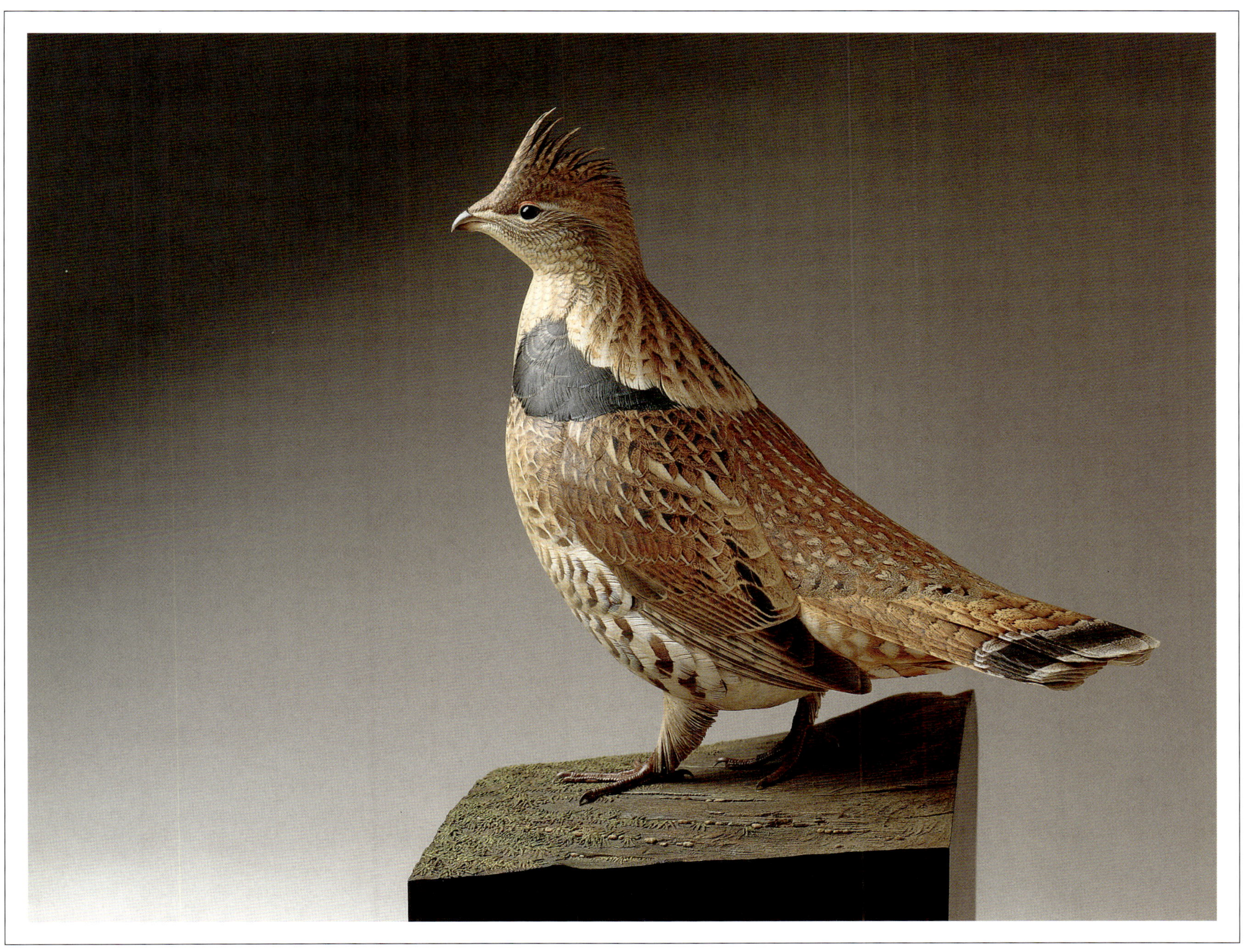

Always searching for a new concept to expand his carving style, Barth takes this life-size sculpture a step further by shaping the ruffed grouse's drumming log into a pedestal for the piece.

Larry Barth
Ruffed Grouse
Forbesway Drummer, 1992

Chris Bonner

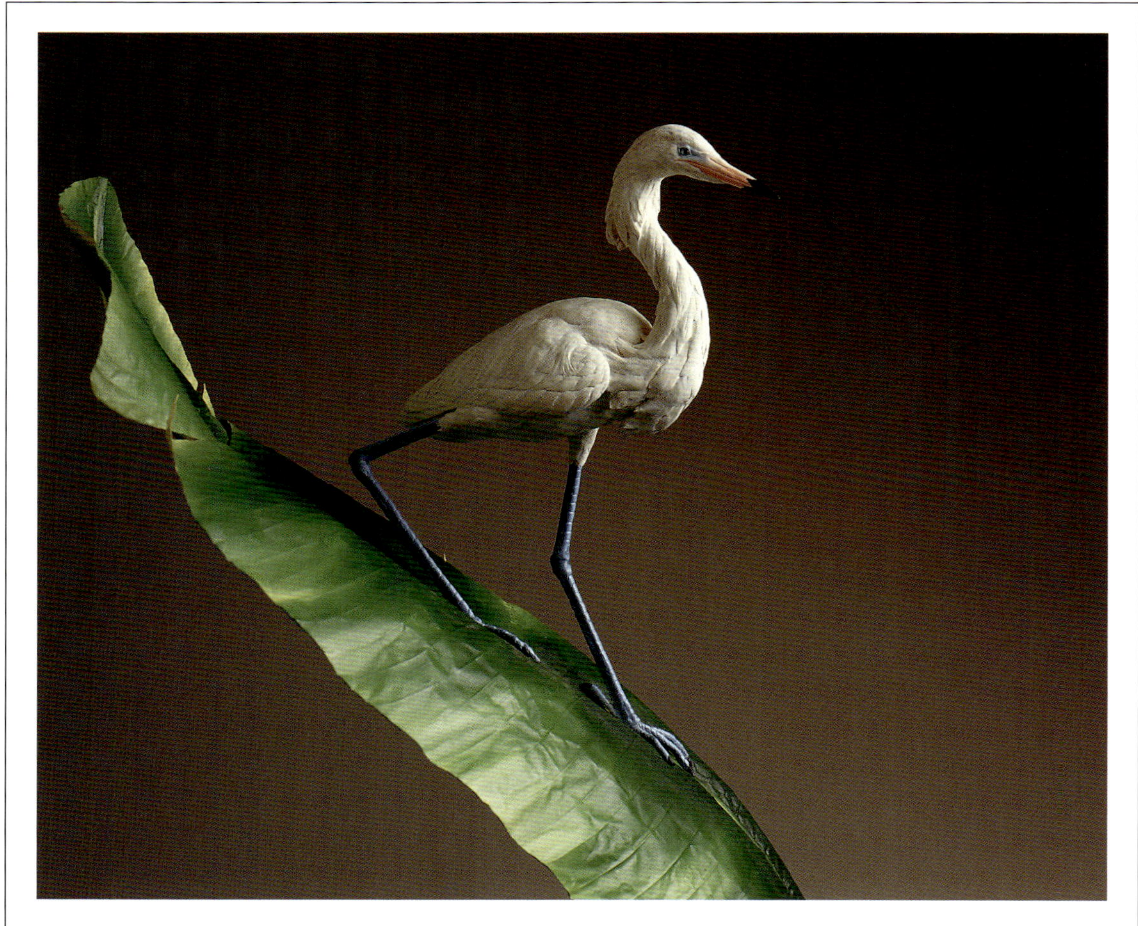

Chris Bonner
Egret, 1994

A white-phase reddish egret strutting on a palm leaf is the subject of this life-size sculpture. In a complete departure from the realistic form, Bonner has created the bird with very little detail, choosing instead to etch deep-relief texture into the wood to create the bird's extravagant plumage.

"Nature is a classical subject," says Chris Bonner. "But it hasn't received a lot of recent attention within the art world."

The Bradenton, Florida, artist began his career in 1983 as an accomplished carver of floating birds, winning the world championship in 1989 with a pair of mergansers. The limitations of that medium, however, motivated Bonner to throw his hat into the decorative life-size ring in 1995.

Loyal to the skills of traditional carving, Bonner belongs to a new generation of wildfowl sculptors who want to liberate wildlife art from the constraints of strict realism. With his premier piece (an eerie barn owl in flight), Bonner massaged the representational style and created an abstract image of grace and speed. "I think it's a better piece of art for that," the 34-year-old carver says of his decision to stretch the exhibition's rules regarding lifelike accuracy. Bonner's sparing use of detail further enhances the moody aura of the sculpture.

Though he takes risks in interpretation, Bonner is not about to leave his classical subjects behind. "Nature is a point of departure for my creativity," he concludes. "There is more that I can do with it, maybe something more original that will let me grow beyond what I have already done."

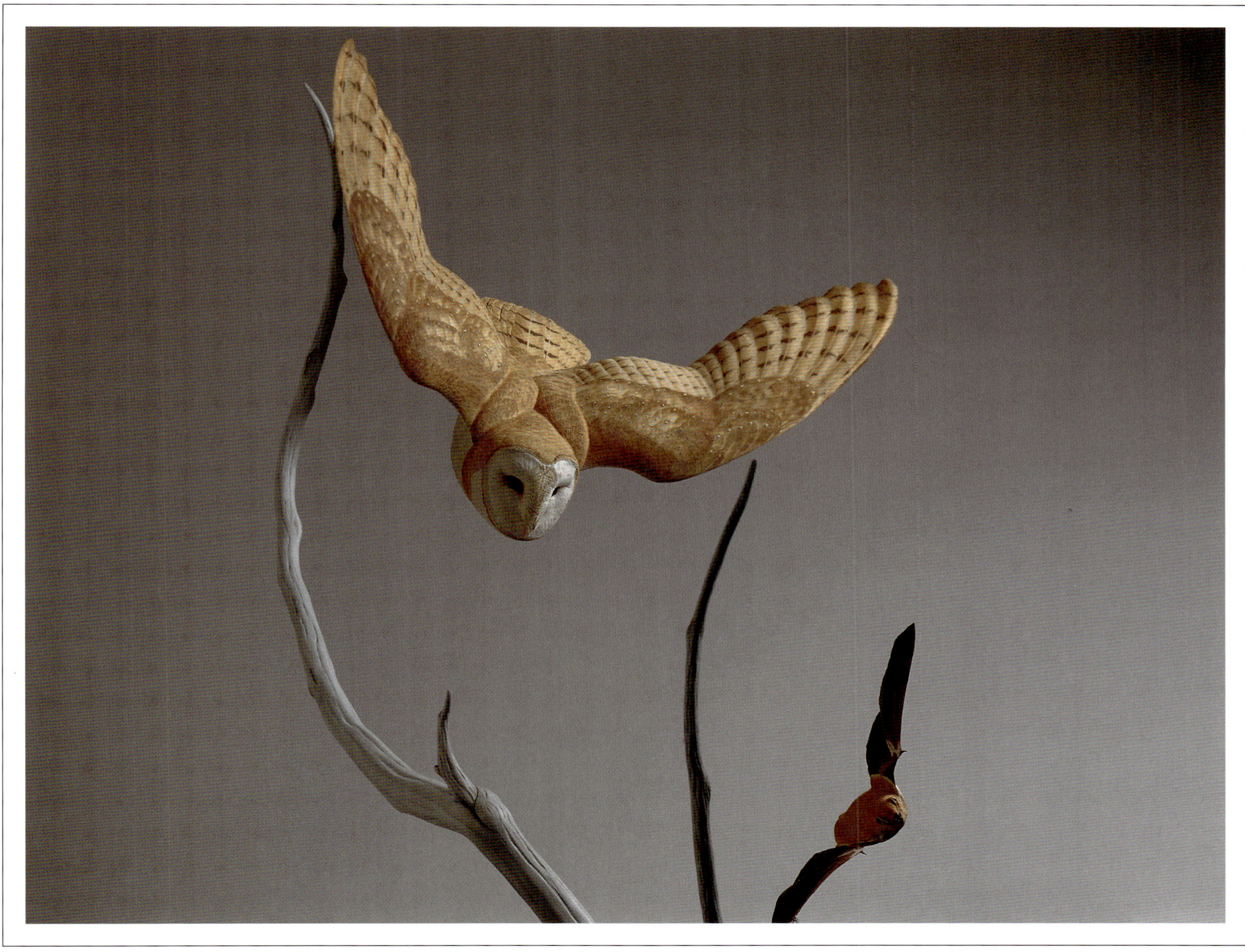

Chris Bonner
Barn Owl With Bat
On Silent Wings, 1995

The asymmetrical composition of Bonner's barn owl in silent pursuit of a red bat gives it a ghostly, dreamlike quality. Painted in impressionistic tones of chamois and tan, the sculpture, which took Bonner two years to complete, earned third place in decorative life-size competition at the world championship. Bonner shaped the owl from three pieces of tupelo that are mortised together at the wing joints. He etched the fine feather detail with knives.

Jett Brunet

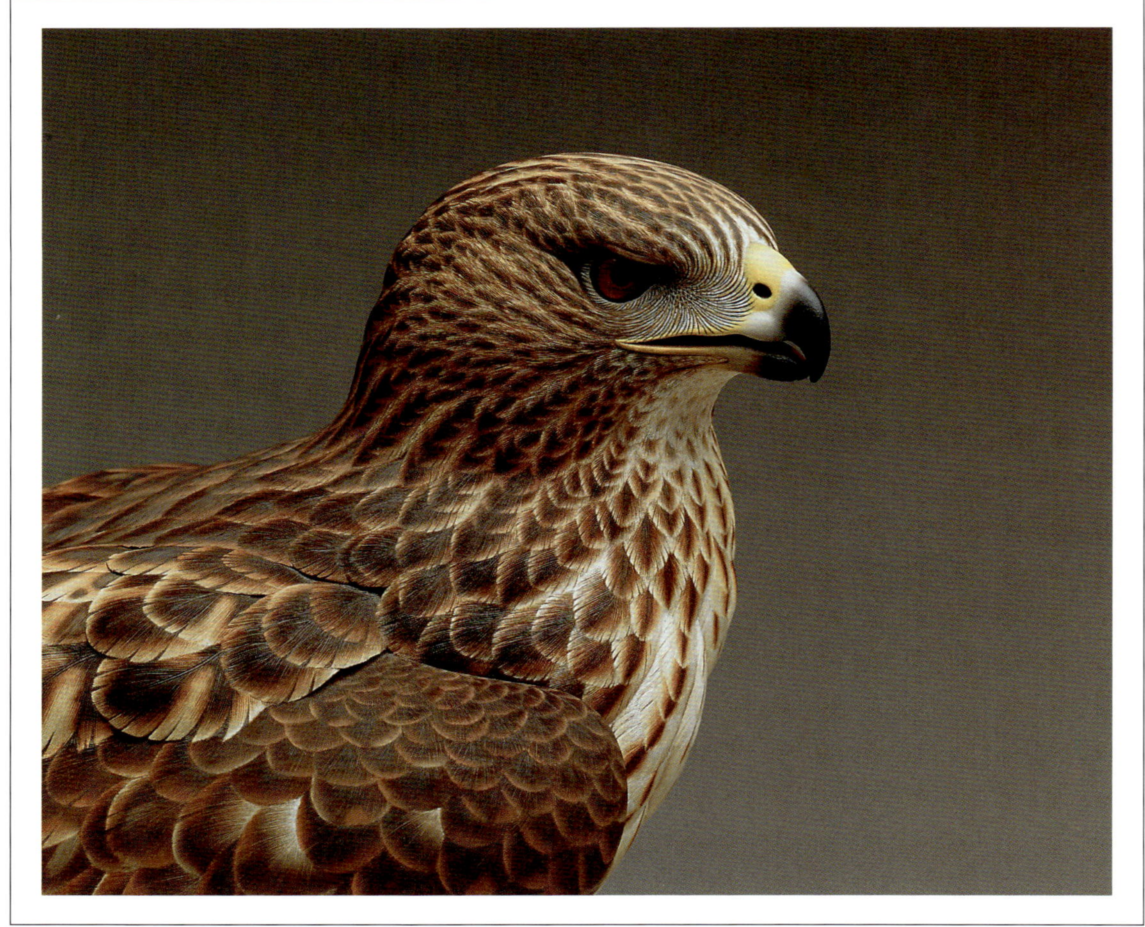

Jett Brunet
Red-Tailed Hawk, 1988 (detail)

Capturing a strong expression in the eyes and face is all-important in creating a convincing bird of prey.

"Watching over Dad's shoulder as a boy inspired me to make decoys," says Jett Brunet. "Similarly, I became interested in decoratives when I saw the life in John Scheeler's birds." Brunet couldn't have admired two more dynamic artists: With his exquisitely artful birds, his father, Tan, established the standard for today's floating decoys, while Scheeler, with his dramatic sculptures, spawned a generation of wildfowl artists.

Filtering the influence of these mentors through his own imagination, the Galliano, Louisiana, artist first established himself as an illustrious carver of animated floating decoys. Nearly 20 years into his career, Brunet has turned his attention to the open field of decorative works. There, he continues to live up to his motto of bringing out the best that a species has to offer while enjoying "the freedom to make different birds with different moods and poses."

The 33-year-old Brunet carves with traditional knives and chisels and paints with artist's oils in a technique pioneered by his father, but his greatest asset is a unique gift for visualization. "I get a really clear picture in my mind of where I'm going before I start," he says. "Then I work to get as close to it as I can."

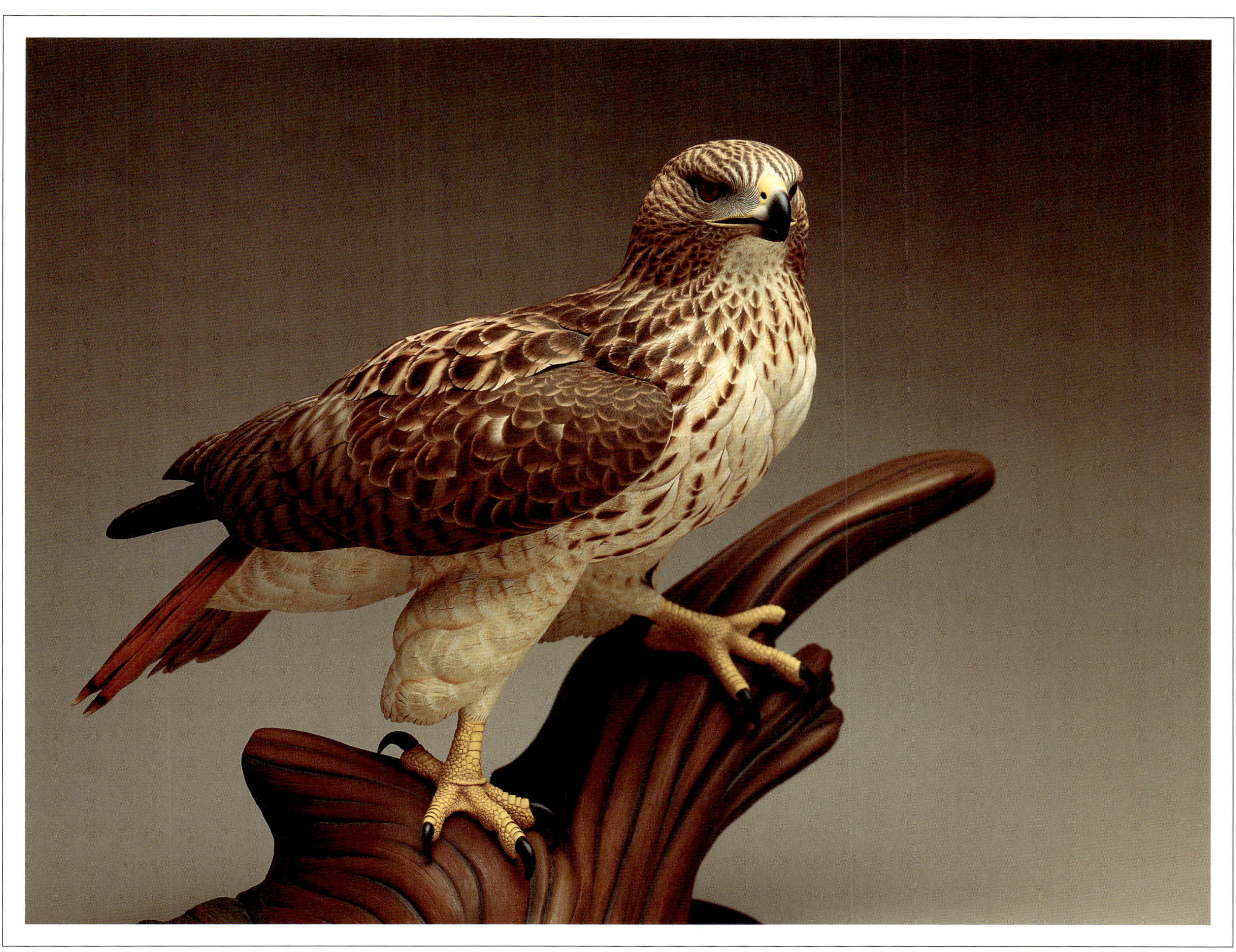

In its fierce stance, Brunet's life-size red-tailed hawk suggests action, frozen in the instant preceding attack or in the moment just before the hunter floats down to a kill waiting beneath him. An avid fan of raptors, Brunet has used his artistic carving and painterly touch to render a perch, reduced in its simplicity to its essential form.

Jett Brunet
Red-Tailed Hawk, 1988

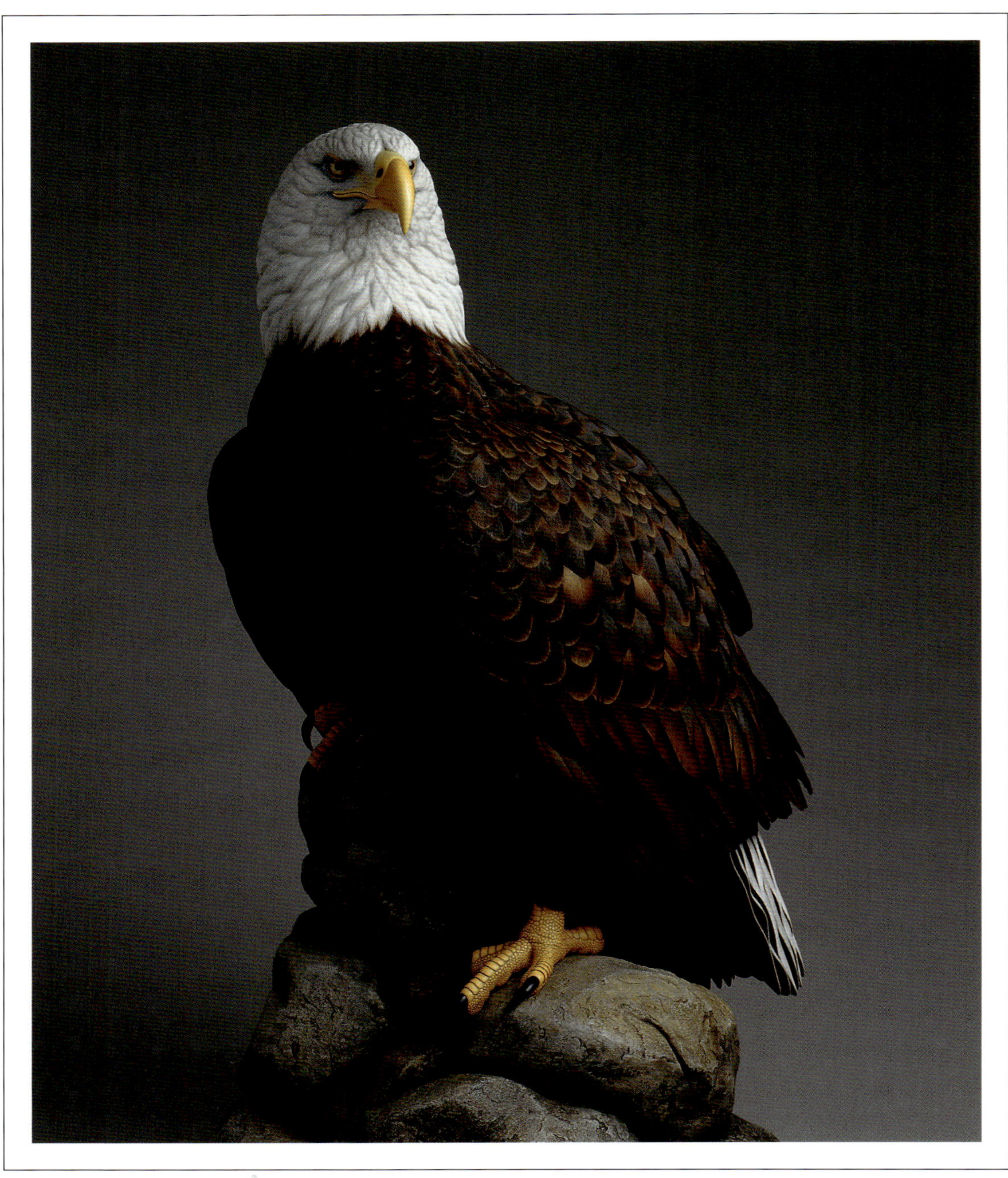

Jett Brunet
Bald Eagle, 1992

Brunet's larger-than-life approach to carving is never realized more fully than in his breathtaking female bald eagle. Brunet relied on a chain saw to shape the rough outline on this impressive four-foot-tall sculpture. He then refined the bird using hand tools, painting its magnificent plumage with oil and pearlescent powders. Unable to find a block of tupelo large enough to accommodate his mighty eagle, Brunet was forced to make the bird and the base from separate pieces.

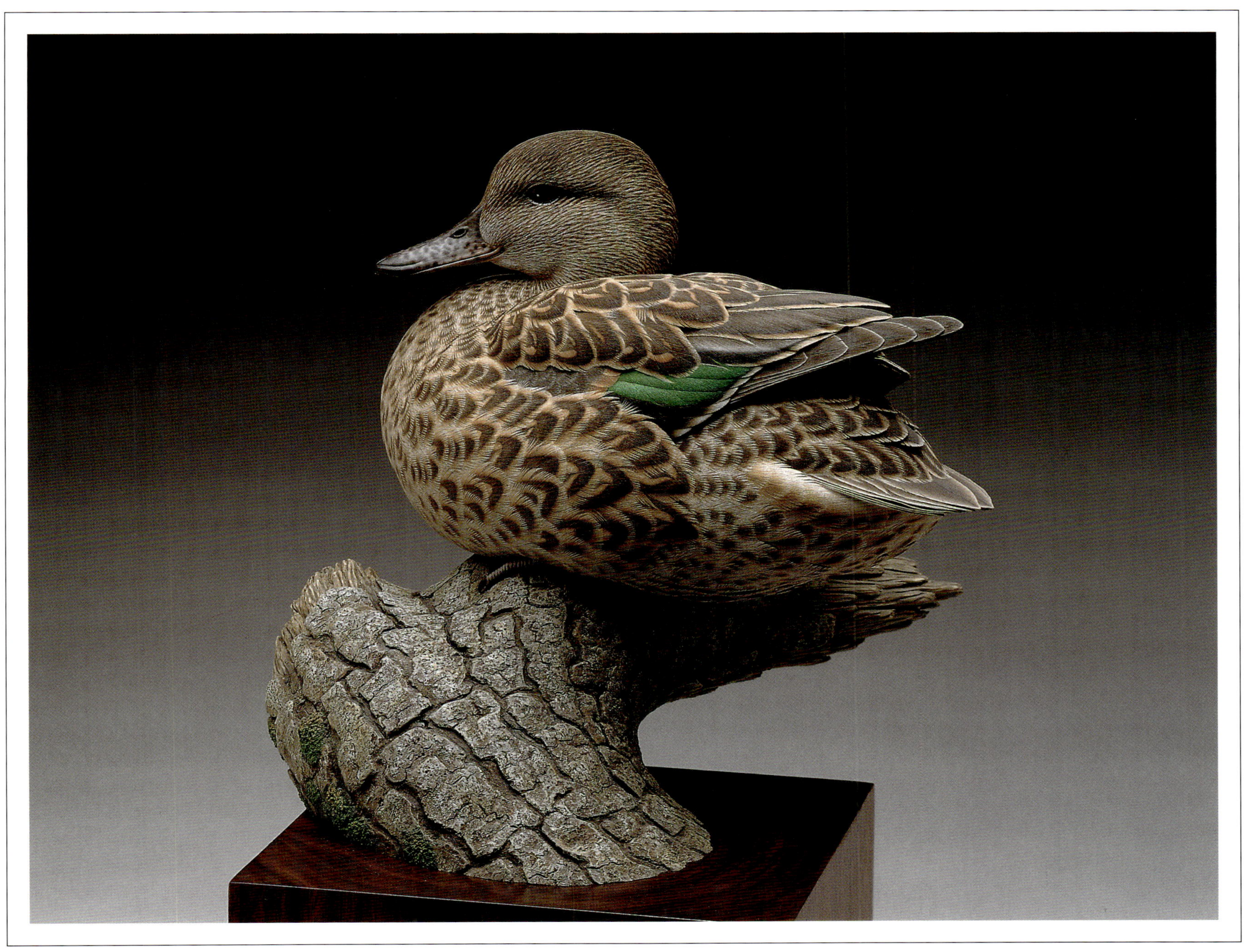

Jett Brunet
Green-Winged Teal, 1993

In sharp contrast to his power birds, Brunet's quiet green-winged teal hen, shuddering as it settles down onto its twisted perch, shows the range of Brunet's artistic abilities. "She is the sweetest and most peaceful little hen, and there is nothing on her that I would change," he says. Among the life-size sculpture's strengths, the circular water pattern, which appeared naturally in the walnut base, allowed Brunet to incorporate the base and pedestal into one.

Philip Galatas

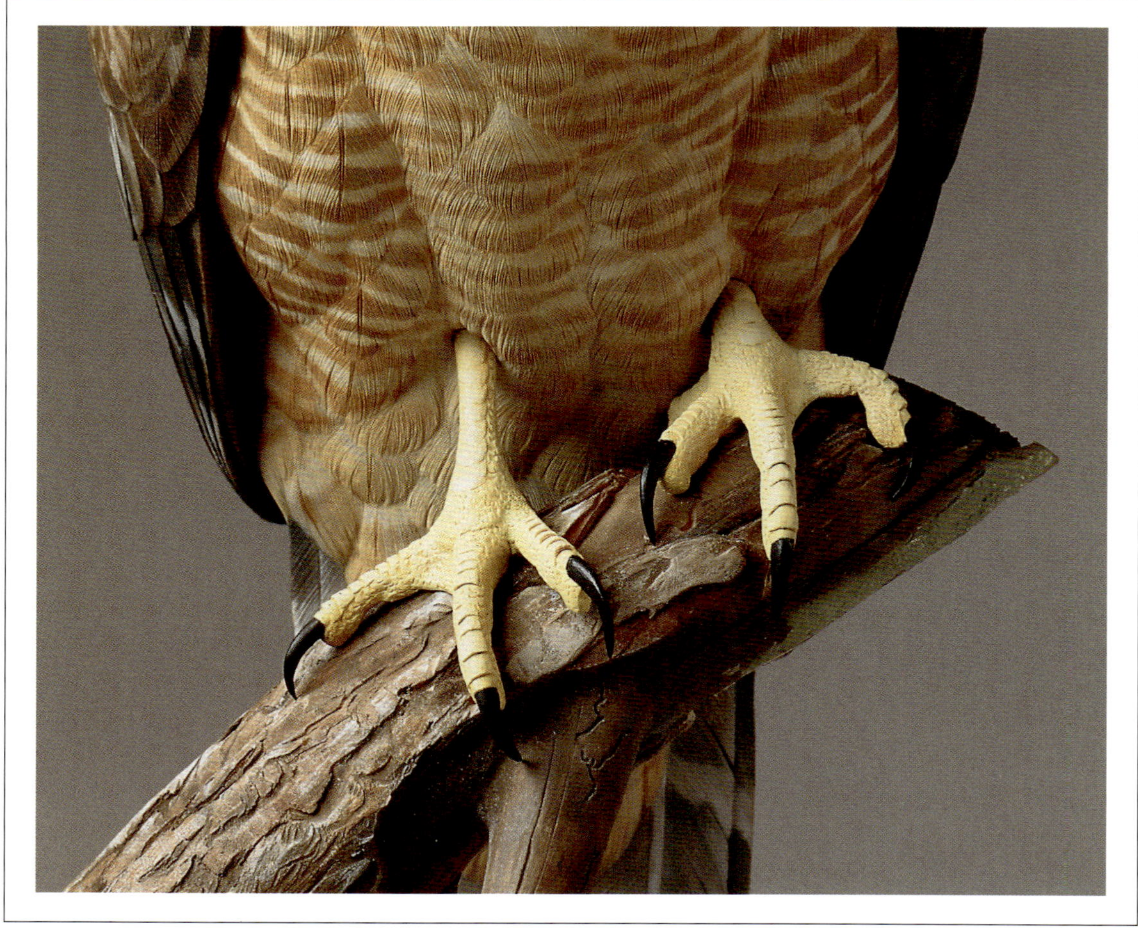

Philip Galatas
Florida Red-Shouldered Hawk, 1995 (detail)

"I want people to feel something when they look at my work," says Philip Galatas. "That's better than a ribbon any day." For Galatas, communicating images of beauty through sculptures of wild birds is a heartfelt artistic adventure, and the powerful emotional response that his work inspires is proof that the journey is on course.

Until 19 years ago, Galatas worked as a commercial artist. But the 45-year-old grew up in a rich waterfowl tradition in Louisiana, and using art to capture its wildlife and sensual landscape was in his blood. It took only a little encouragement from an art instructor for Galatas to take up carving in 1977. Since then, he has put his heart into creating lifelike, stylized designs.

Steadfastly sincere about the integrity of his work, Galatas, who now lives in Humboldt, Nebraska, respects the ebb and flow of his own creativity, often retreating for two or three years to find fresh inspiration. Each time, he comes back strong: a 24-month hiatus from world competition concluded with back-to-back best-in-world miniature honors in 1989 and 1990. "When I start a piece, I think to myself, 'I'm going to dig deep for this,' " explains Galatas. "But until I'm finished, I never really know where it's going to take me."

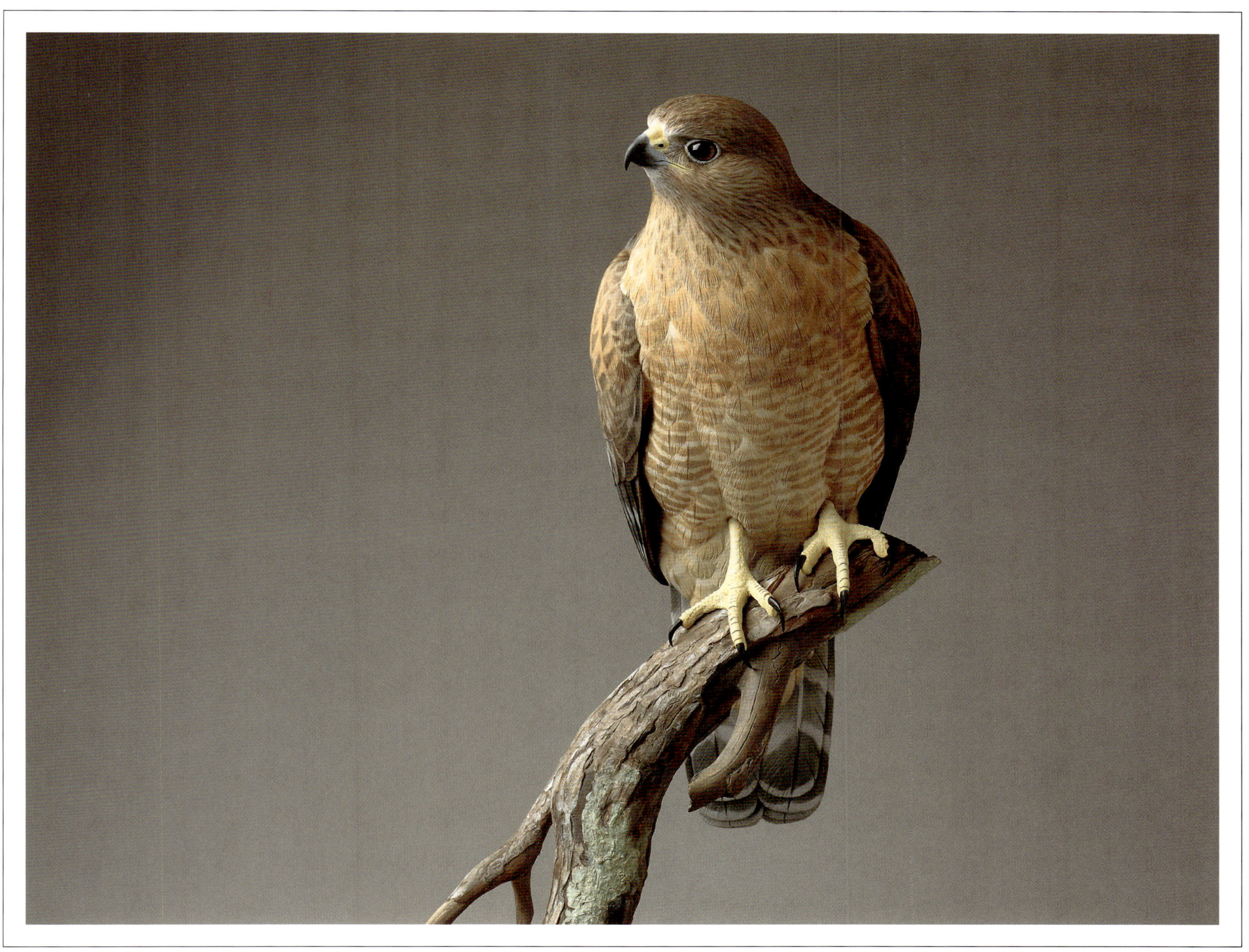

Philip Galatas
Florida Red-Shouldered Hawk, 1995

Projecting the poignant longing that the artist feels for his Louisiana home, Galatas' life-size red-shouldered hawk perched on the swamp-soaked bark of a southern pecan tree captivates and touches audiences wherever it is displayed. By focusing his efforts on the bird's face, Galatas has portrayed a kinder, gentler raptor. He has created the warm and richly blended colors of the bird's orange-phase plumage using artist's oils and small brushes.

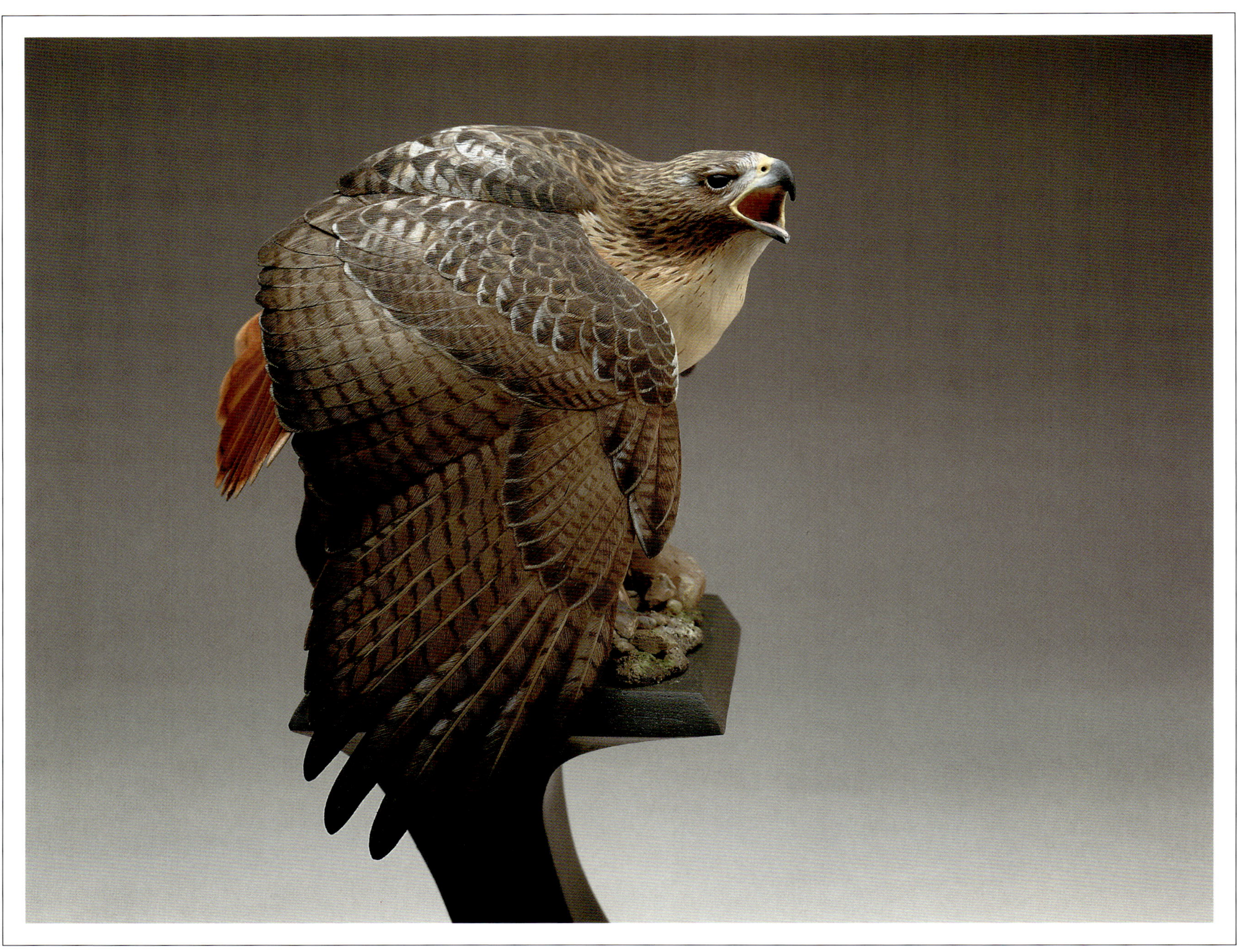

Philip Galatas
Red-Tailed Hawk
Highland Defender, 1990

"This was the hardest bird I ever did," says Galatas. "Everything was completely conscious." Taking great pains to perfect the design and composition of this miniature red-tailed hawk, Galatas positioned the bird sheltering its prey from competition and its habitat from human encroachment. Its massive outstretched wings reveal the hawk's elegant contours and rich colors.

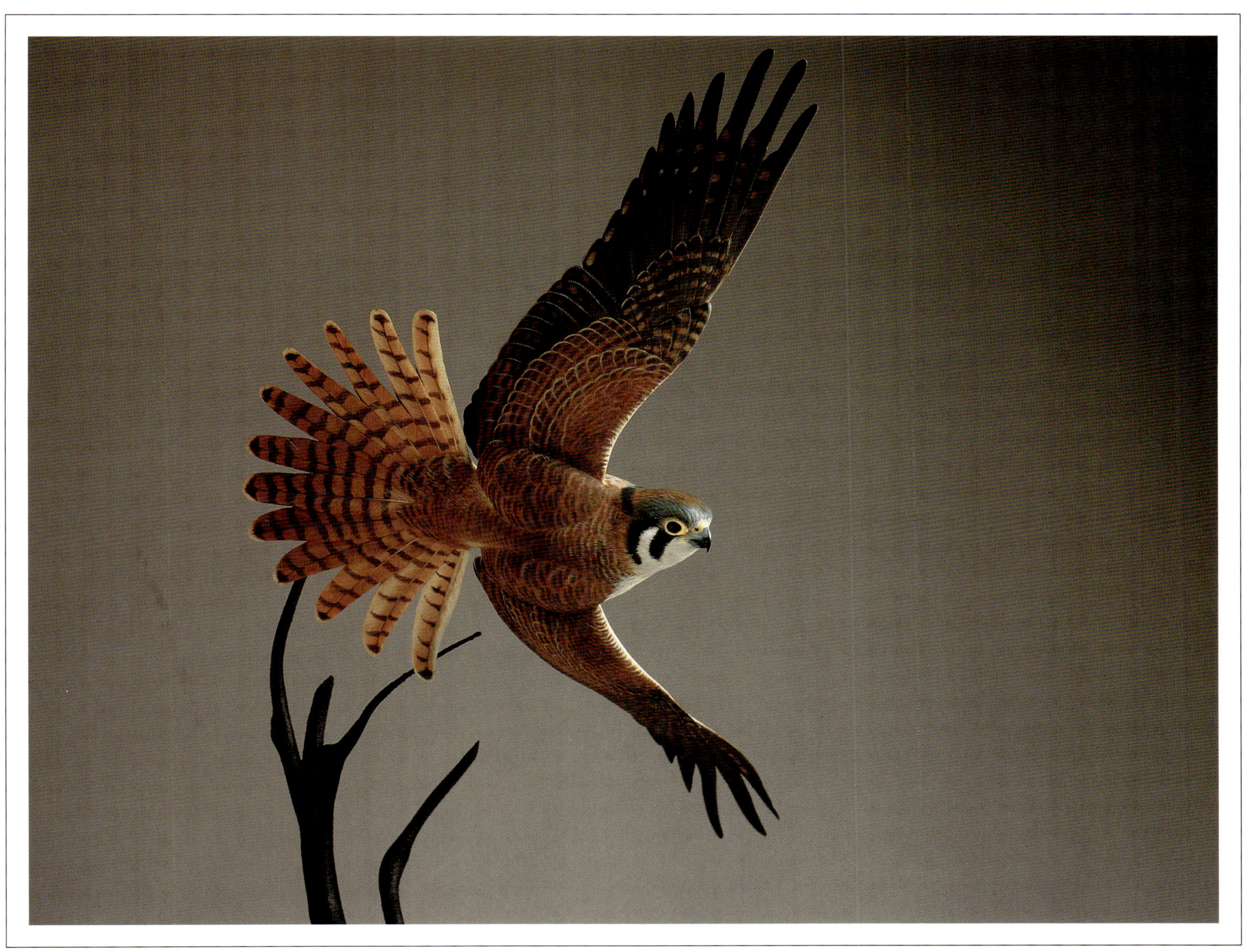

Before finding a composition that pleased him, Galatas took his cutting torch to this life-size American kestrel and removed a snake from its talons and some marsh grass from the background. With this simpler carving, he has created a freewheeling bird of prey soaring effortlessly on fully spread wings.

Philip Galatas
American Kestrel
Wind Rider, 1992

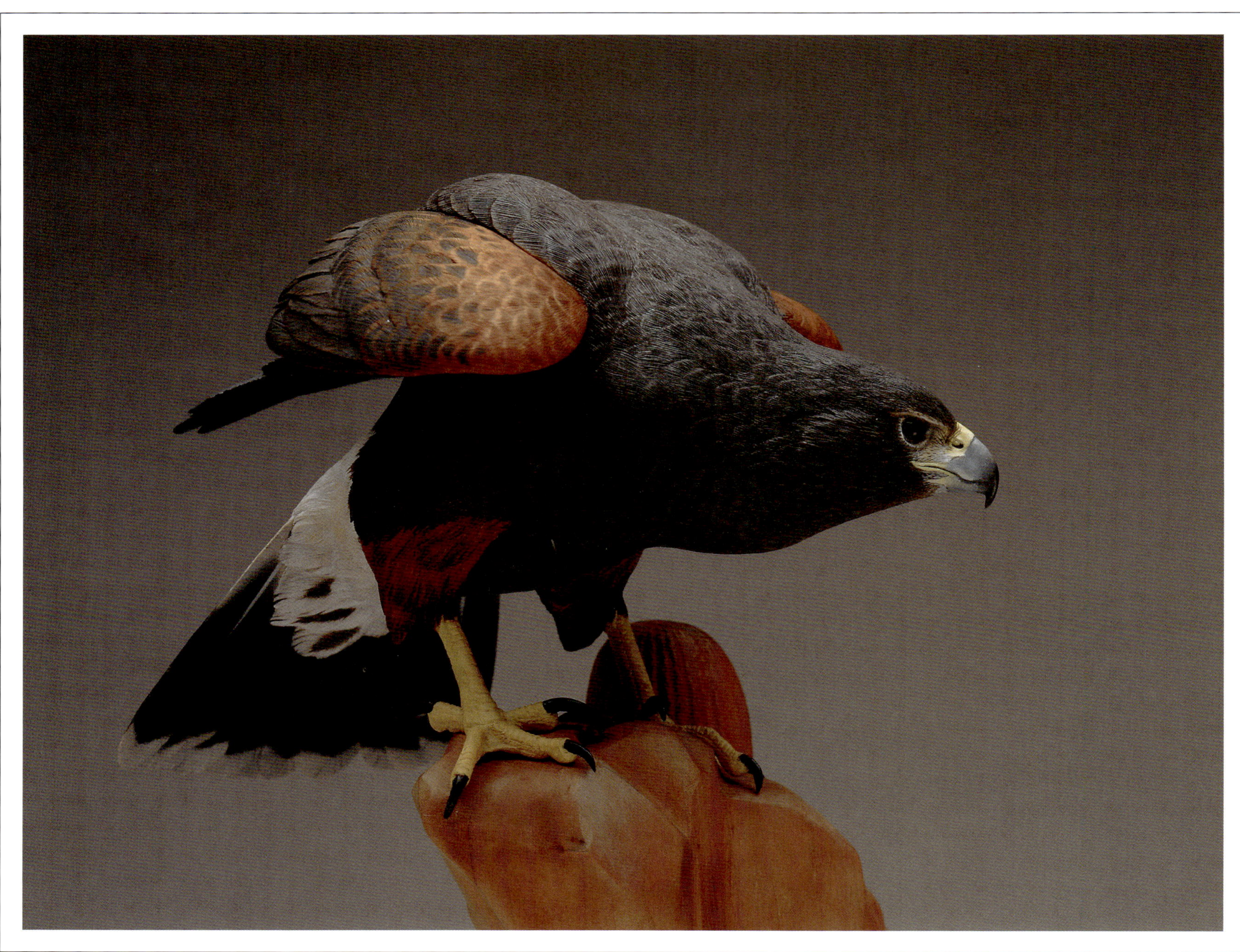

Philip Galatas
Harris' Hawk, 1995

With its head snaking down and its rear feathers ruffled as they catch a breeze, Galatas' eight-inch bird of prey looks as if it is about to lift into the air. The miniature Harris' hawk, perched on an abstract cactus made of cherry, captures the mood of the Southwest. To create an unadorned look for the sculpture, Galatas brushed stain on the wood to enhance its natural color.

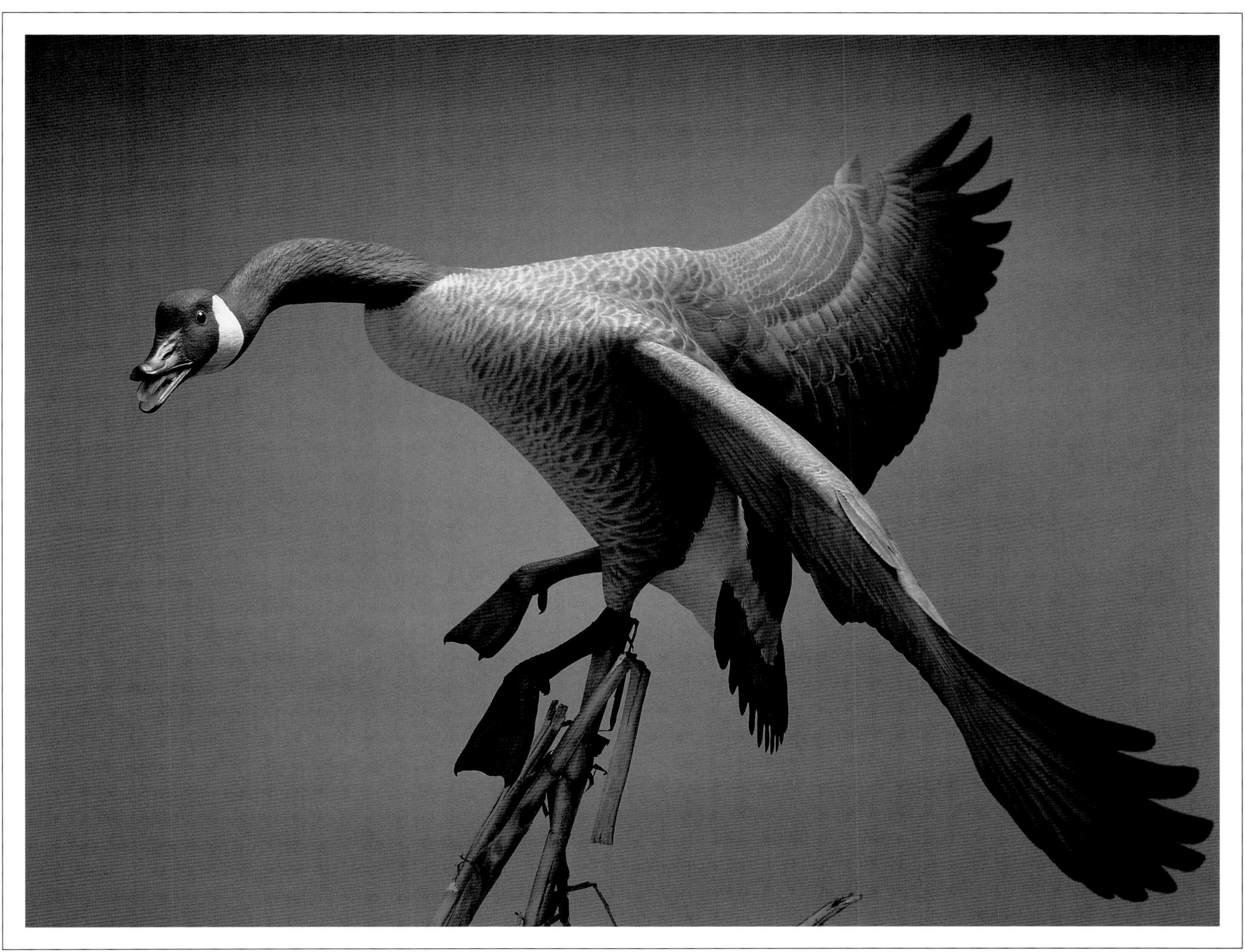

Galatas' gangly life-size Canada goose, with its daunting six-foot wingspan, took more than two years to complete. The sculpture, which was the featured centerpiece at the Easton Waterfowl Festival, was assembled from three pieces of tupelo.

Philip Galatas
Canada Goose
Ballet on the Wind, 1989

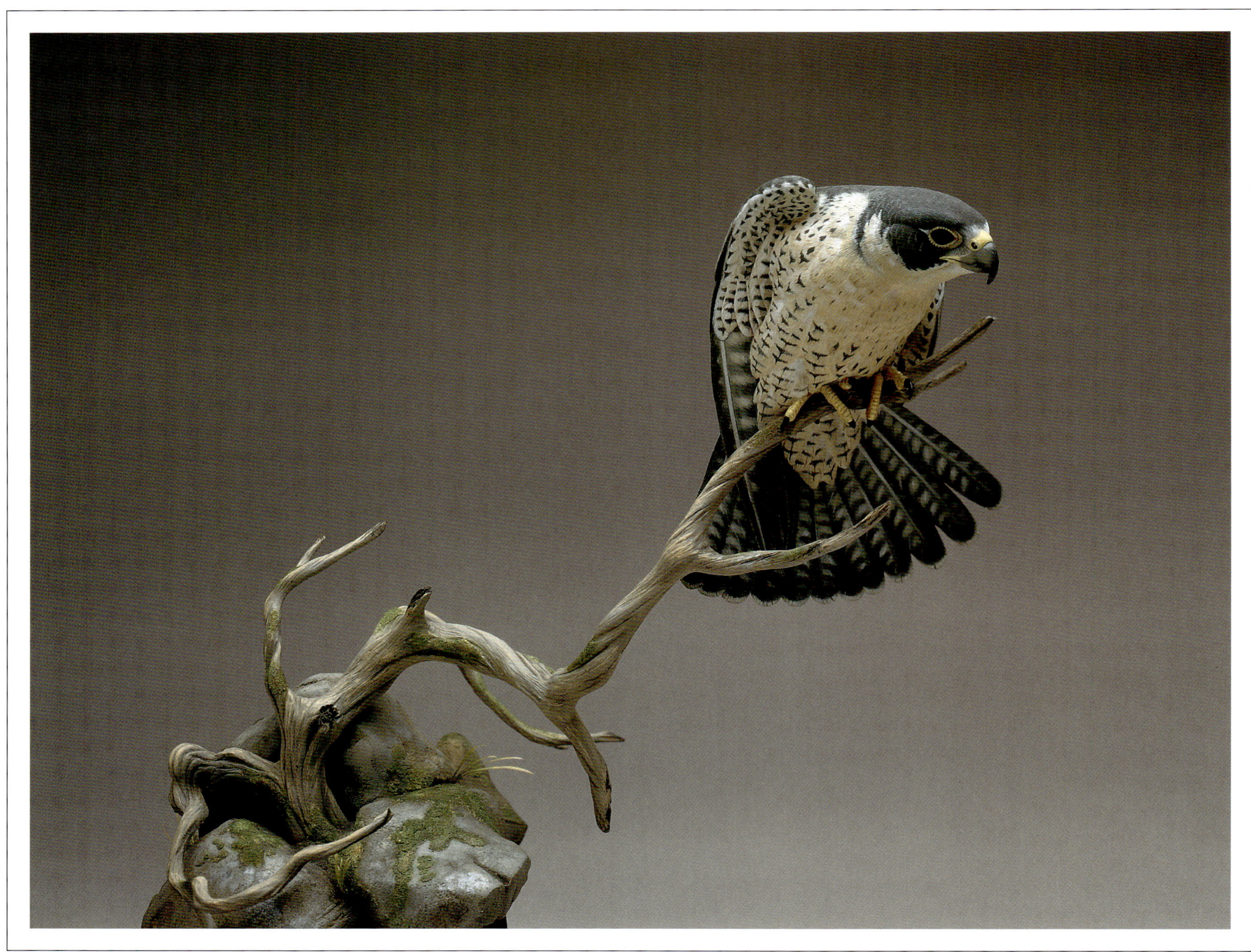

Philip Galatas
Peregrine Falcon
Watch On, 1989

By positioning the miniature peregrine falcon off-center from the base, Galatas establishes the bird as the focus for his piece and increases its airborne feeling. Field studies, sketches, photographs, visits to avian rehabilitation centers and study skins provide the background for Galatas' work, and a combination of knives, gouges and power grinders allows him to bring his ideas to life.

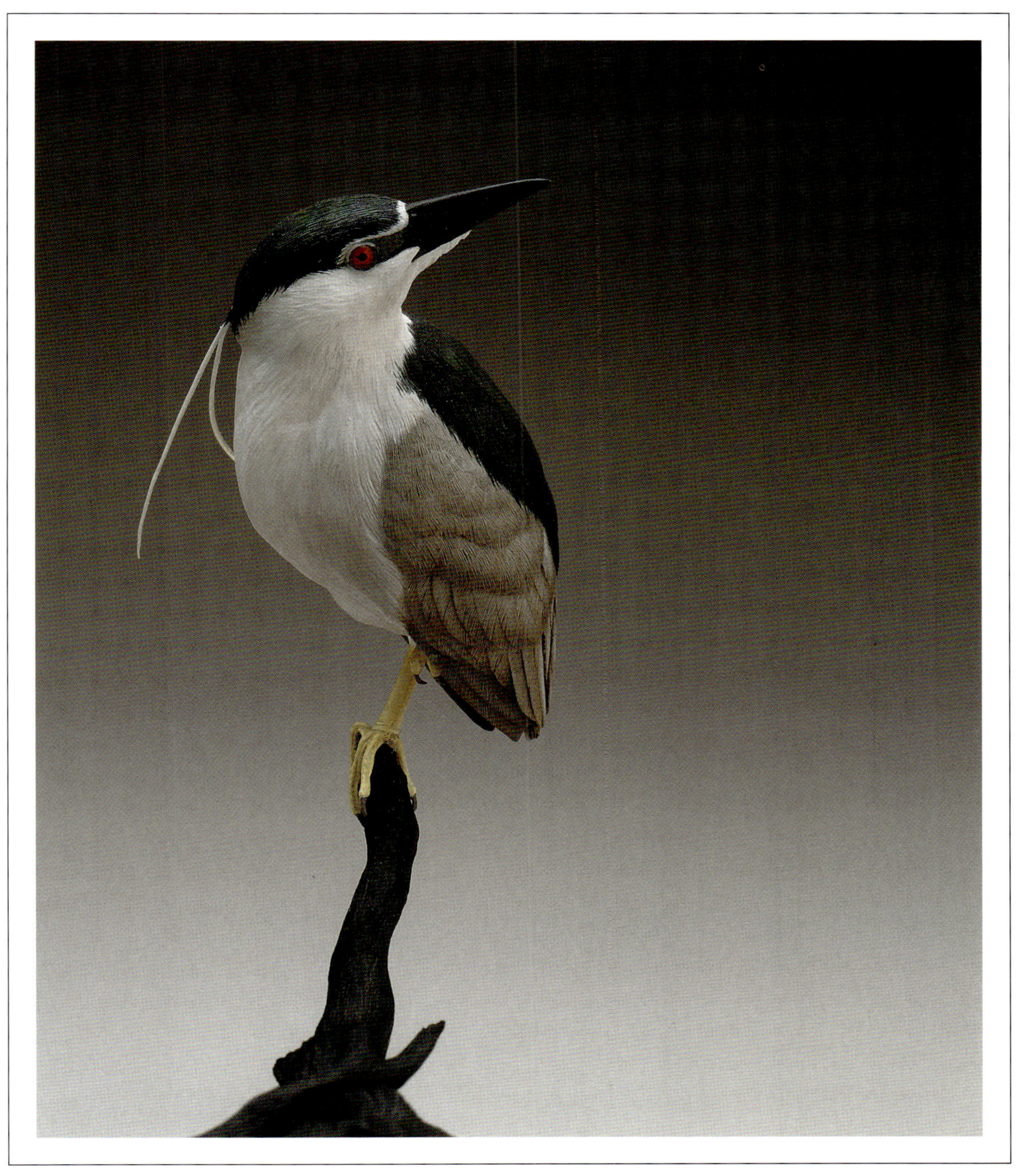

Philip Galatas
Black-Crowned Night-Heron, 1996

Galatas returns to his Louisiana home once again with a miniature sculpture that deftly captures the sly skill of a black-crowned night-heron on the hunt. Blackish green tones transform the moss-covered deadfall, which emerges from the still water of a Southern bayou in day's waning light, into an elegant perch for the artist's statuesque fisher.

Patrick Godin

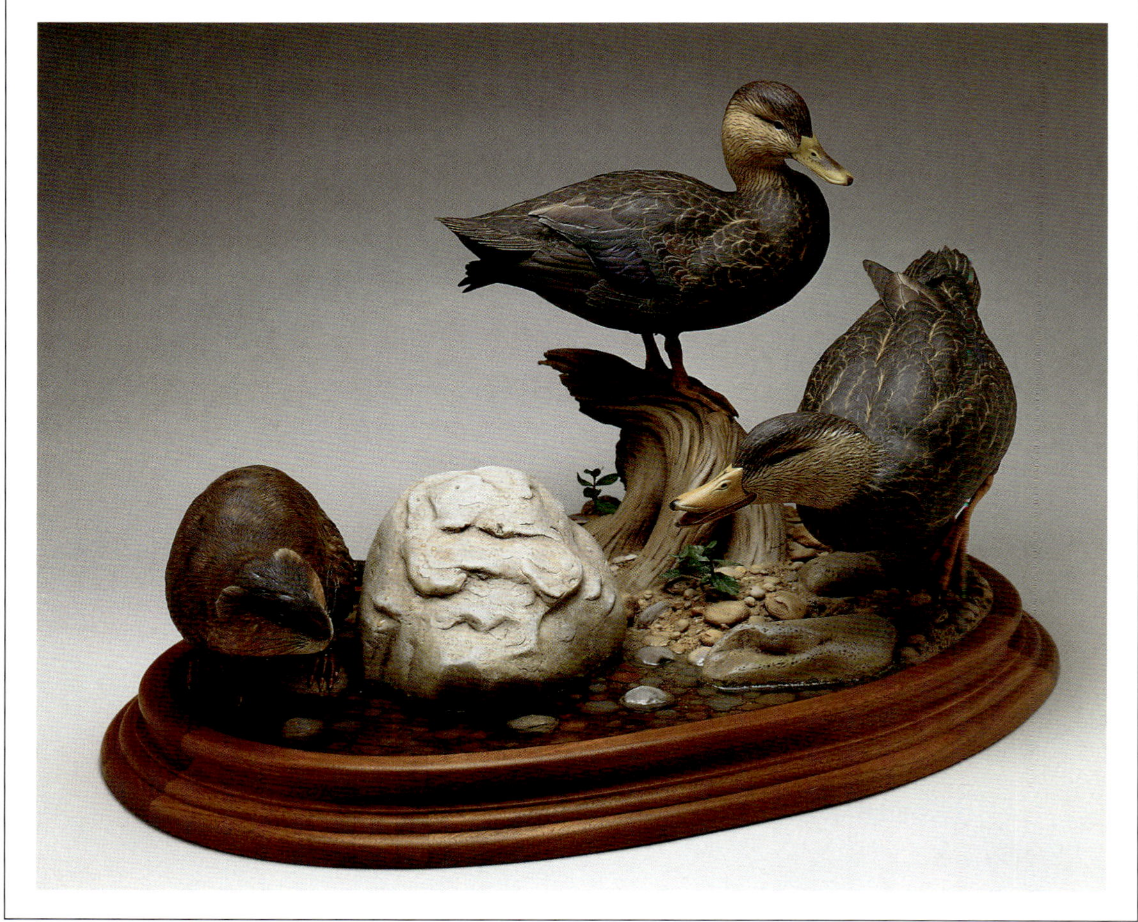

Patrick Godin
Black Duck Pair and Muskrat
Along the Grand, 1982

Godin's life-size sculpture was inspired by boyhood days spent skipping stones and building rafts along Ontario's Grand River. Even in this simpler style, he distinguishes himself as an artist. The carving is designed around a descending spiral that flows from the hen's bill through the back of the territorial drake to the muskrat. To energize the scene, Godin has incorporated concentric rings and rebounding water droplets on the river's surface.

"The unique aspect of a bird is sometimes very subtle," admits Patrick Godin. It comes as no surprise, then, that the Paris, Ontario, artist often turns to understated subjects, such as waterfowl or game birds, to project his enlightened ornithological insight.

The meticulous finish on Godin's sculptures—the feather detail and lifelike painting—forms the foundation for his classical, realistic style, which is rooted in a childhood fascination with birds. His enthusiasm for avian subjects initially found expression in decoy making when he was 14 and became the focus of his studies at university, where he specialized in waterfowl ecology. Since launching his career as a wildfowl artist in 1979, Godin has consistently created ground-breaking sculptures that have helped expand the boundaries of traditional carving by reflecting innovation in concept, composition or materials.

As the 43-year-old artist expands his vision of nature, he treats his audiences to increasingly intimate ways of seeing wild winged species. "Ideas separate the artist from the accomplished carver," explains Godin. "After a certain point, there are no technical challenges left, so you turn your attention to the message you want the carving to convey."

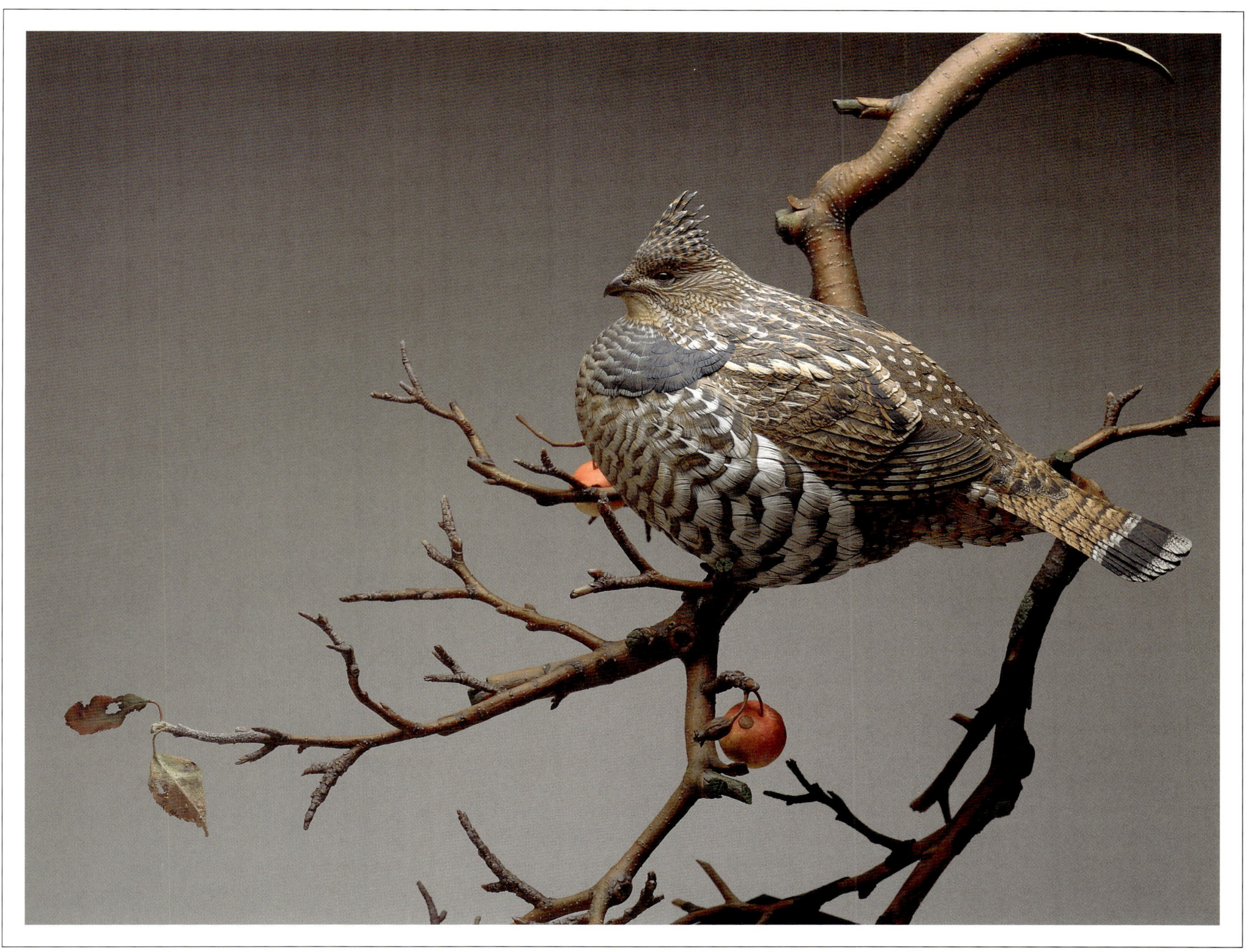

Perched in a neglected apple tree, Godin's life-size ruffed grouse conveys the familiar forlorn feeling of a deserted rural homestead. Unpicked ripened red fruit highlights the cryptically colored bird that defensively ruffles its plumage against the late-autumn chill. Godin draws from an assortment of reference materials—live birds, photographs, sketches and clay models—in his painstaking execution of the detailed sculpture.

Patrick Godin
Ruffed Grouse
Abandoned Orchard, 1994

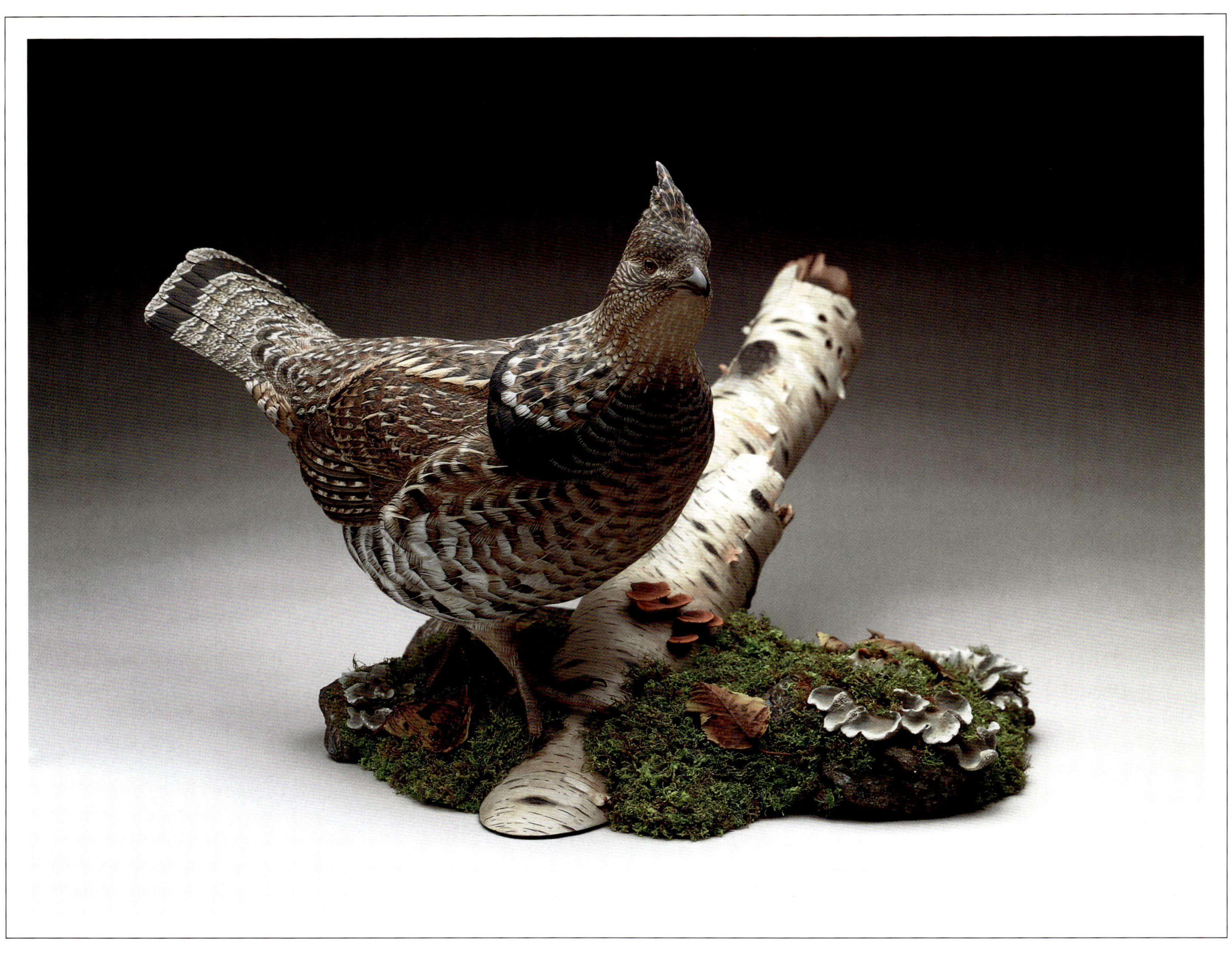

Patrick Godin
Birch Lake Ruffed Grouse, 1993

Godin's life-size ruffed grouse reflects the full measure of his mixed-media style. In addition to carving the bird, birch bark, lichen and small rocks from tupelo, Godin fashioned paper for the leaves and used granite for the large rocks, copper for the feet and chemically treated nylon scouring fibers for the moss. A wooden form supporting the sculpture base lends an undulated natural shape to the forest floor and animates the bird.

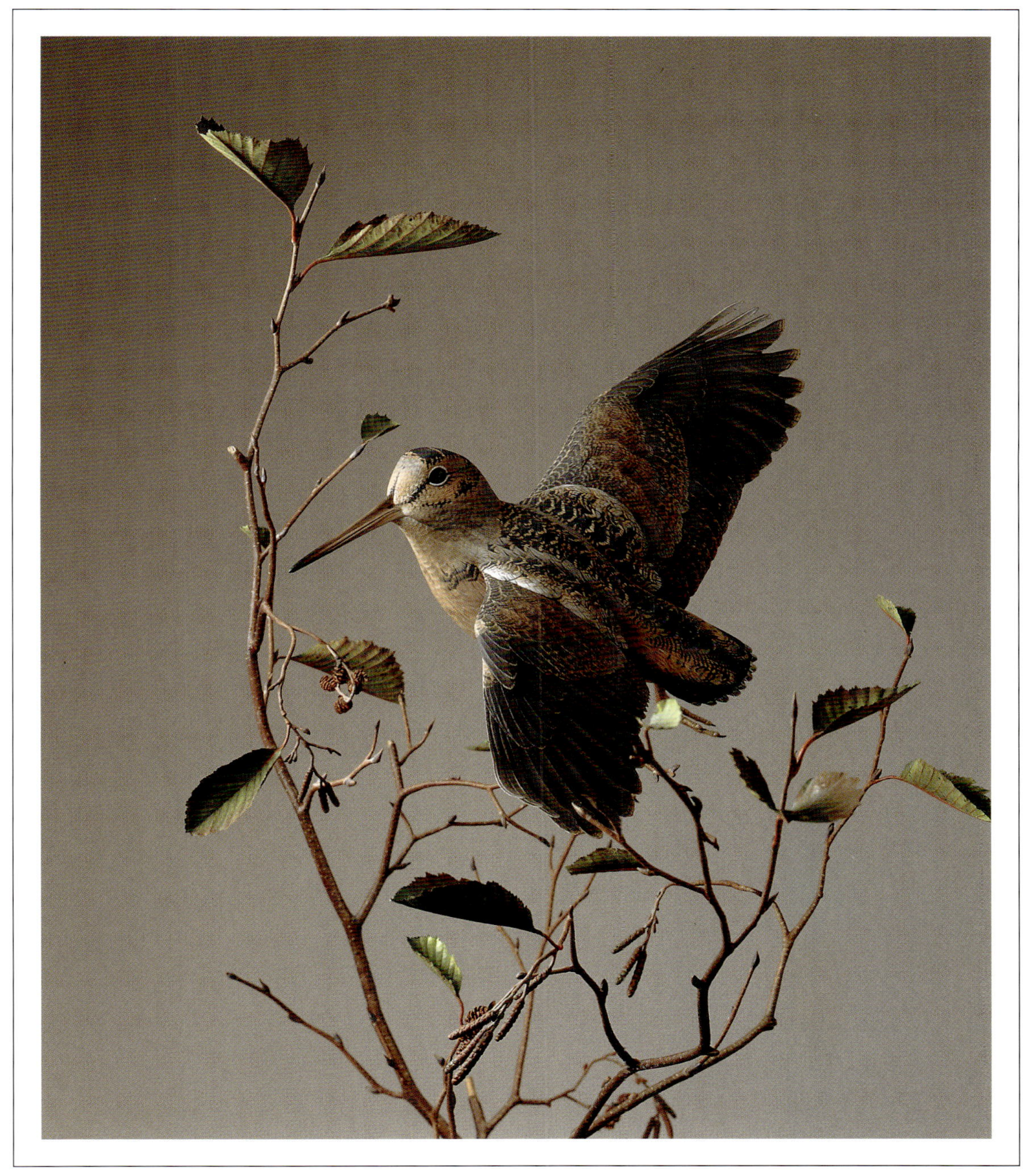

As though it had been flushed from the underbrush, Godin's American woodcock magically floats past the tips of tender alder branches before landing. Using knives and power grinders to carve the life-size bird and undercut its feathers, Godin then etched the fine detail with wood-burning pens. Applying acrylic paints in multiple washes, he was able to create the luminous texture of dappled sunlight on the bird's plumage.

Patrick Godin
American Woodcock
Descent Through the Alders, 1995

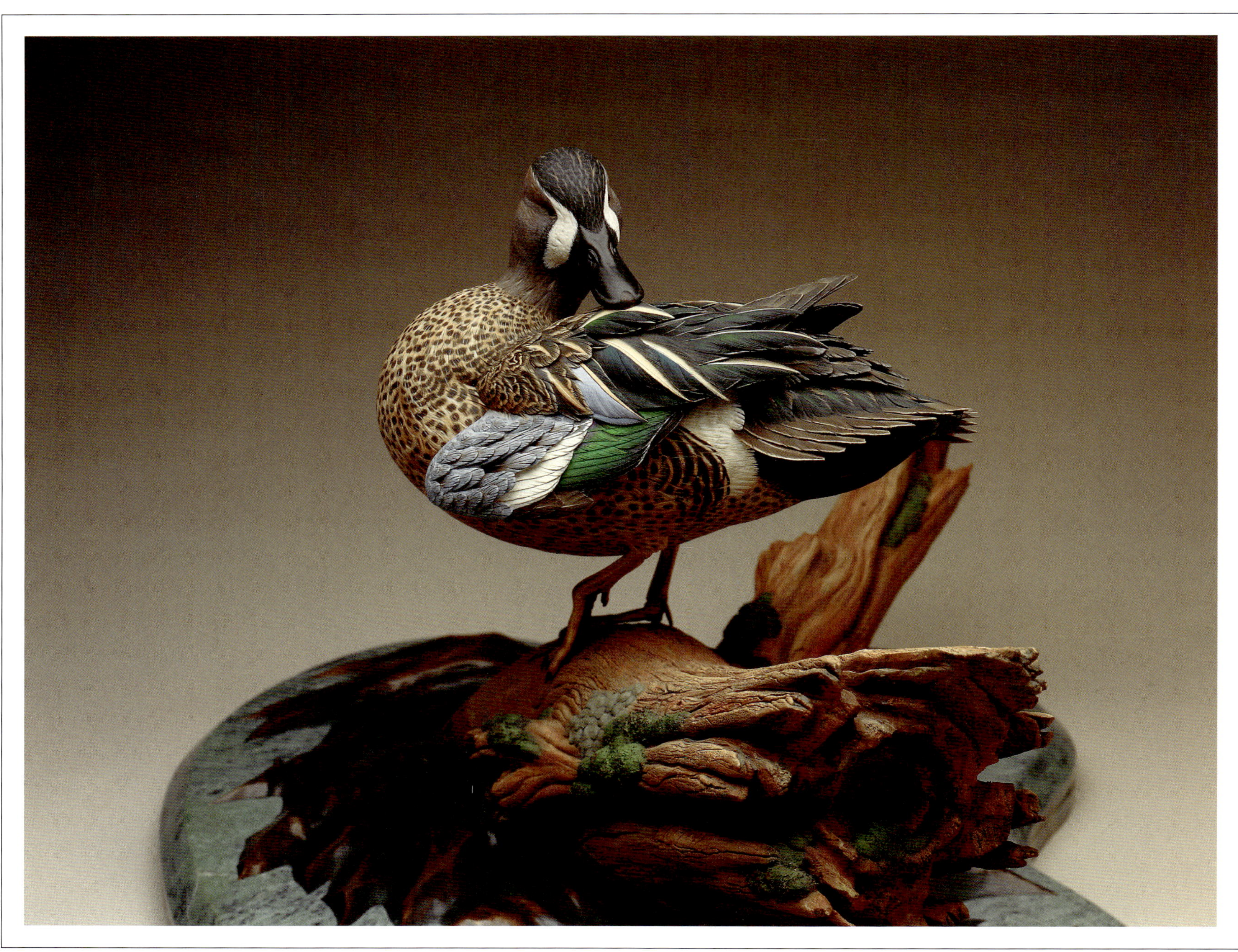

Patrick Godin
Blue-Winged Teal
Pond Edge, 1991

This life-size preening blue-winged teal standing on a partially submerged log represents an important transitional work for Godin, whose career until this point had been almost exclusively dedicated to creating floating decorative decoys. The artist made an innovative decision to use cast bronze as the rippling water; the bronze was treated with chemicals and heat to achieve the patina and the foamy finish.

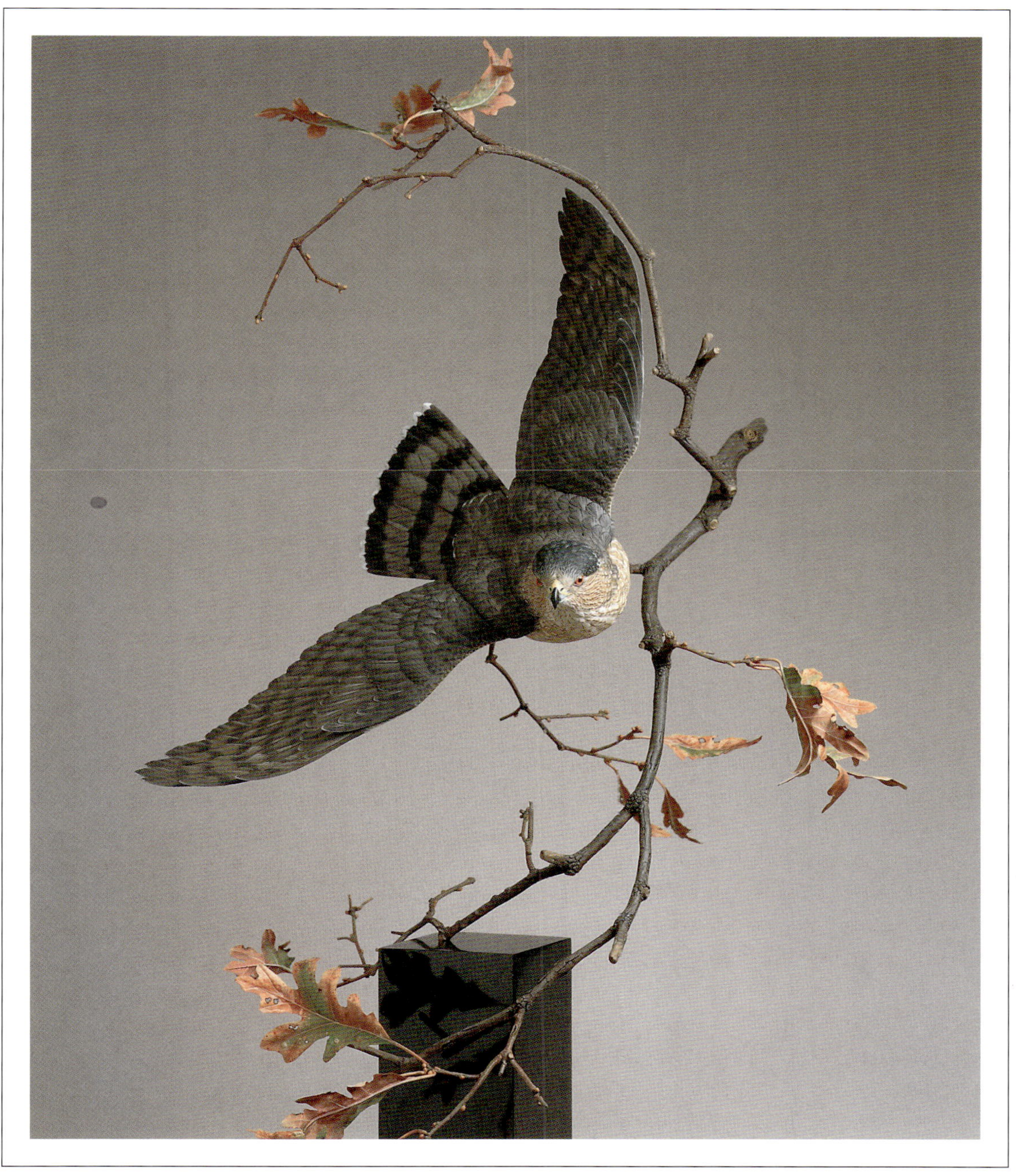

Patrick Godin
Cooper's Hawk
The Chase, 1996

An arc of delicate oak branches elegantly frames the curve of Godin's life-size Cooper's hawk in flight. To emphasize both the control and the dynamic energy of the bird on the hunt, Godin turned the tips of its wing feathers up and fanned its tail. After forging the branches from bronze, reinforced with a steel infrastructure, Godin cut the autumn oak leaves out of paper-thin sheets of brass and burned them with a soldering torch to create the look of decay.

Bob Guge

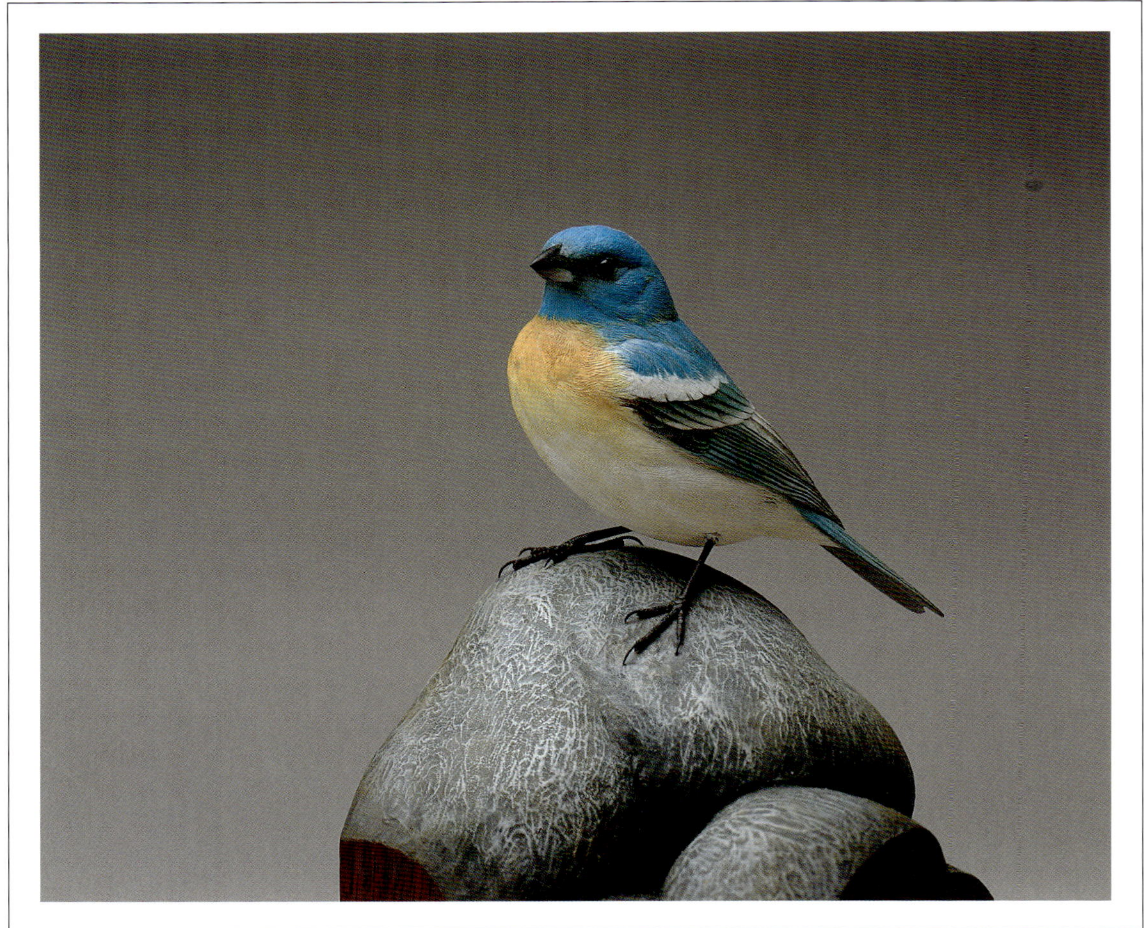

Bob Guge
Lazuli Bunting, 1995

In Guge's life-size sculpture of the western bunting, the bird's cold, gray rock perch gradually becomes the walnut base. Guge makes the bird the focus of his sculpture with a simple style, unadorned with other elements that might act as a distraction. Disciplined painting with acrylics highlights the colorful turquoise plumage on the bird's back.

"I'm always looking ahead," explains Bob Guge. "Constantly doing different things allows me to keep fresh." Variety is the spice of Guge's endless creativity. The four-time world champion divides his time between decorative sculptures, teaching carving classes to beginners and creating "smoothies"—carvings that are painted in detail but lack the undercuts and feather renderings of decoratives.

Guge began his full-time carving career in 1979, the offshoot of a hobby that he had shared with his father as a boy. After starting with floating decoys, Guge soon added songbirds to his carving repertoire as a means of expanding his artistic options.

Guge's sculpture is grounded in a fundamental love and understanding of the subject that he nurtures with hours of field study near his Sleepy Hollow, Illinois, home. "You need to look at birds to know how to carve them," he says. "I spend the time that it takes to understand a species, and then I can imagine it in my sculpture."

The artist, 44, is completely self-taught, and his hard-won knowledge makes him a compassionate and empathetic teacher. According to Guge, his interaction with students creates a synergy that makes him a better artist: "I learn more about carving from teaching than working on my own."

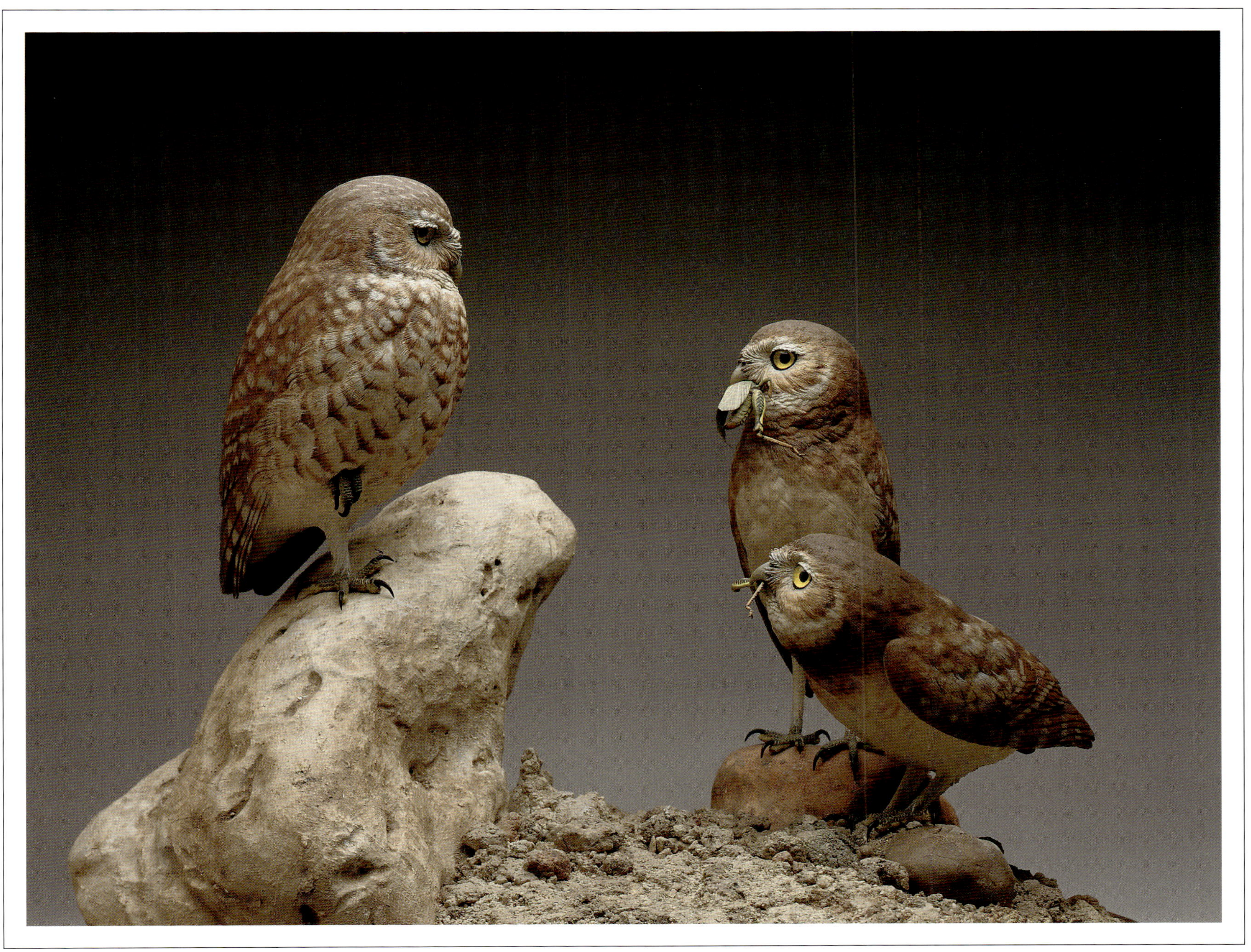

Two juvenile burrowing owls return to the nest with their first catch in Guge's life-size family portrait. By mixing putty to shape the loose soil and carving all other elements from wood, Guge has created a sculpture that projects the ease and spontaneity typical of his work.

Bob Guge
Burrowing Owls
Two for Approval, 1988

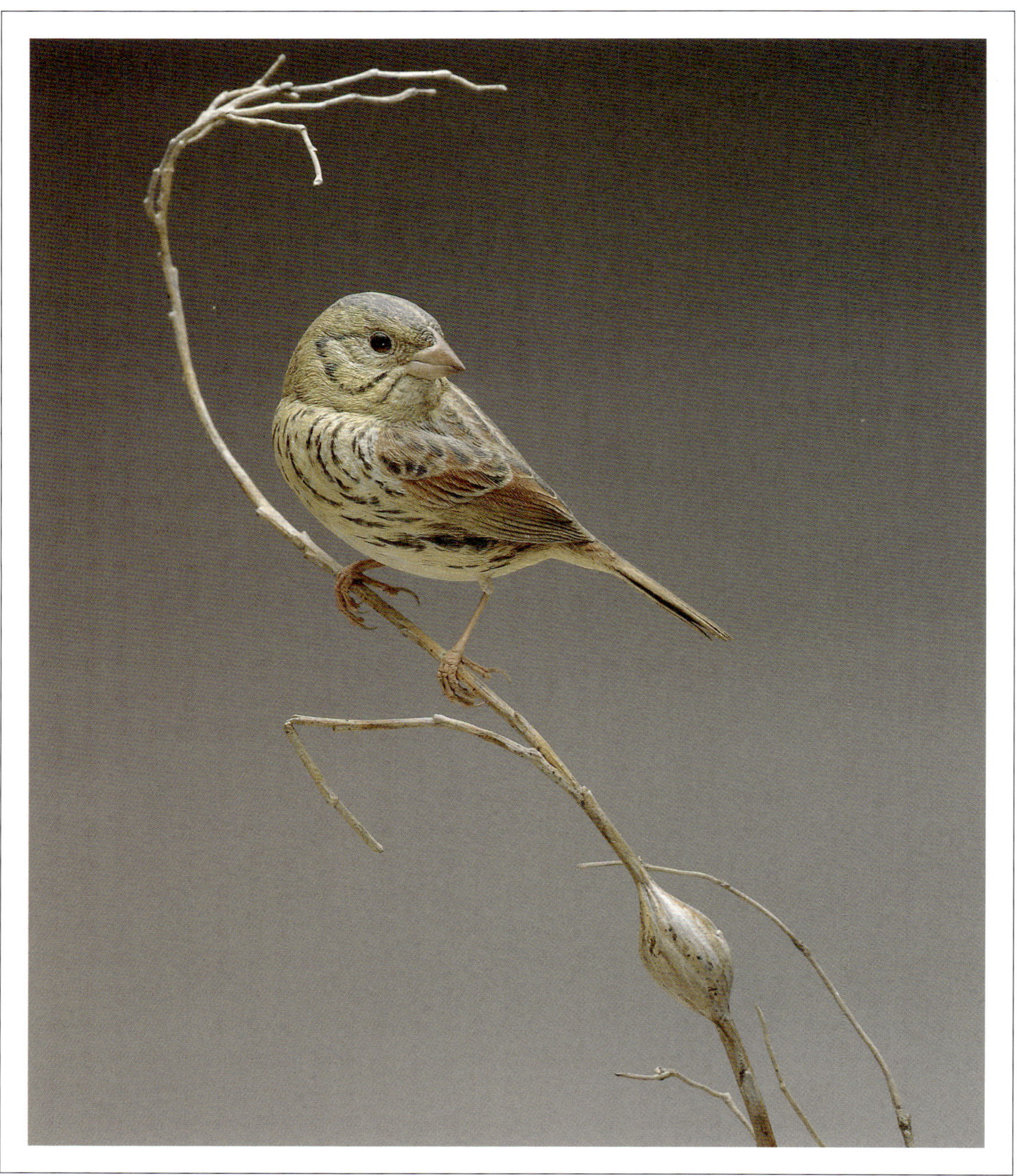

Bob Guge
Henslow's Sparrow, 1989

Fingerlike fronds of goldenrod form a halo around the sparrow's head in Guge's life-size songbird sculpture, the first of two works in a series. With his sophisticated use of color, Guge has transformed the humble bird into a breathtaking wildlife model.

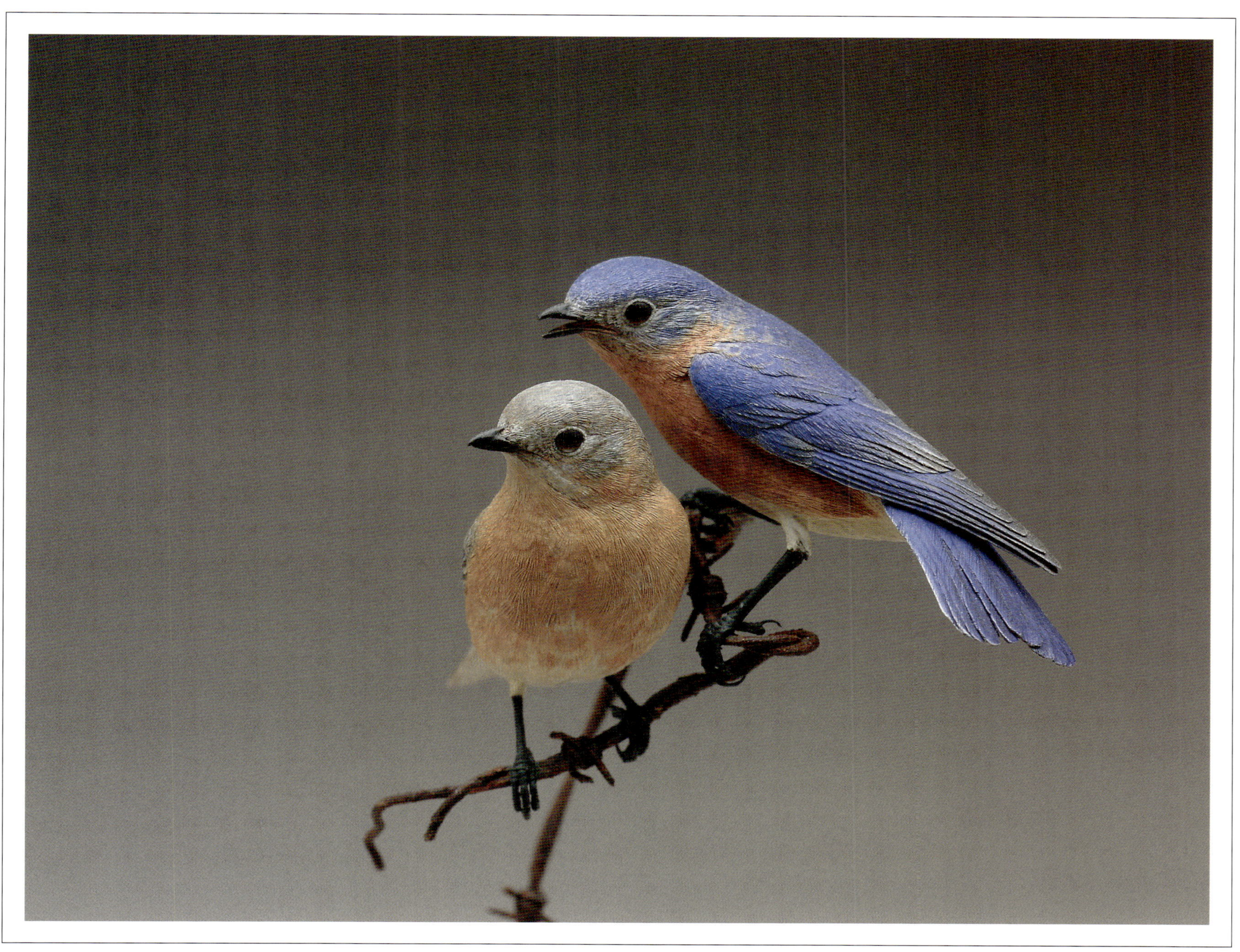

Perched on a rusty barbed-wire fence, Guge's miniature bluebirds look quizzically off into the distance of the Northeastern countryside. A power carver, Guge uses modern tools to create his tupelo carvings, roughing out samples of each step in wood. To achieve the aged and corroded look of the birds' perch, Guge fashioned brass wire and coated it with sawdust before painting it.

Bob Guge
Eastern Bluebirds, 1987

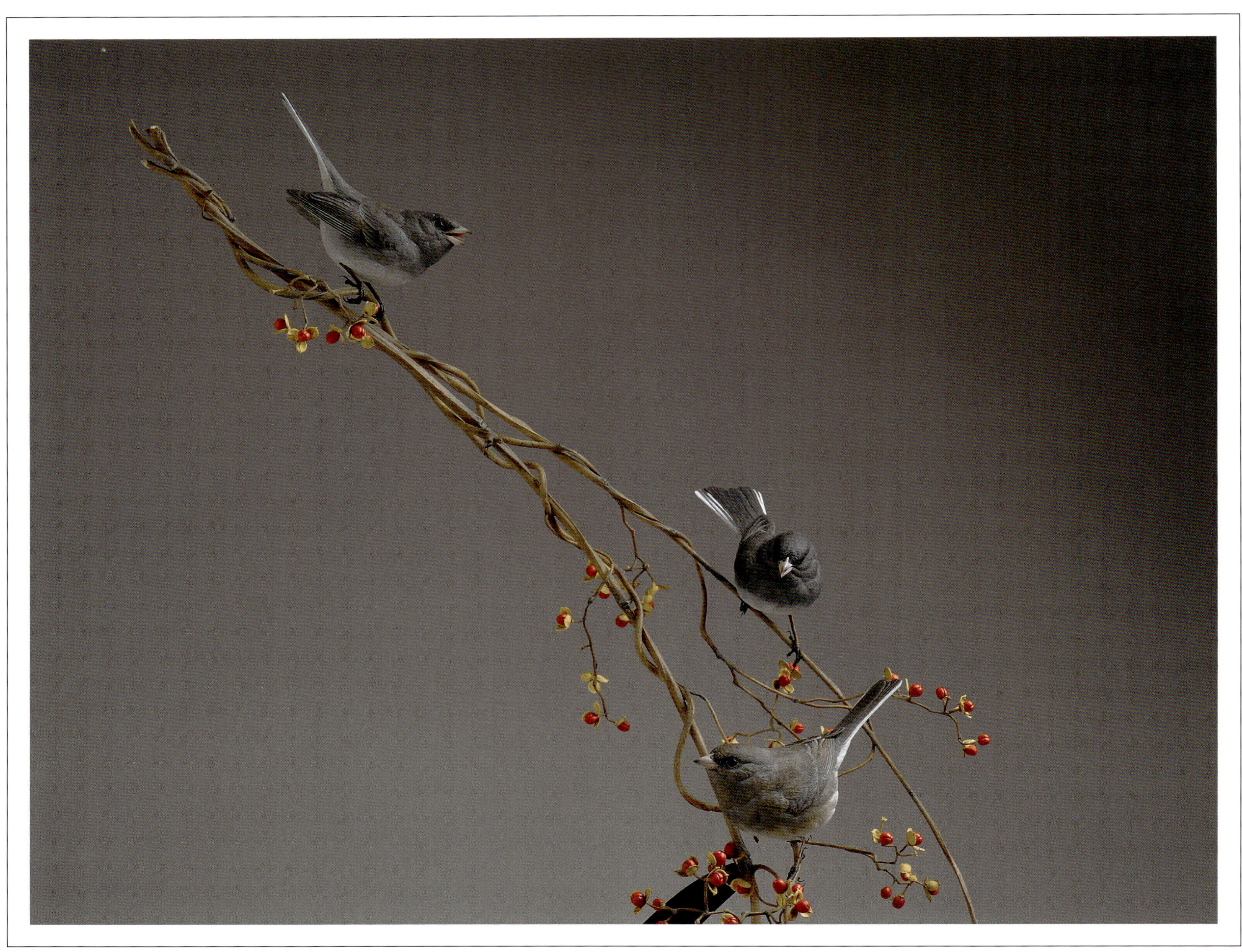

Bob Guge
Juncos and Bittersweet, 1995

Buff-colored birds highlighted by colorful clusters of bittersweet set the stage for the animated flirtation among strutting dark-eyed juncos. Guge first roughed out the life-size sculpture in wood, establishing its composition, then carved the birds from tupelo, forging the branches from brass and copper and shaping the berries from epoxy. The yellowish shells of the berries were made from metal stamped out in cookie-cutter fashion.

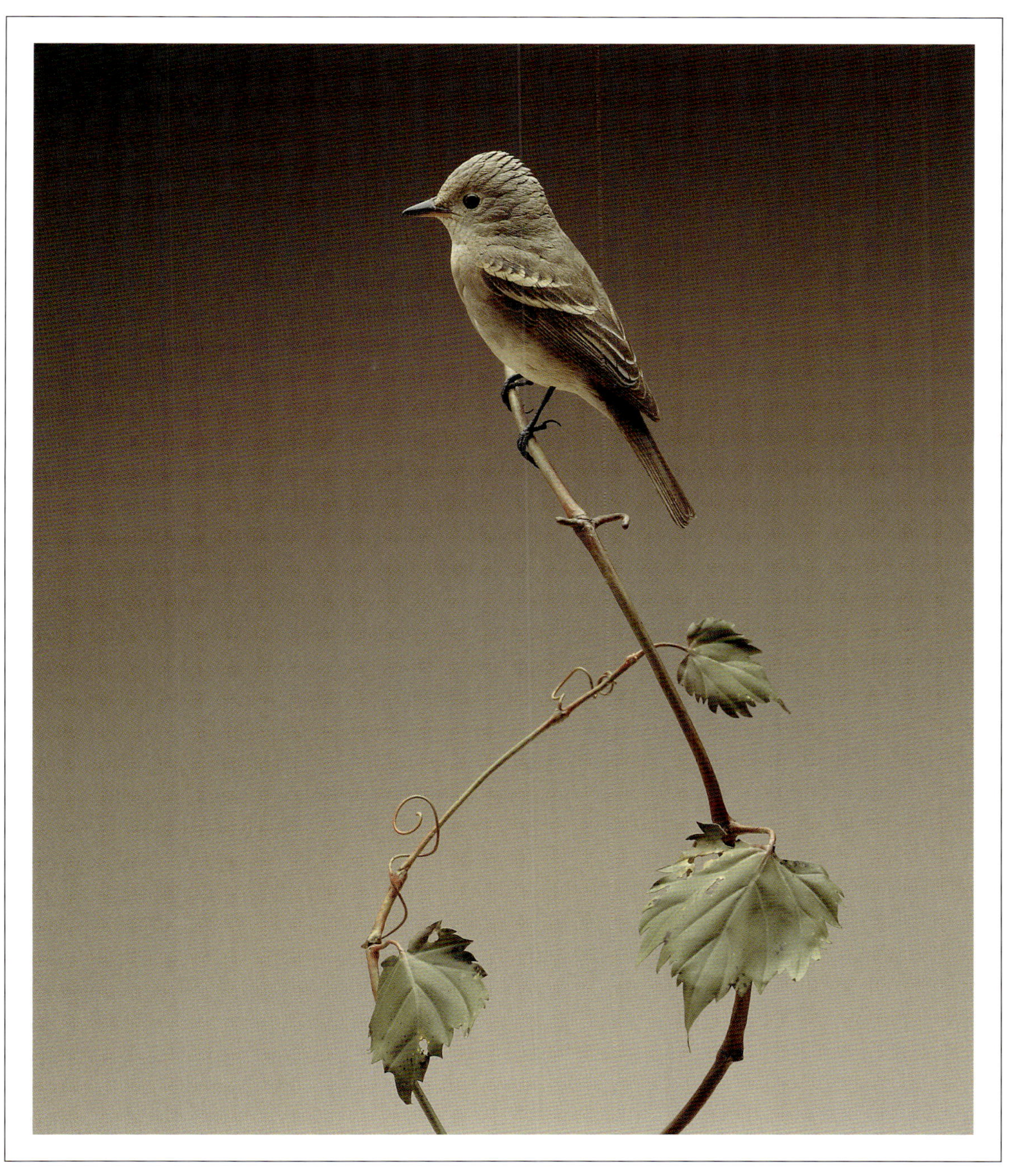

Perched atop a sinewy wild grapevine, Guge's tawny-colored willow flycatcher with its yellow-tipped wings is the picture of grace and elegance. During the year that Guge worked on this life-size sculpture, a willow fly-catcher frequently visited his yard; its presence—and its distinctive call—offered the artist regular inspiration.

Bob Guge
Willow Flycatcher, 1994

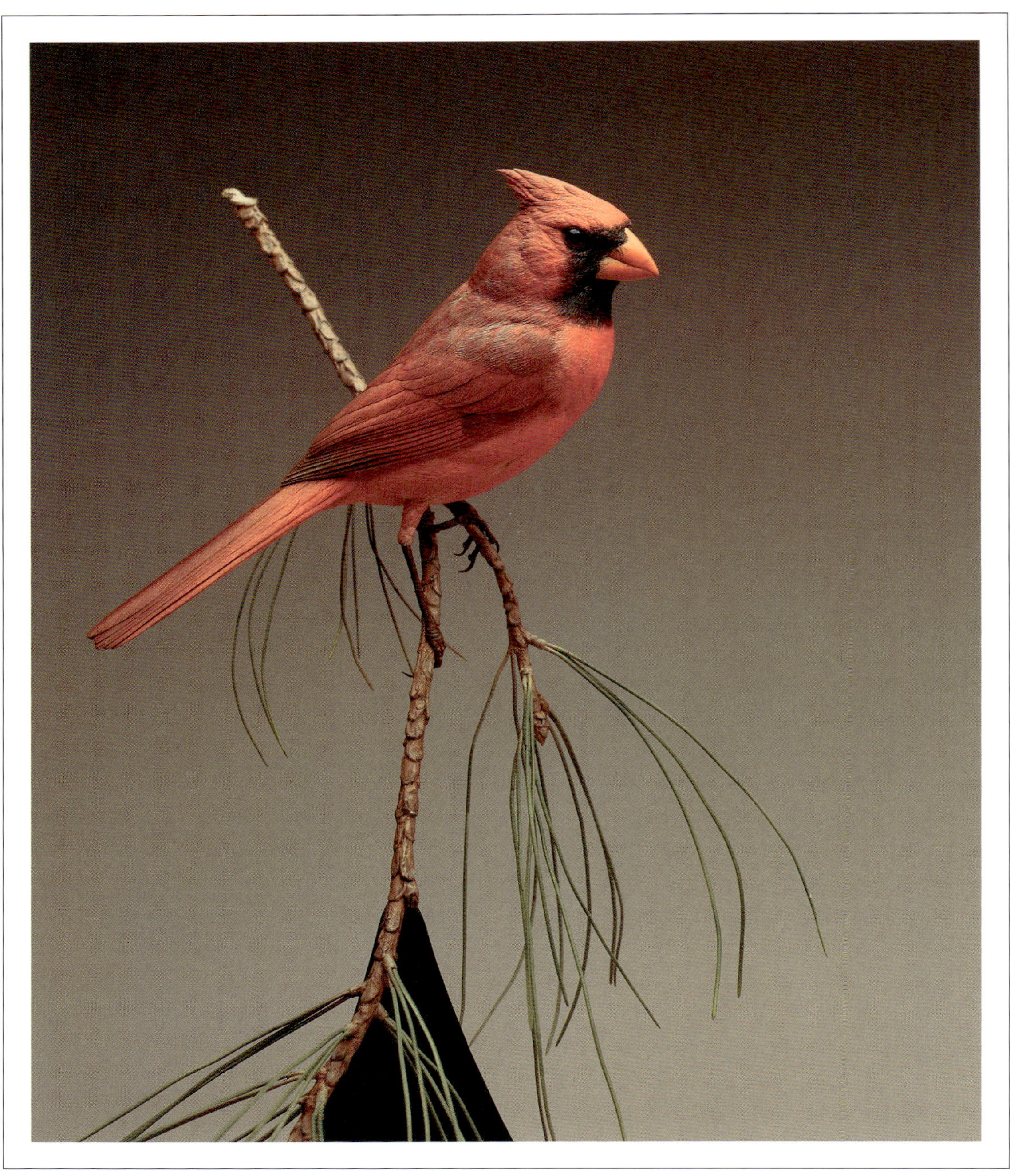

Bob Guge
Cardinal, 1996

A loblolly pine is the Southern-style perch which signals viewers that the dramatic scarlet cardinal is not just a bird of the Northeastern woodlands. While Guge has chosen a subtle composition for his life-size sculpture, the bird's raised crest, large eyes and seed-crushing bill give it an animated mood. Delicate stoning on the nape of the cardinal's neck creates the ruffled texture of individual feathers.

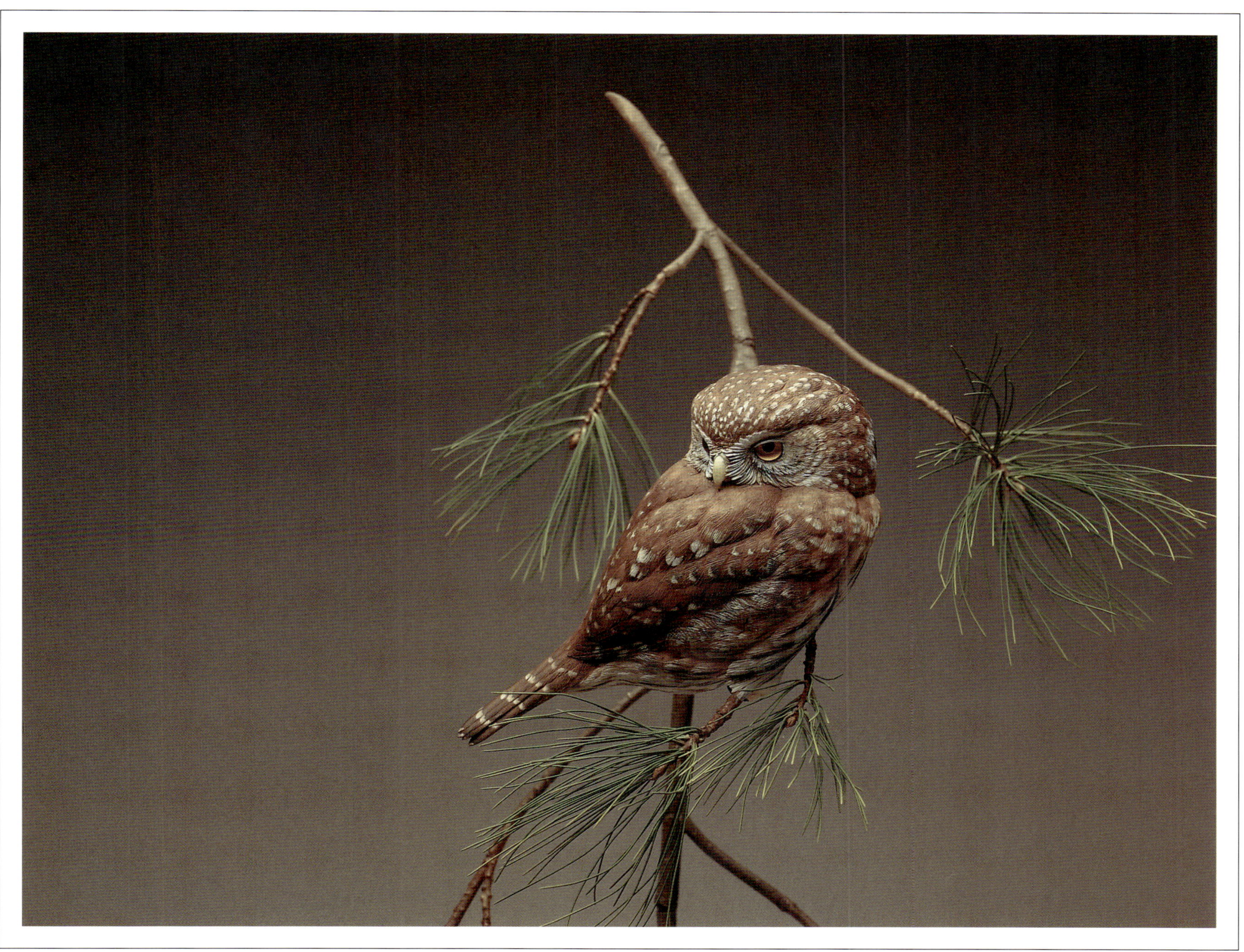

Framed by the fine needles of a white pine tree, Guge's life-size pygmy owl dozes in its daytime roost. The artist relies on power tools to carve his tupelo birds, forming the pine needles from brass. Guge captures the stealth of this tiny bird of prey by giving it heavily shadowed but brilliant yellow eyes.

Bob Guge
Pygmy Owl, 1996

Gordon Hare

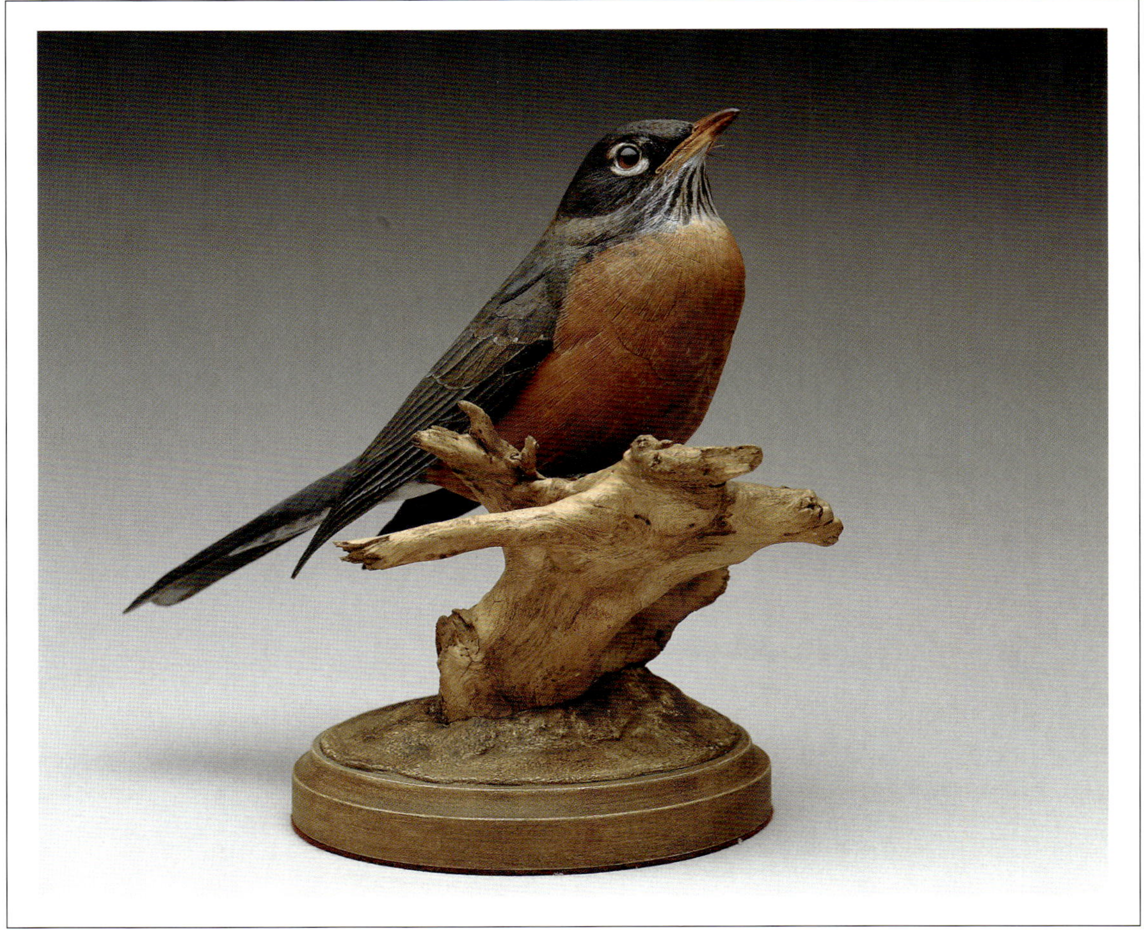

Gordon Hare
Robin, 1985

Hare's premier piece for the Ward World Championship earned the then novice carver a best-in-show ribbon. While his solitary life-size robin on an apple blossom is typical of the birds he might see around his Ontario home, Hare also enjoys close encounters with exotic species in zoos and avian rehabilitation centers.

"I'm not interested in power birds or power poses," says Gordon Hare. "My style is to create quieter pieces." Hare's decision to use understated subjects, such as the blue jay and the American kestrel, has been the hallmark of his string of victories as a professional carver.

Hare began to paint and draw birds at the age of 5 and was carving by the time he was a teenager. His lifelong interest in animals led him to study biology at university, where he intended to take a degree in veterinary science. But it was Hare's artistic rather than his medical treatment of birds that eventually won out.

Like many wildfowl sculptors of his generation, Hare, now 40, is largely self-taught. He produced his first decorative sculpture in 1976, but his gradual segue into full-time carving took a quantum leap after his 1985 premiere at the Ward World Championship earned him best-in-show honors.

"Composition and the effect of the piece are as important as the subject you choose," says the Rockwood, Ontario, resident. With their minimalist style, rarely adorned with elements other than the central avian subject, Hare's sculptures deliver a soft-spoken message that resounds throughout carving circles.

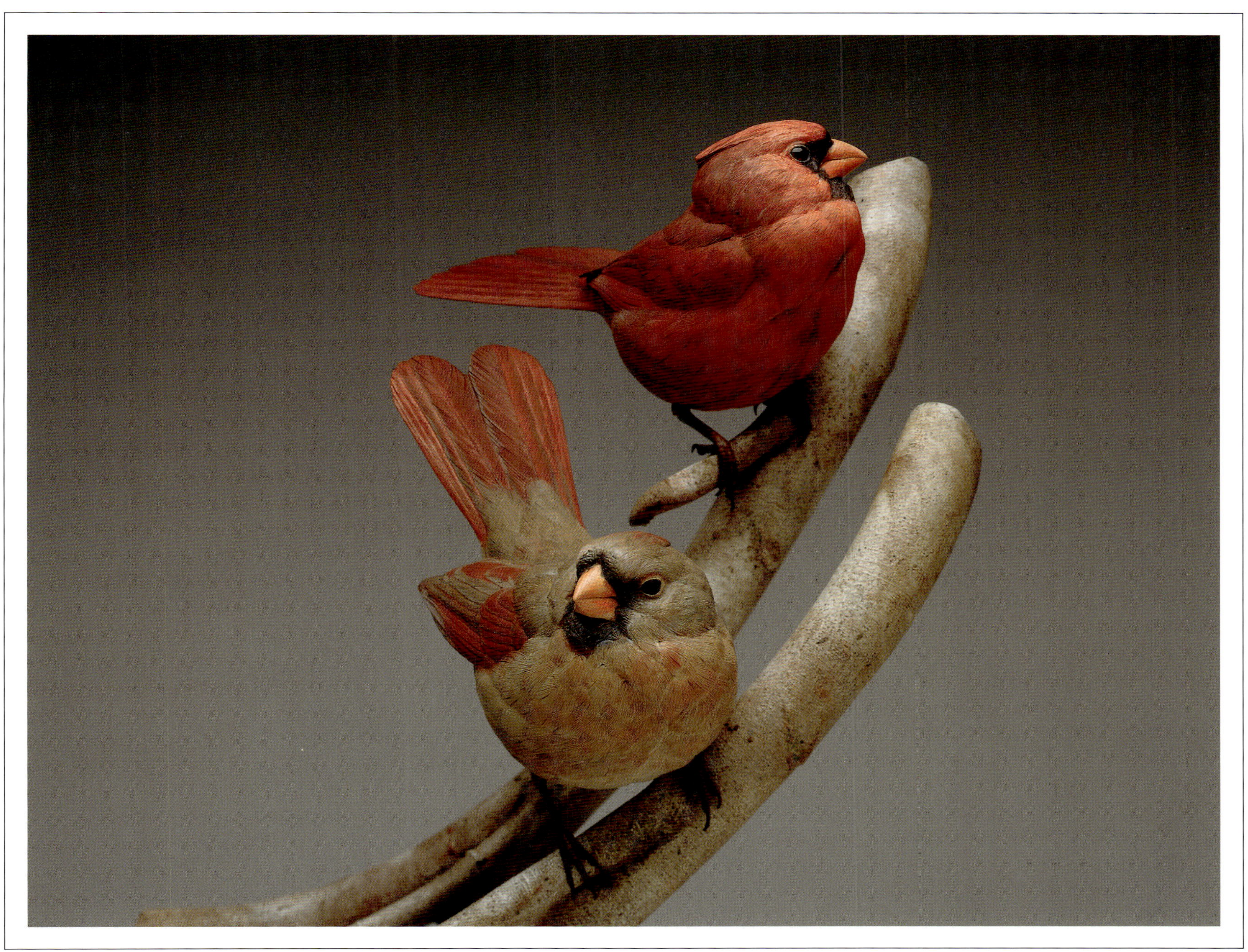

Hare relied on clay models to establish the composition of his cardinals and on two "skins" to help guide him when making decisions about feather groupings and colors. With acrylic washes, he created the rich plumage of his life-size cardinal pair, and by using a limited palette, he derived a complementary range of colors.

Gordon Hare
Cardinal Pair, 1994

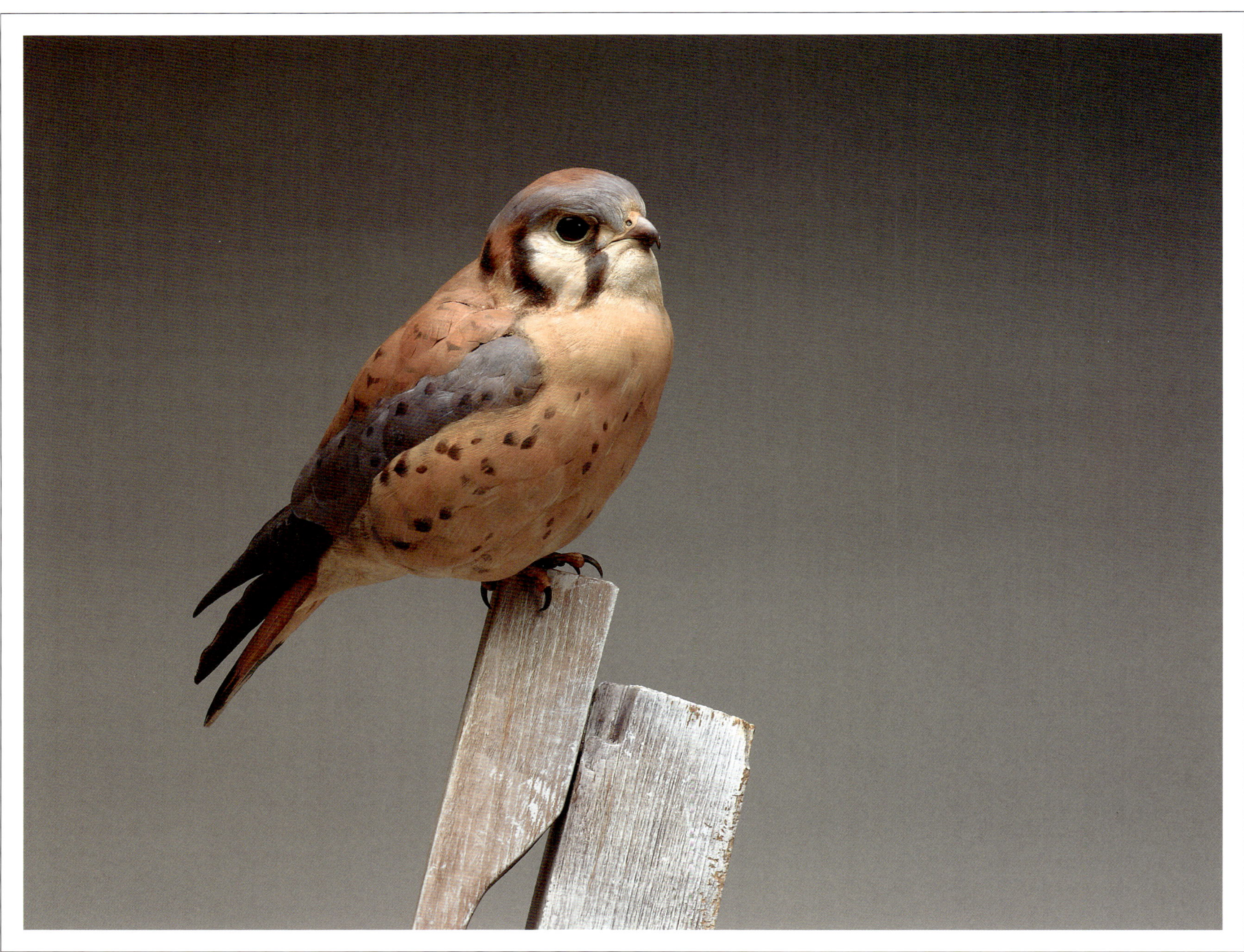

Gordon Hare
American Kestrel
Circles and Arrows, 1988

Human constructions and a species' ability to adapt to them are the theme of Hare's life-size sculpture. The weathered fencepost, a circle on top of a square, mimics the basic silhouette of the American kestrel and accentuates the softly blended colors in the plumage of this tiny bird of prey.

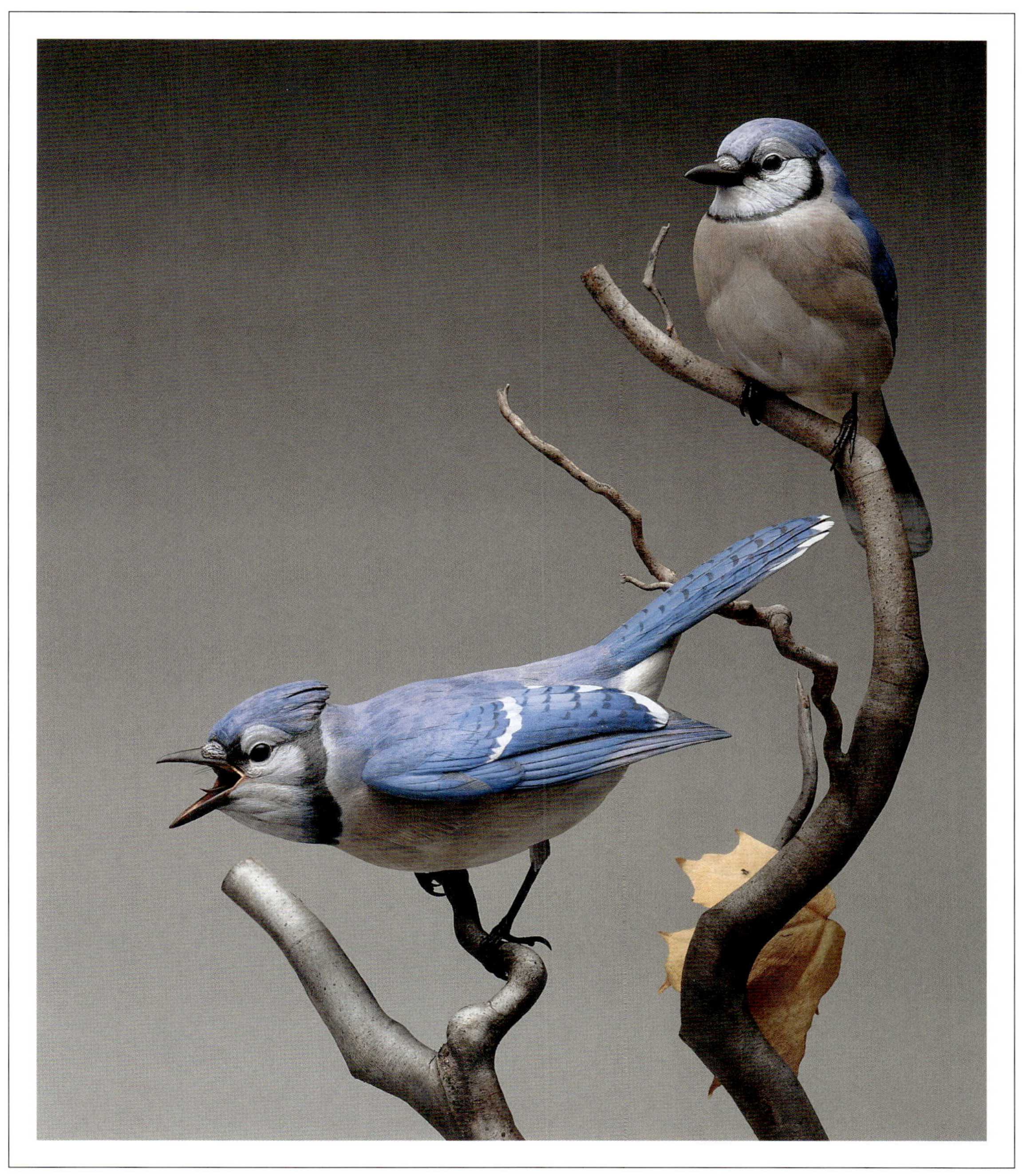

The quiet and the cacophonous meet in Hare's life-size treetop vignette. To overcome the limitations that a static base imposes on animated subjects, Hare's innovative championship carving has no formal base. Instead, its movable tangle of fingerlike branches allows the birds to be placed in more than one configuration. Hare used basswood to carve the branches and the blue jays, whose feet were sculpted from aluminum.

Gordon Hare
Blue Jays
Hue and Cry, 1987

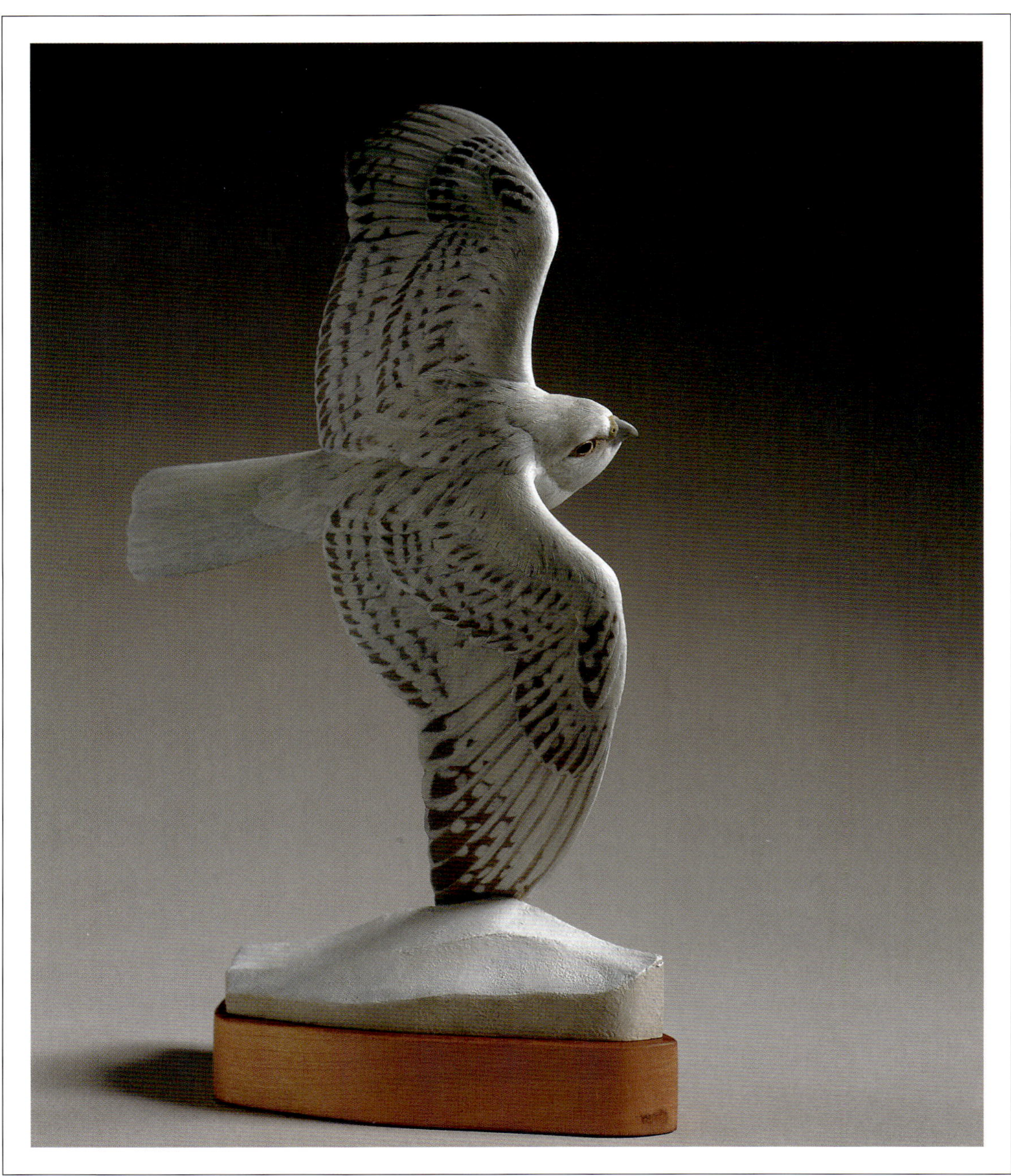

Gordon Hare
Gyrfalcon
North Wind, 1995

Capturing form, light and color, Hare brings a very particular perspective to this miniature carving, reducing detail in the plumage of this gyrfalcon to suggest distance. Whether he is creating miniature or life-size works, Hare uses a host of tools (band saw, adz, chisels, rotary tools and grinders) and a range of "tricks of the trade" to sculpt the shape and texture of his carvings.

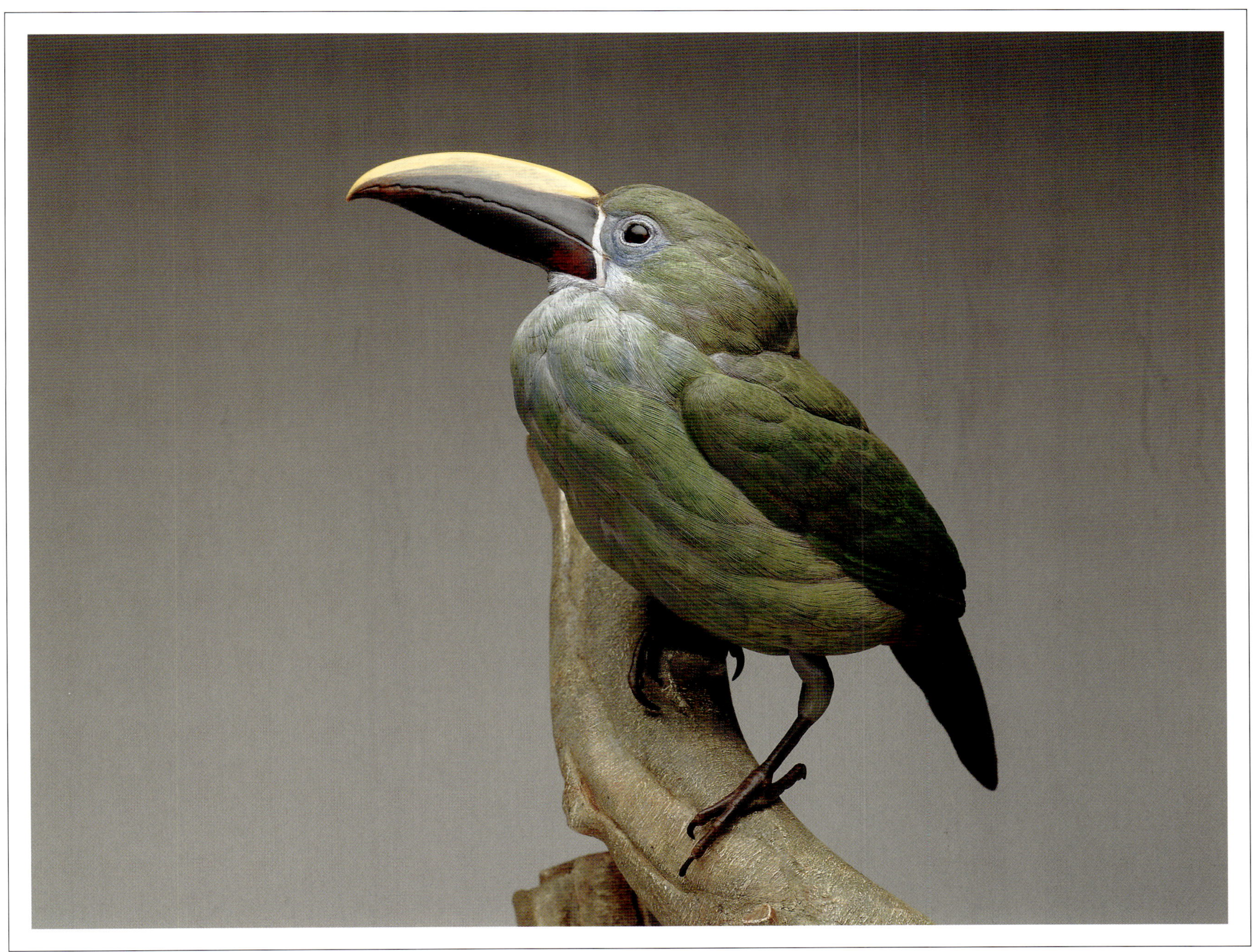

Nowhere is Hare's awareness of light more evident than in his dazzling life-size emerald toucanet. This sculpture, which showcases Hare's most dramatic painting and represents his first and only tropical bird, was inspired by a captive bird at the Metro Toronto Zoo.

Gordon Hare
Emerald Toucanet, 1993

Glenn Ladenberger

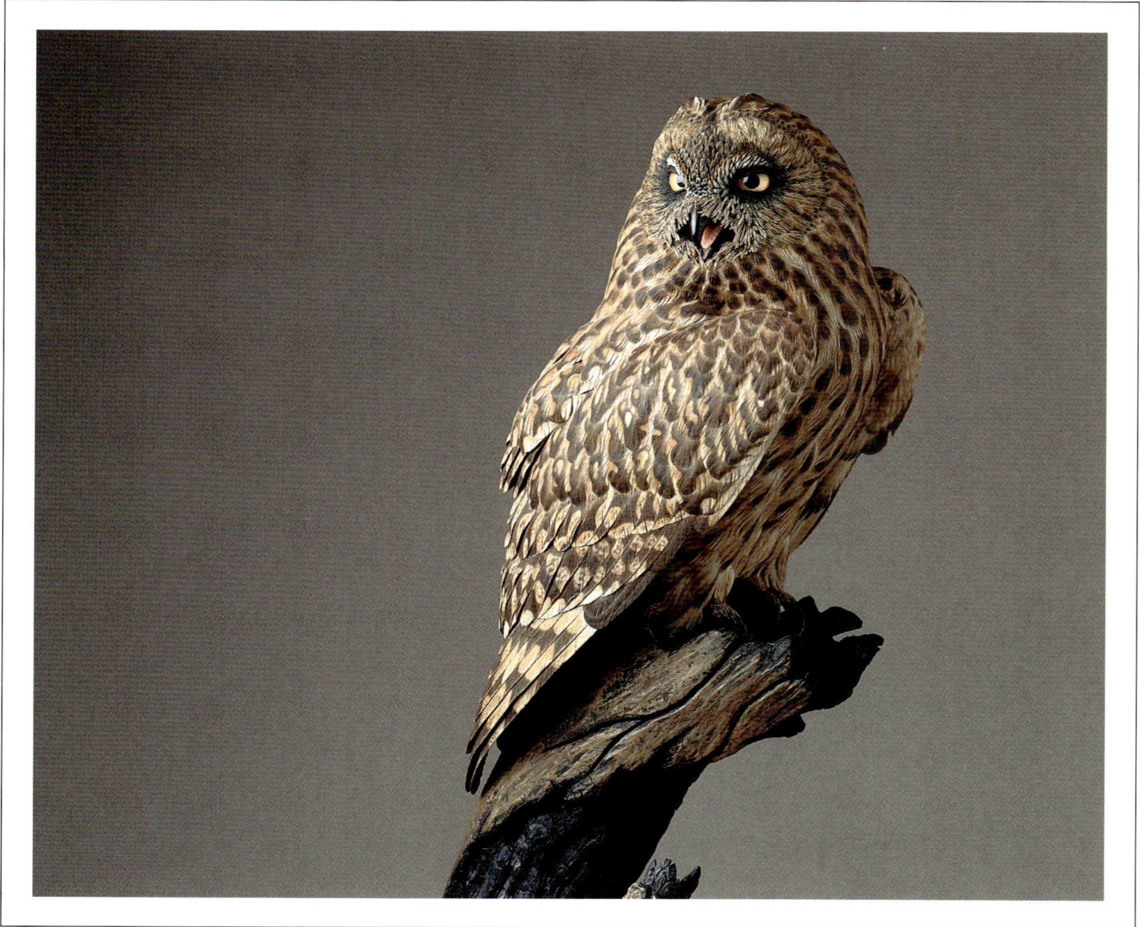

Glenn Ladenberger
Short-Eared Owl, 1993

Ladenberger's pine-tree stump—carved and painted to look charred—re-creates the natural open habitat of his life-size short-eared owl. The feather tufts on the owl's flexible facial disk animate the bird and capture its distinctive character. Ladenberger often presents his raptors with open bills to emphasize their voracious nature.

"I like duplicating life the best that I can," says Glenn Ladenberger. Putting vitality and energy into wildfowl sculpture is what has kept the artist inspired since he began carving.

Ladenberger dabbled in carving as a youngster, but in 1985, when the Niagara-on-the-Lake, Ontario, artist entered his first bird in a Canadian competition, he was an overnight sensation. "Nobody had a clue who I was," he recalls, "but they kept telling me I should be competing as a professional." By his third event, the novice wildfowl artist was going head-to-head with carving's elite.

Focusing his energy on birds of prey, Ladenberger creates majestic sculptures interpreted with mesmerizing precision, and he is unanimously admired among other carvers for his undercuts—individualized feather groups—and detailed feather barbs. To create these effects, Ladenberger uses power tools and fine wood-burning pens, but to reach the hidden crevices and corners of the upturned feathers and undercuts, he is often forced to improvise with homemade mini-saws, emery boards and hundreds of strips of sandpaper.

"That's the look of the real bird," explains the 42-year-old artist. "Even if it takes 10 times as long, I can't cut corners. I can't work any other way."

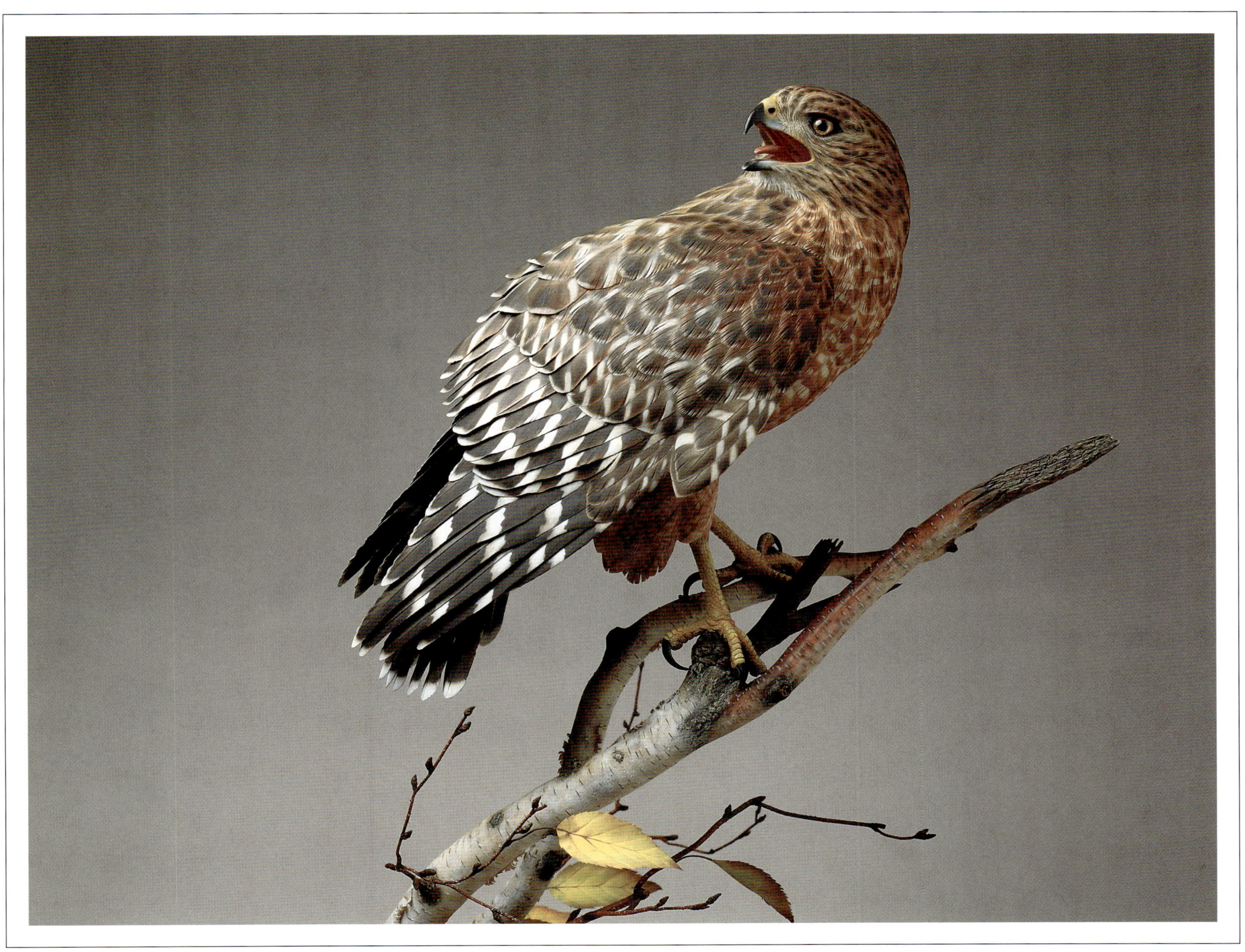

Glenn Ladenberger
Red-Shouldered Hawk, 1995

With a wing dropped to showcase the colors on its back feathers, Ladenberger's hawk casts a startled glance in the direction of an observer. Deep undercuts of six or seven inches on the tail feathers, without inserts, provide the technical centerpiece of the challenging life-size work. "Once you take care of what you can," Ladenberger explains, "the unknowns have a way of working themselves out."

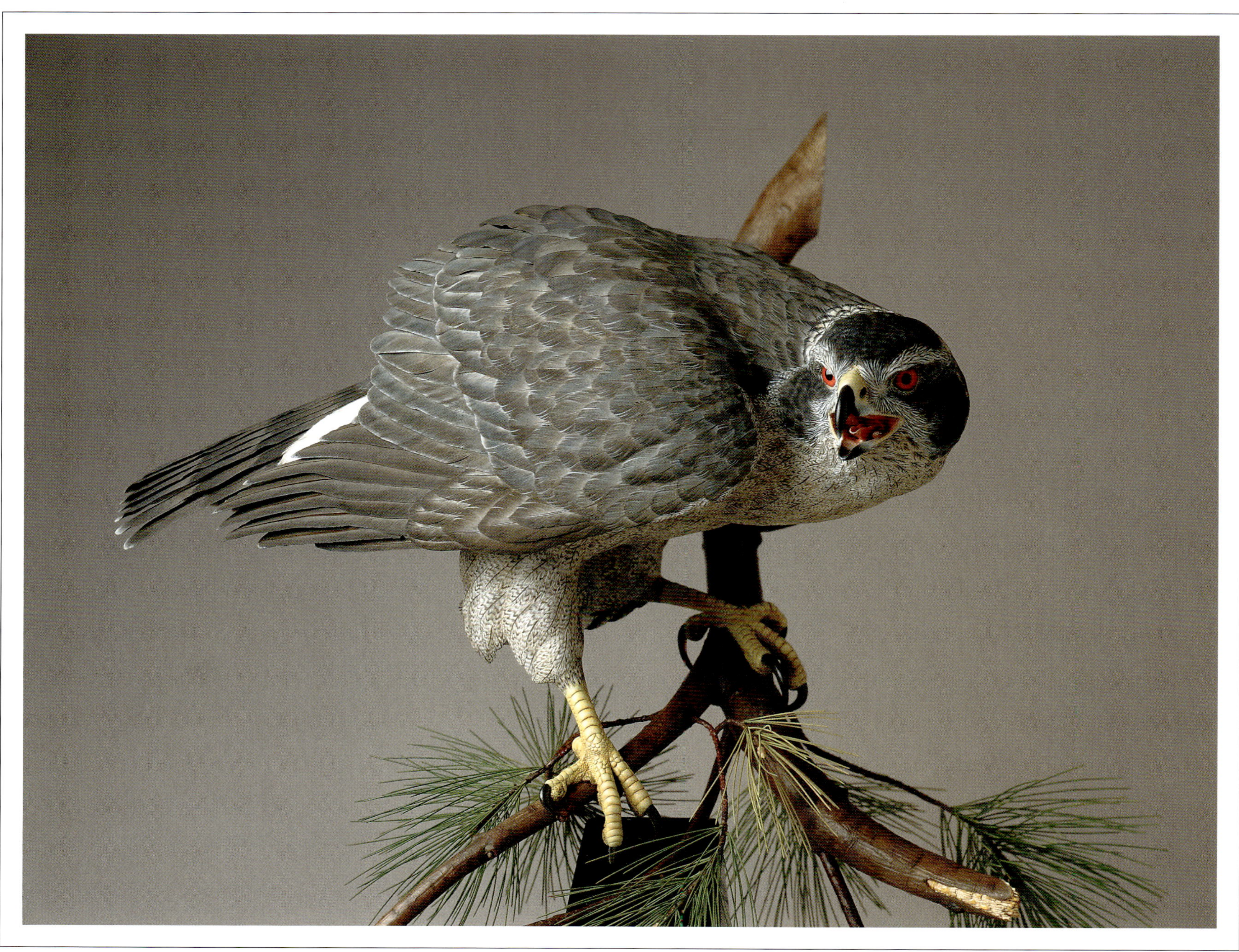

Glenn Ladenberger
Northern Goshawk, 1994

With its blood-red eyes aflame, Ladenberger's best-in-world life-size sculpture captures the spirit of this winged force of the North. Toiling 10 hours a day, 7 days a week for 11 months, Ladenberger completed the bird in three pieces, assembling them using a carbon-tracing technique and painting the goshawk with some 15 shades each of acrylic blues and grays.

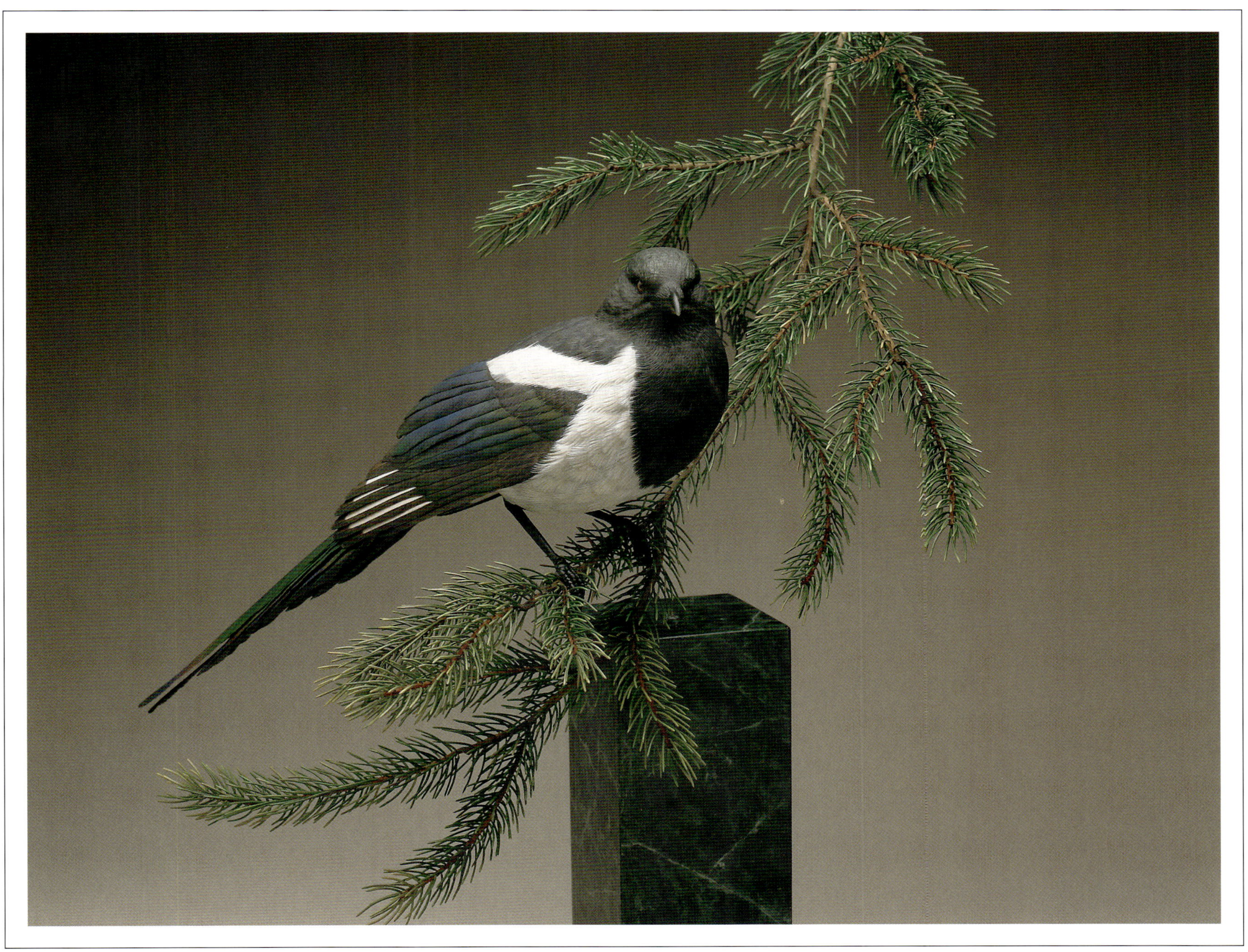

Glenn Ladenberger
Magpie on Spruce Branch, 1996

To elevate the humble magpie to a new, elegant status was the motivation behind Ladenberger's detailed life-size carving. Viewed by many as a nuisance species, the handsome bird is perched on a spruce-tree branch adorned with more than 4,600 needles forged from steel and individually painted. Despite the creative challenge that such backgrounds present, Ladenberger argues that "branches are the free and fun part of carving."

Ernie Muehlmatt

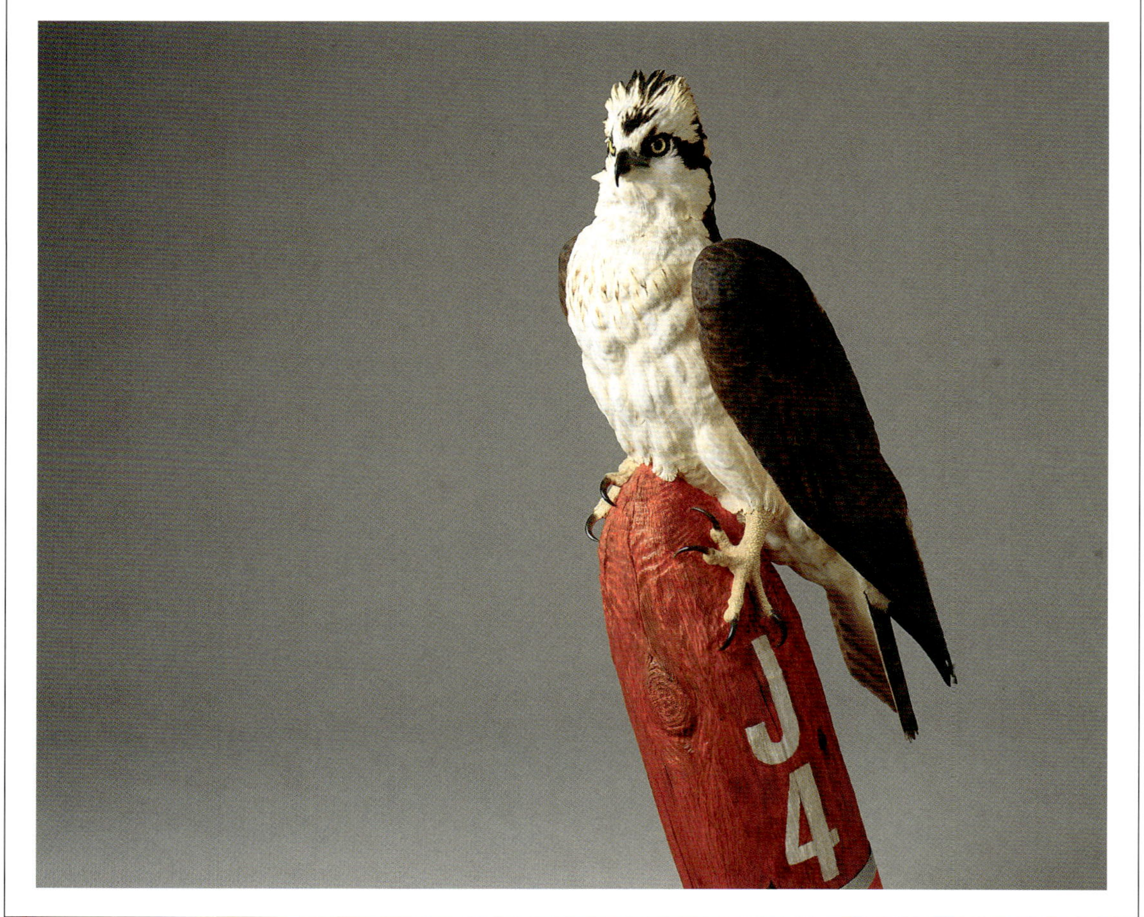

Ernie Muehlmatt
Osprey
Red Right Return, 1994

Perched on a buoy, Muehlmatt's impressive osprey stands five feet tall. The artist began with a 2-by-2-by-$4\frac{1}{2}$-foot block of grainless tupelo, carving the head in near-perfect detail before working his way down the wood to shape the rest of the body. Requiring some 640 hours of work, the sculpture bears a title that alludes to both the rules of the sea (positioning the red buoy to the right as you return to dock) and the osprey population's recent recovery from the perils of DDT.

"It's like a person peeling off a bulky sweater and revealing the true shape underneath," says Ernie Muehlmatt of his signature carving style. In a class by himself, the Springfield, Pennsylvania, artist creates true subtractive sculptures, carving from a single block of wood and shearing the excess away from the top to the bottom—without the aid of feather inserts or rough models—to complete even his most detailed pieces. "When I work this way," he adds, "the bird comes to life bit by bit."

Muehlmatt's unique method for releasing the bird trapped in the wood has its basis in his firm knowledge of avian anatomy, although the artist, a lifetime birder, began his career as a floral designer. When Muehlmatt stumbled across a carving show in the mid-1960s, however, he had a revelation about his options. "Birds are just flowers that fly," he says.

Since selling his first piece in 1968 for $3, the 69-year-old carver has produced more than 4,000 sculptures. Now specializing in raptors and game birds, Muehlmatt is a power carver who relies only on a sketch to guide him to the finished sculpture. "The bird talks to me as I carve it," he says. "It is the greatest feeling of freedom to create this way. Whatever you can envision, you can do."

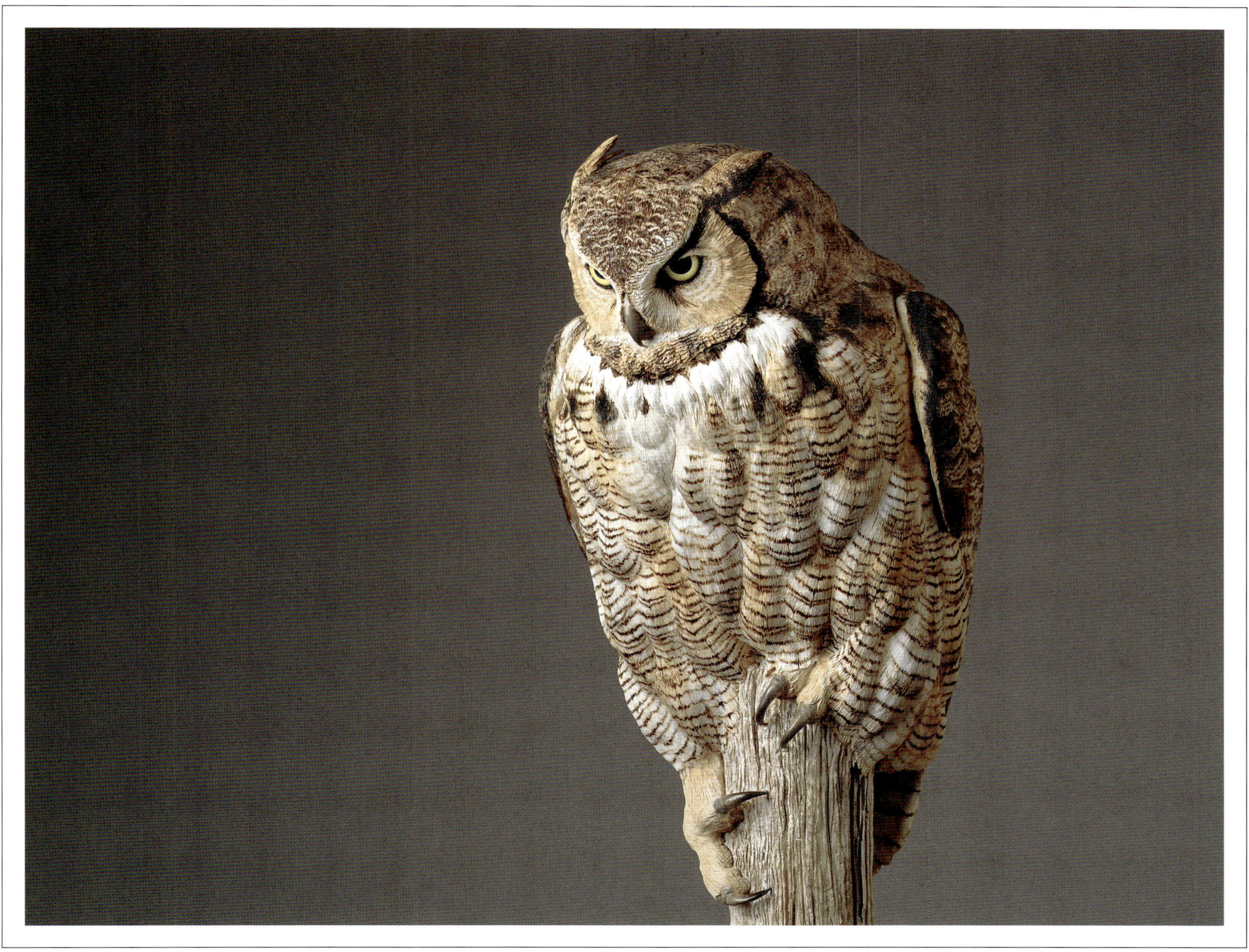

Ernie Muehlmatt
Great Horned Owl
Snag, 1995

Anchored by its rapierlike talons to the broken spire of a decaying pine tree, the great horned owl casts a dramatic look downward from its elevated perch. Working with only an owl skin for feather references, Muehlmatt carved the four-foot-tall sculpture from a single piece of tupelo. A three-time world champion, Muehlmatt employed his wood-burning technique to render the brown barred feather vermiculations in the owl's plumage, using two muted acrylic tones on the finished piece.

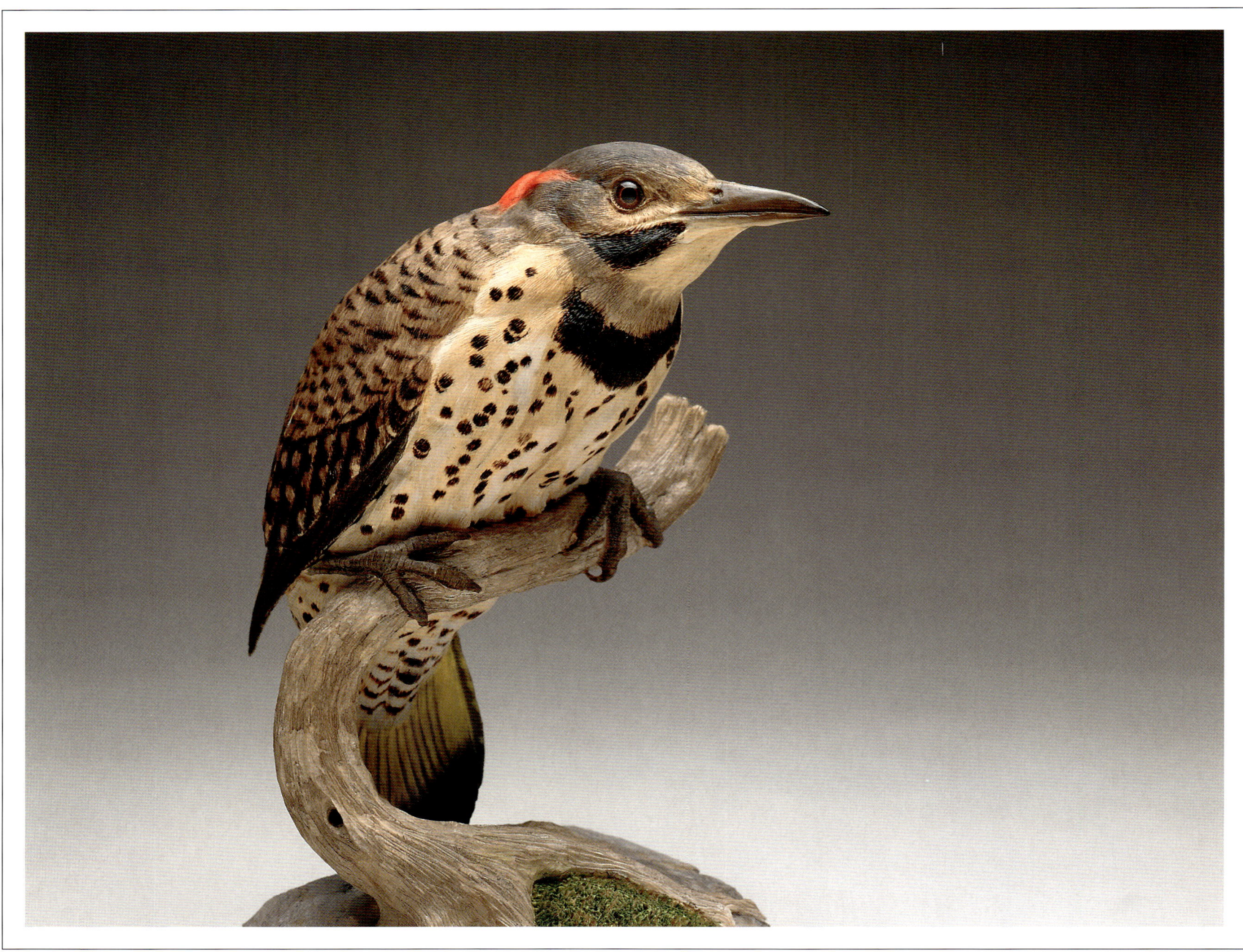

Ernie Muehlmatt
Northern Flicker
Yellow Hammer, 1995

Muehlmatt's yellow-shafted northern flicker is a fine example of the artist's "burning for color" technique, which involves using numerous wood-burning pens, each set at a different temperature, to create various shades of brown on the bird's plumage. Looking much like a black-and-white photographic print, the life-size carving is then highlighted with colors selected from a limited palette that includes ultramarine blue, burnt umber and burnt sienna.

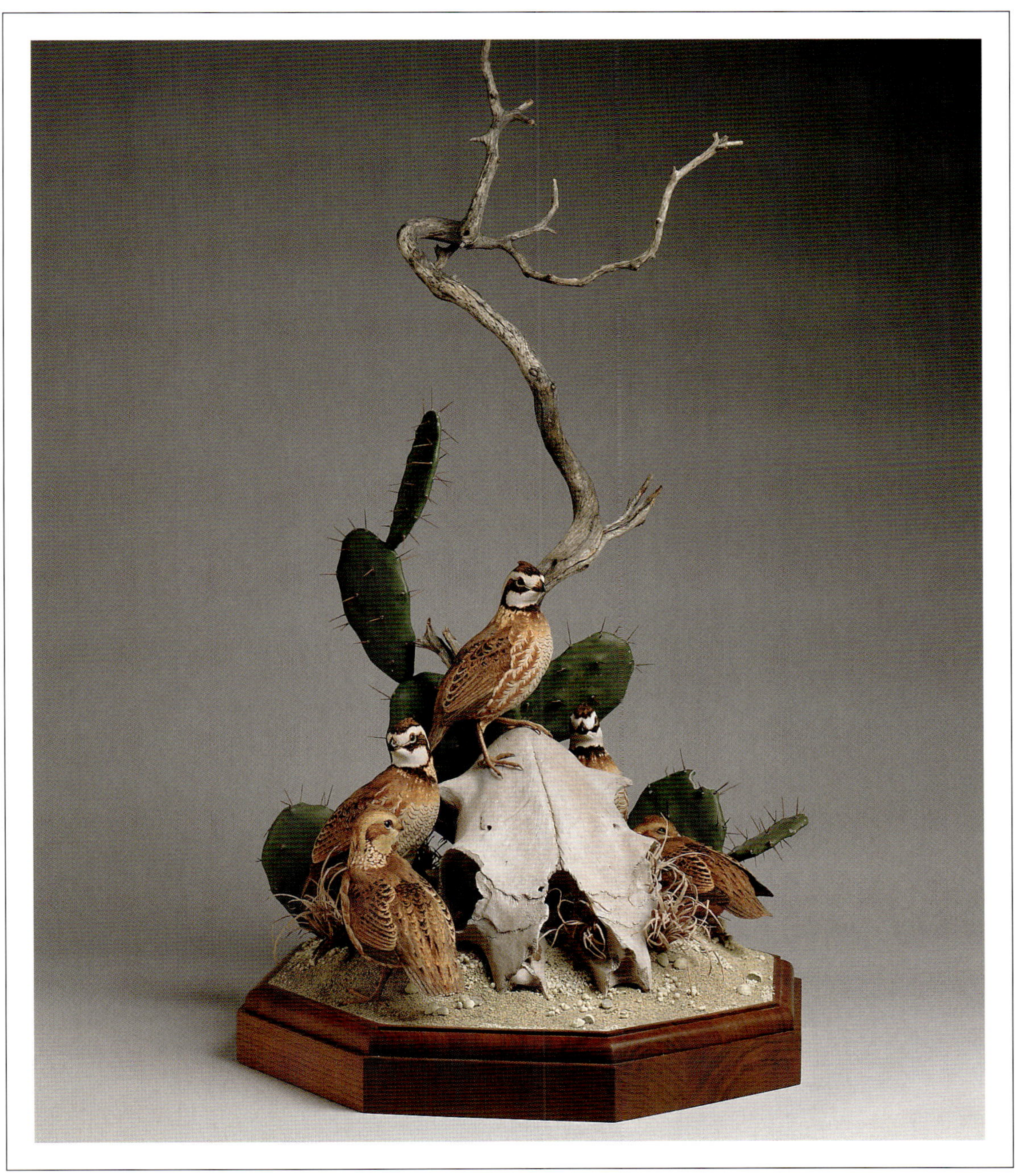

Five life-size northern bobwhite quail perch atop a steer skull in Muehlmatt's sculpture, which is reminiscent of a natural-history diorama. Muehlmatt used wood to carve all elements of the piece—from the birds and the cactus to the steer skull and the toad hidden in the eye socket—then dusted it with marble powder to convey the bone-dry look of the desert.

Ernie Muehlmatt
Northern Bobwhite Quail
Needle, Feather and Bone, 1984

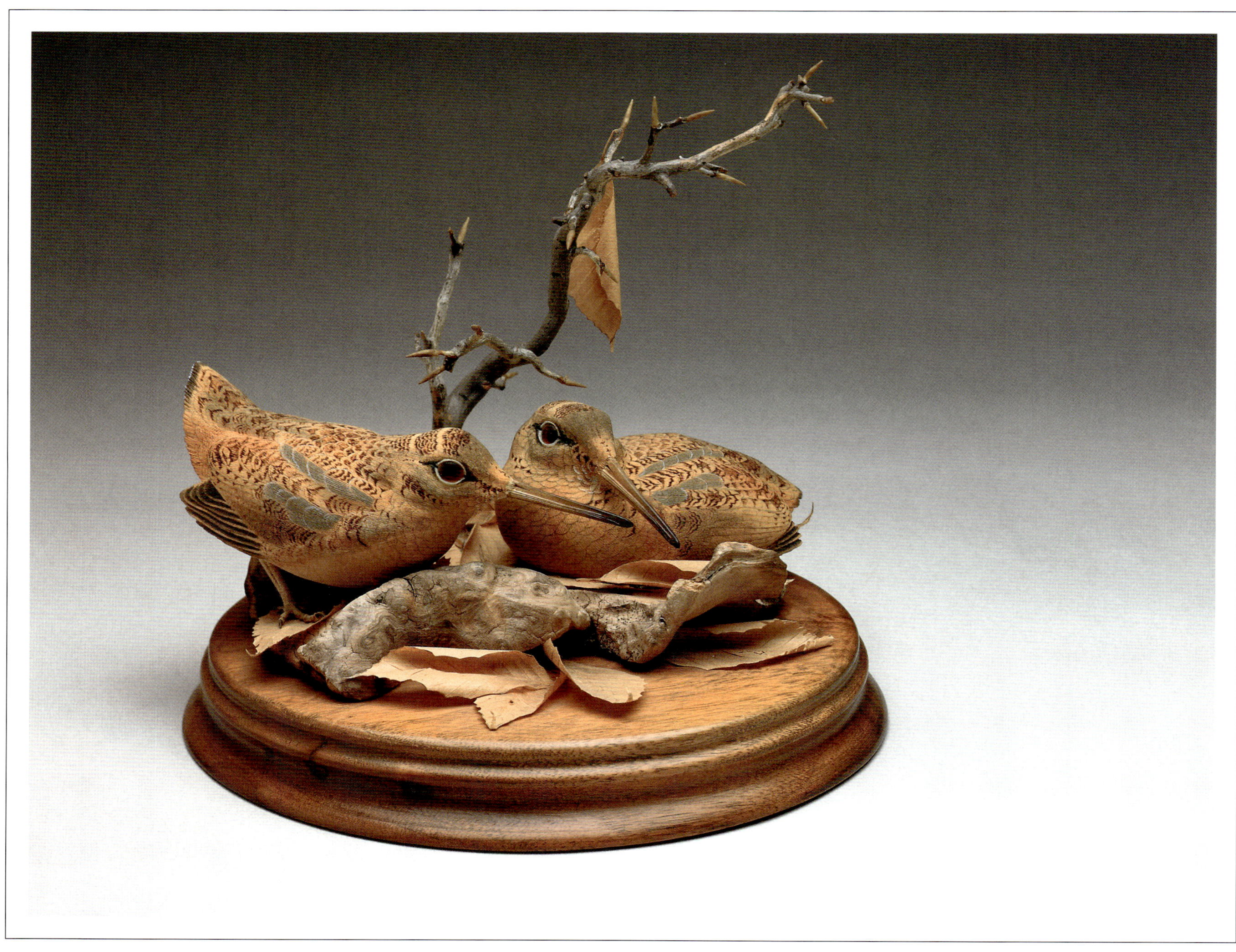

Ernie Muehlmatt
Woodcock Pair, 1979

Inspired by fluttering birds that he saw as he knelt by a backyard pond to fetch water for his studio, Muehlmatt created a cryptically colored miniature woodcock pair concealed in the litter of fallen leaves, just as they appeared that night on the property where he has spent his entire life. Their caramel-colored plumage, painted with acrylics, shows the artist's earliest experiments with undercut feather detail.

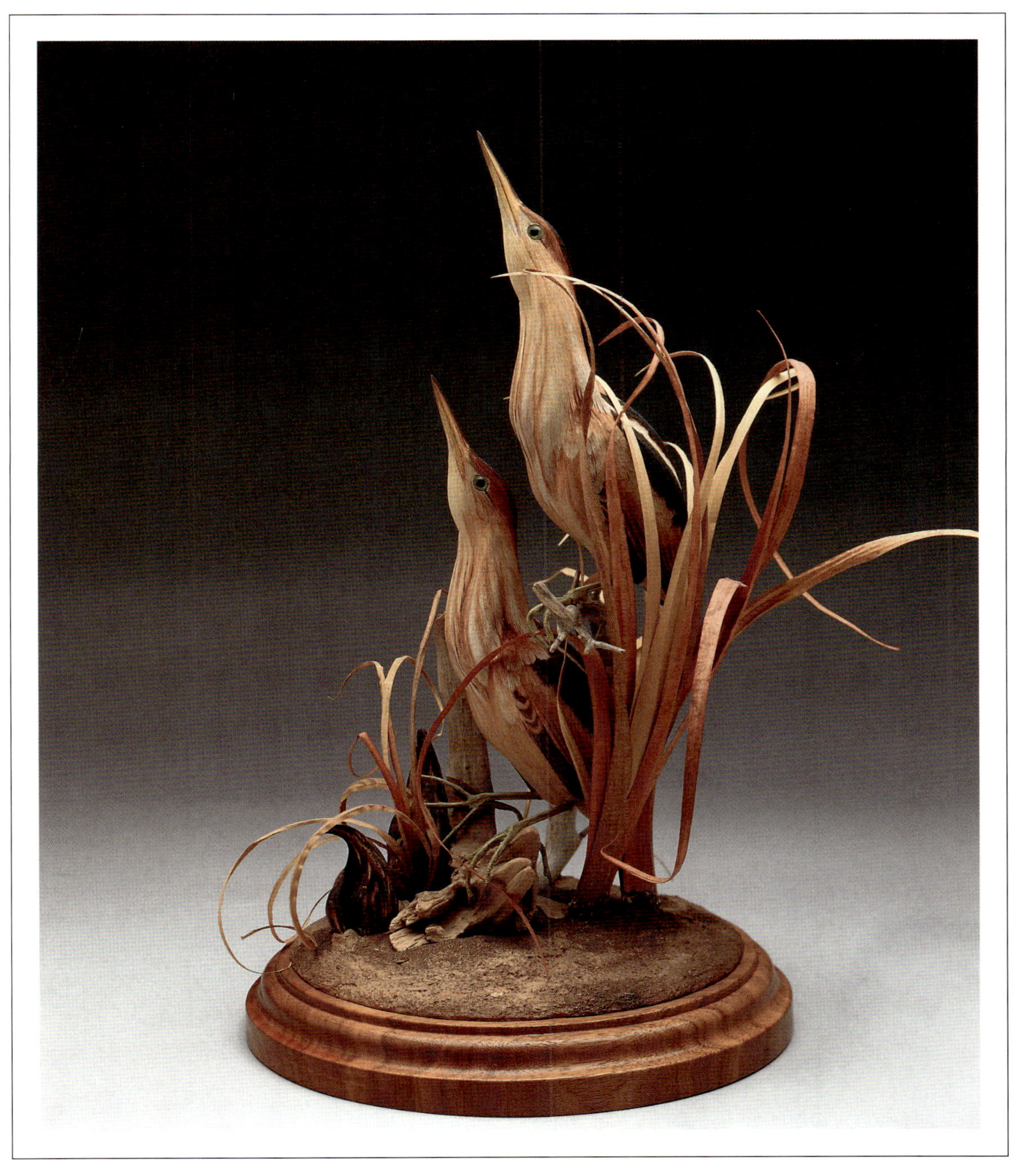

Muehlmatt's miniature bittern pair strikes a familiar "freeze" pose that helps the birds hide from danger—and survive—amid the tall grasses of a marsh. The second of the artist's best-in-world championship miniature works, the sculpture is now housed in the permanent collection of the Ward Museum of Wildfowl Art in Salisbury, Maryland.

Ernie Muehlmatt
Bittern Pair, 1981

Floyd Scholz

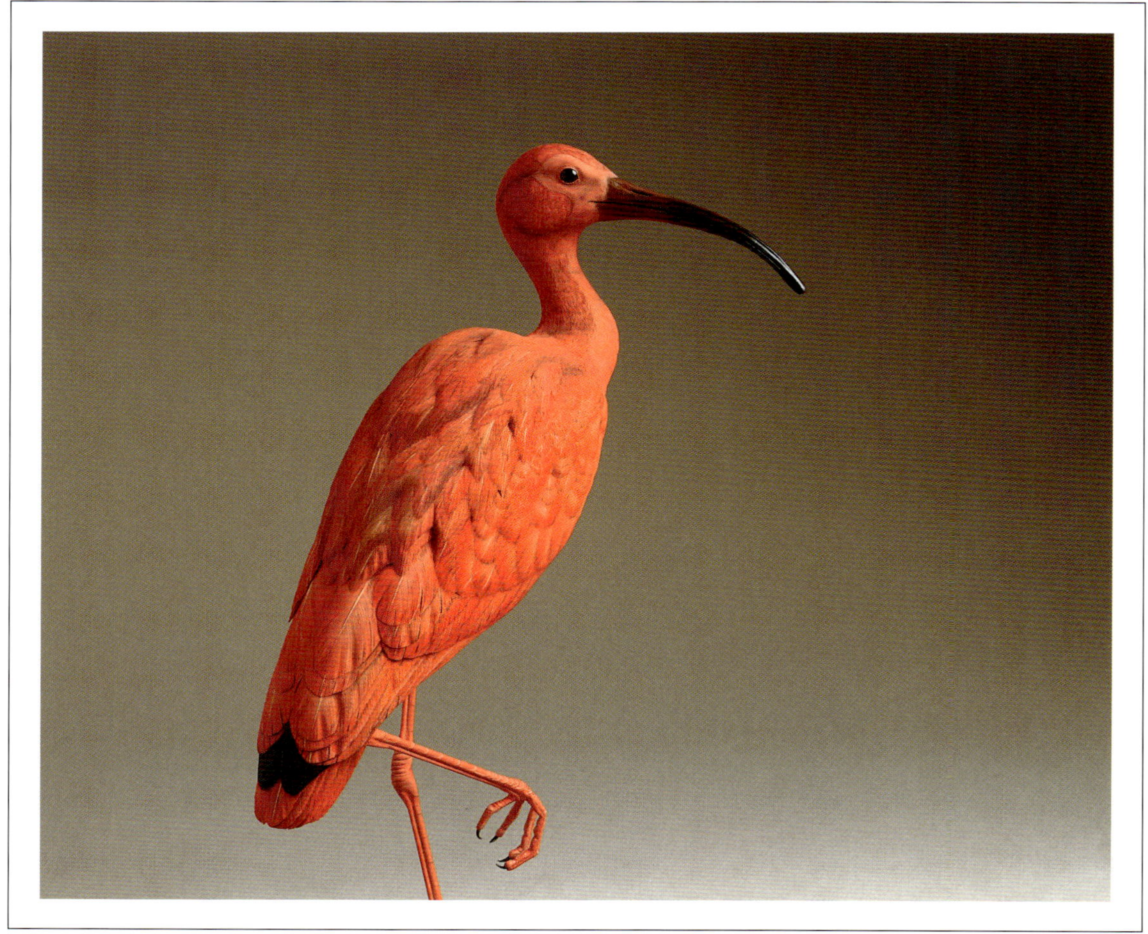

Floyd Scholz
Scarlet Ibis, 1995

Tiptoeing through the watery flats of an imaginary estuary, Scholz's statuesque scarlet ibis sports the same iridescent plumage of the living bird, which comes from water-resistant preening oil carefully distributed throughout its feathers. After carving the body from wood and sculpting the legs in brass, Scholz created the iridescent effect on his life-size sculpture by mixing pearlescent powders with his paints.

"Just as the musical composer combines soprano, tenor and bass," explains Floyd Scholz, "I take the disparate elements of a subject and unite them in a meaningful way to tell a story." Relying on the passions of his life—wood, sculpture and birds—Scholz constructs visual narratives about the natural world around him.

Over the course of his 14 years as a professional carver, Scholz has distinguished himself as a fearless master of the art form. Although he has earned a reputation for creating daunting birds of prey, however, the 38-year-old carver is not constrained by that expertise. Scholz is among the first of the eastern-flyway artists to bring lesser-known tropical species to the competitive arena.

A self-described fanatic for detail, Scholz creates carvings whose composition transcends anatomical minutiae and reflects the flow and balance of the animated avian subjects. "A bird's anatomy is a given," he explains. "It is simply a means to an end." That end is Scholz's artistic accord with life in three-dimensional color, rendered in wood with chisels and grinders and born from a love of nature which is nurtured in the woods near his Vermont home, on excursions with regional conservation associations and on regular trips South.

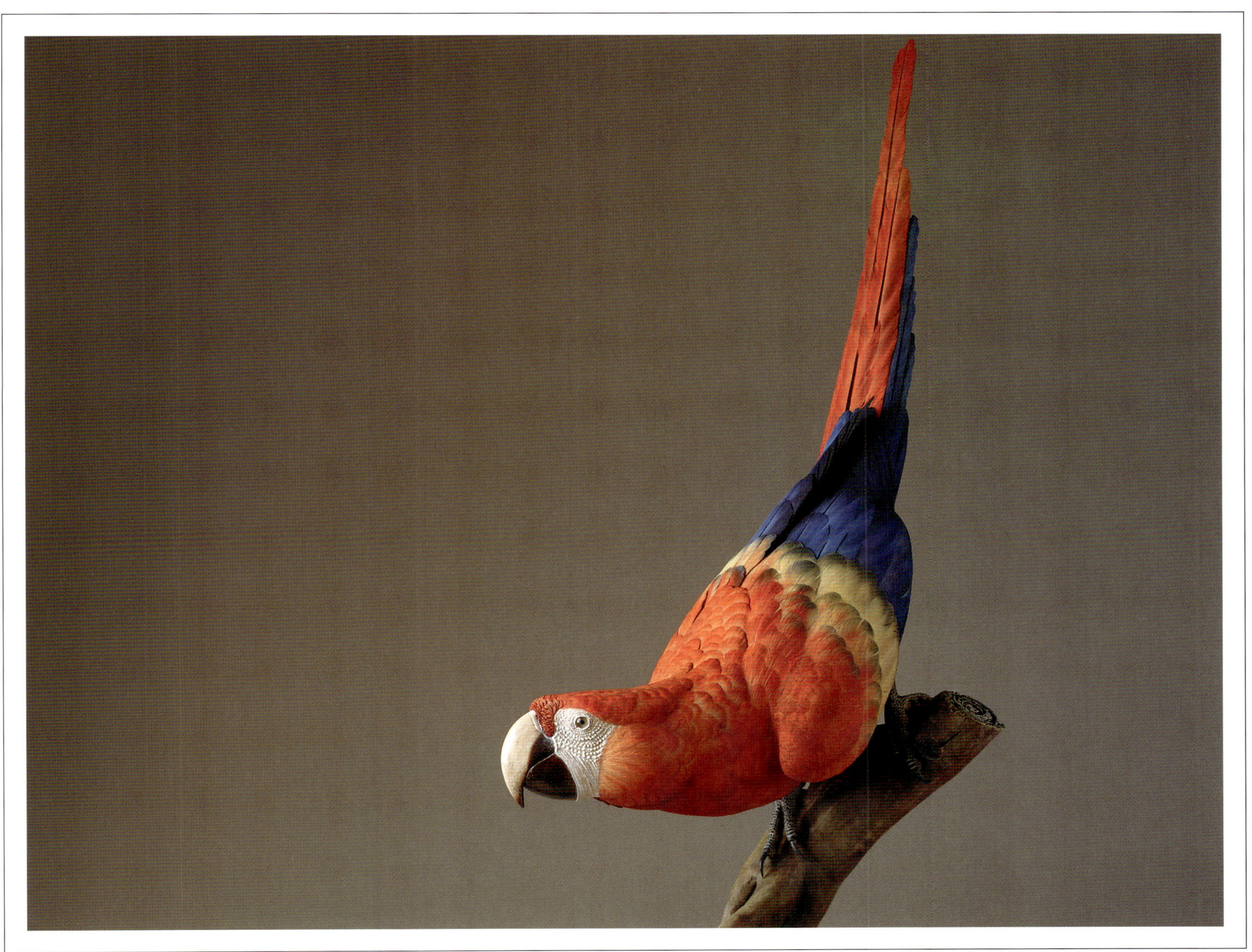

Frequent visits to the tropical forests of Venezuela inspired Scholz to tackle this brilliant scarlet macaw. Life studies, sketches and photographs form the conceptual foundation of the dramatic sculpture, whose graceful, arcing lines and strong colors reinforce the contrasts of elegance and raucousness inherent in the three-foot-long bird. Thirty washes of color (including seven shades of red) lend richness to the flamboyant plumage of this wildly energetic species.

Floyd Scholz
Scarlet Macaw
Flame, 1995

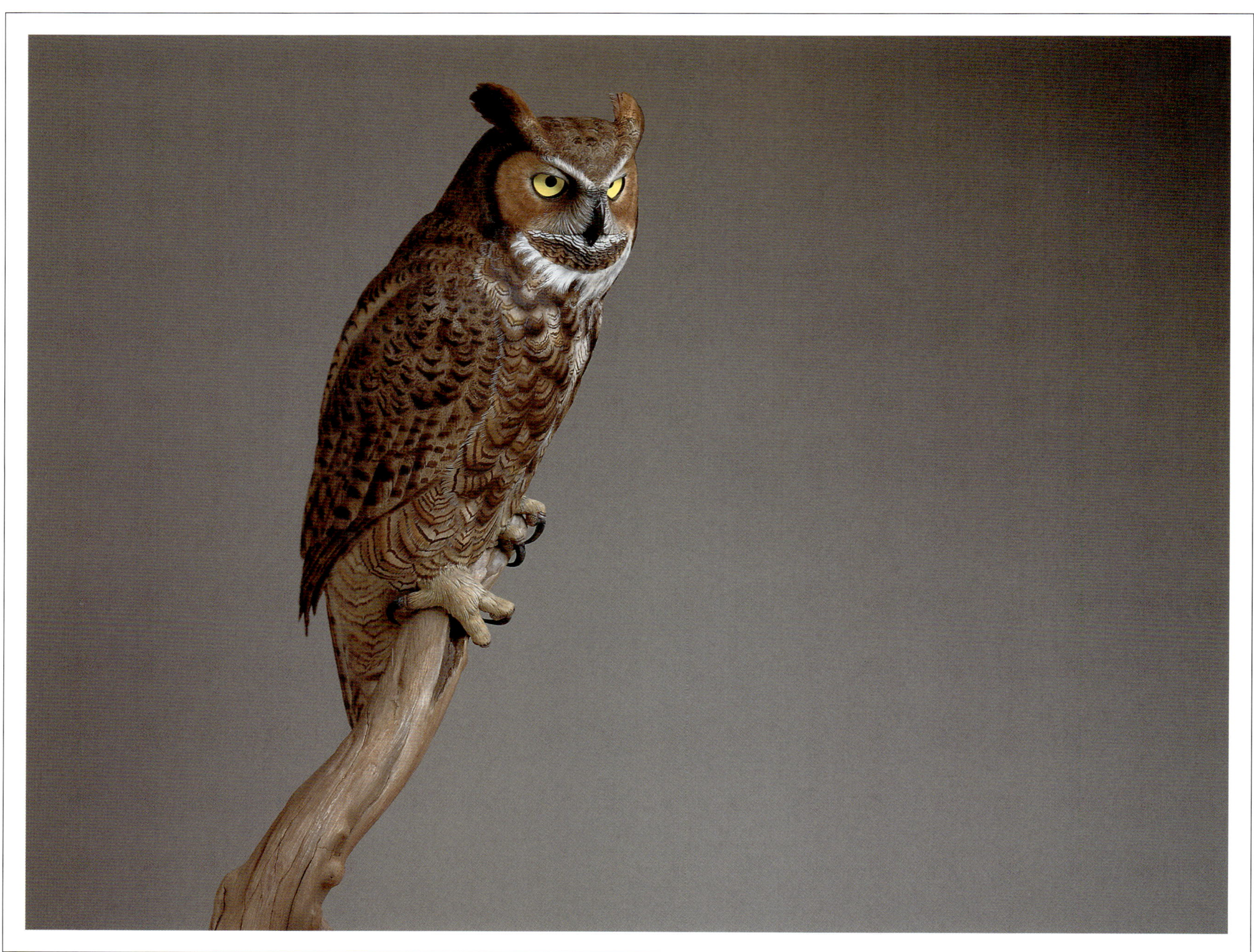

Floyd Scholz
Great Horned Owl
Moonlight Observer, 1991

Large golden eyes illuminated by the evening moonlight guide the way for Scholz's serene life-size great horned owl. Scholz uses wood-burning pens to render the fine feather vermiculations, and he relies on several values of acrylic paint (for each shade of brown) to wash the soft, warm colors into the owl's plumage.

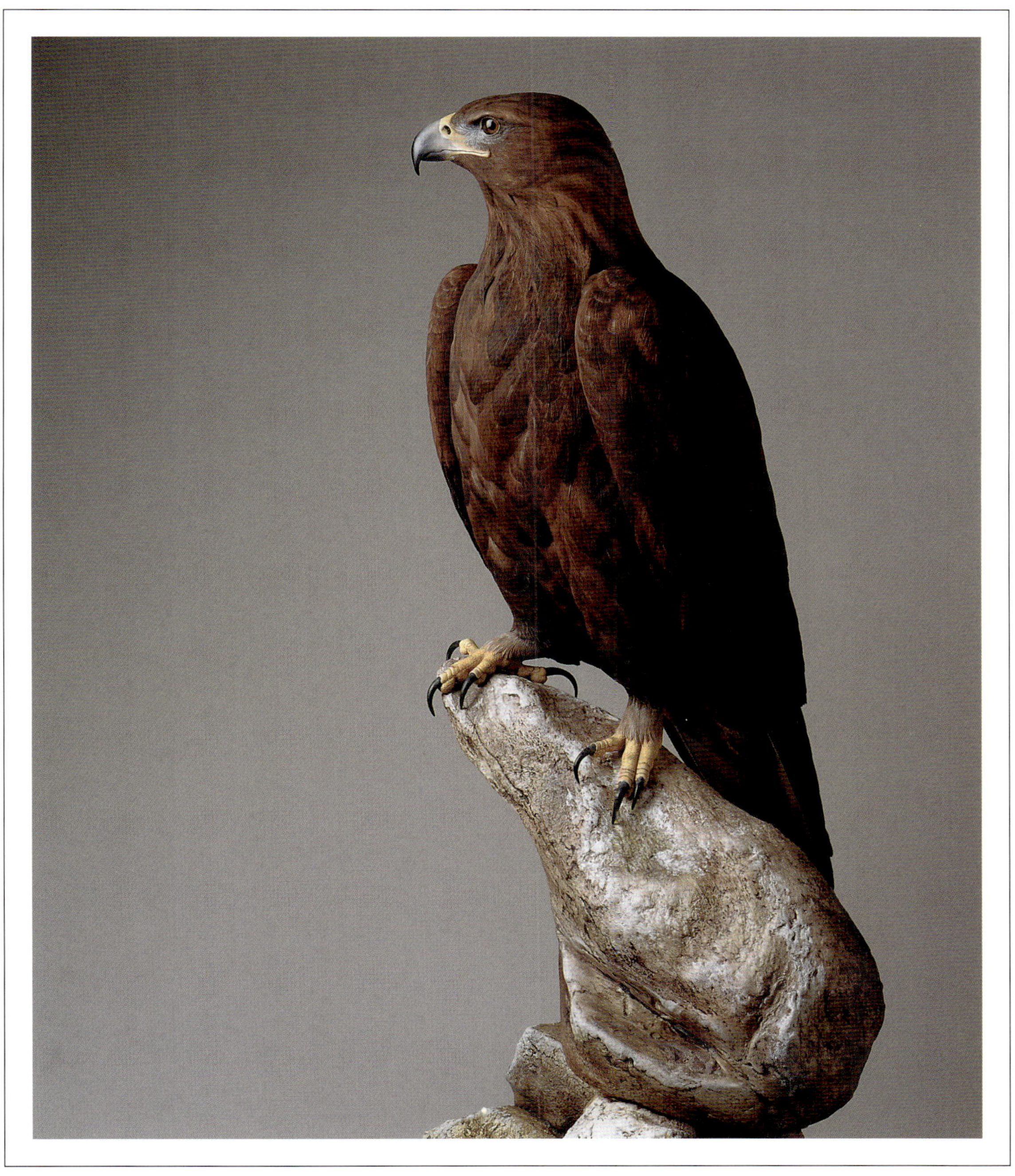

Its feathers flowing like armor across its breast, Scholz's life-size golden eagle stands proud, like a Roman centurion, conveying the raw power of this hunting species. Scholz perches the bird in its mountainous habitat, which emphasizes its aloof and unassailable character.

Floyd Scholz
Golden Eagle
Majesty, 1995

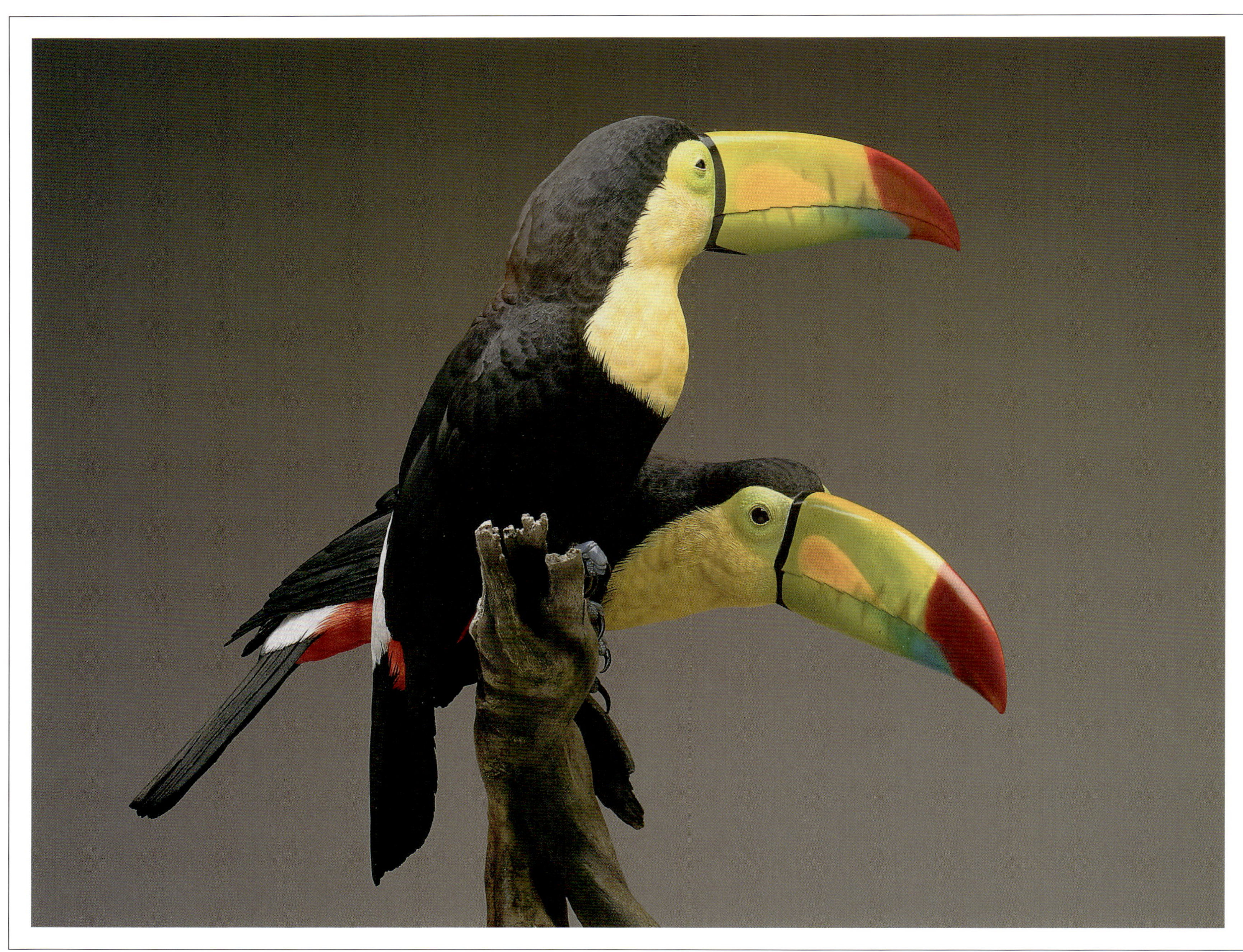

Floyd Scholz
Keel-Billed Toucans
Rainforest Symphony, 1996 (detail)

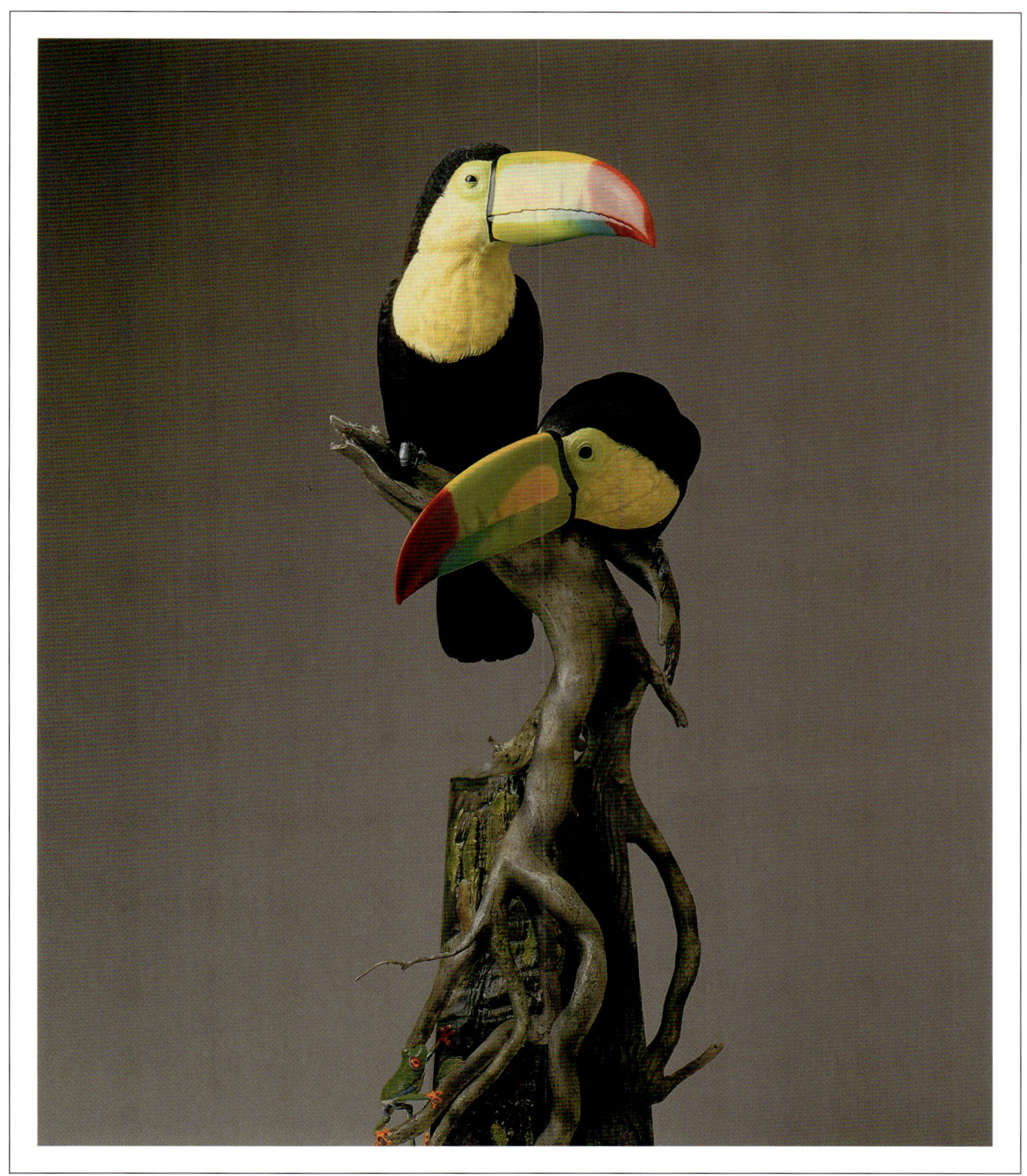

Floyd Scholz
Keel-Billed Toucans
Rainforest Symphony, 1996

With their long tails and enormous serrated bills, keel-billed toucans provide a kaleidoscope of primary hues to challenge the wildfowl artist. To offset the potential monotony of these radiant birds, Scholz has created a tension between the life-size pair, with the drowsy female a counterpoint to the inquisitive male leaning forward to investigate an approaching red-eyed tree frog. The slick tree stump, shaped like rivulets of water streaming through the rainforest canopy, is rendered in walnut.

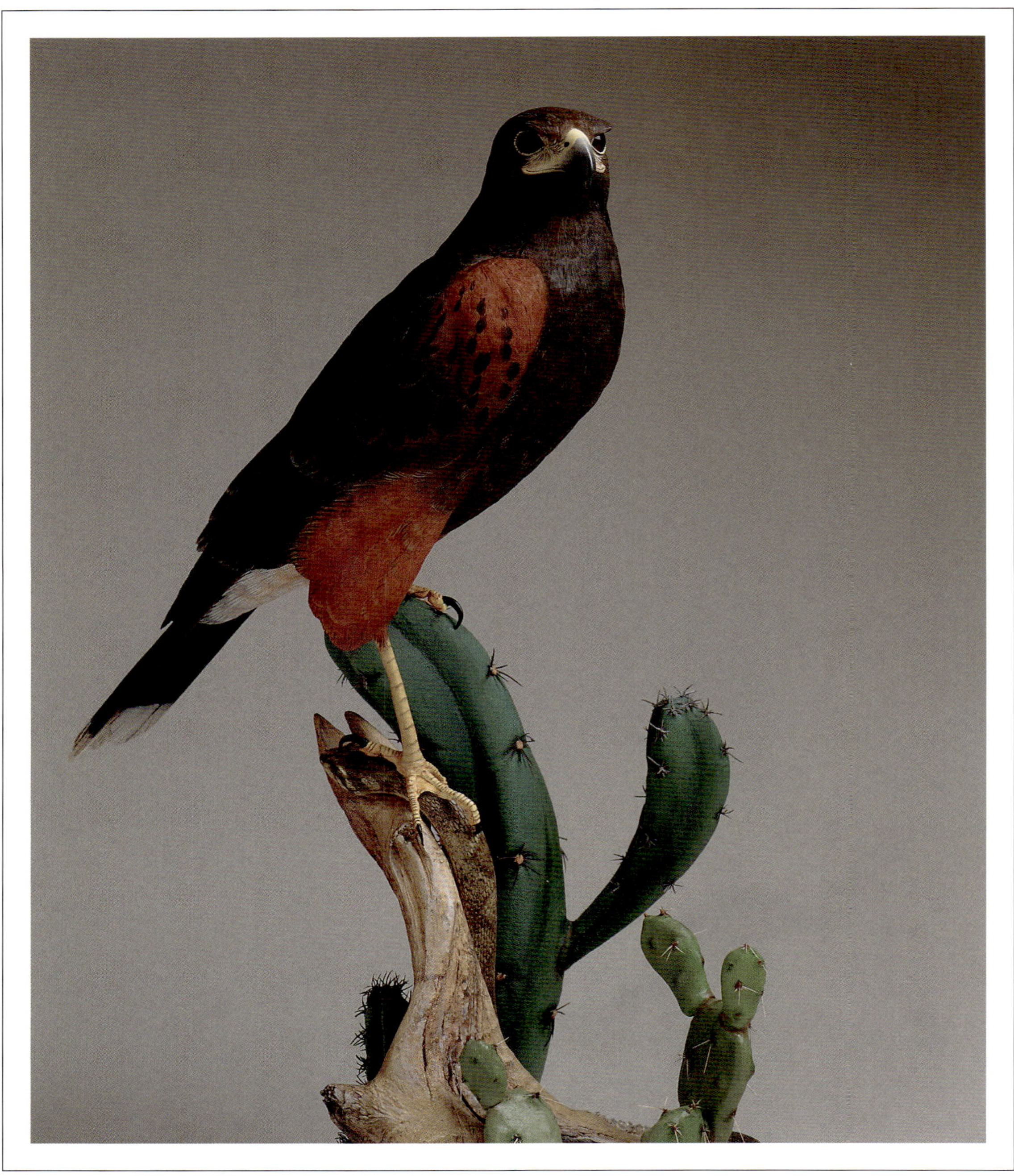

Floyd Scholz
Harris' Hawk
Desert Arrow, 1995

With a deadly western diamondback rattlesnake pinched underfoot, Scholz's wide-eyed life-size Harris' hawk is a portrait of pent-up energy. Scholz relies on detailed sketches to help him formulate the complex composition of his works, which, in this case, elegantly incorporates the slithering reptile woven around the cactus and the sculpture base.

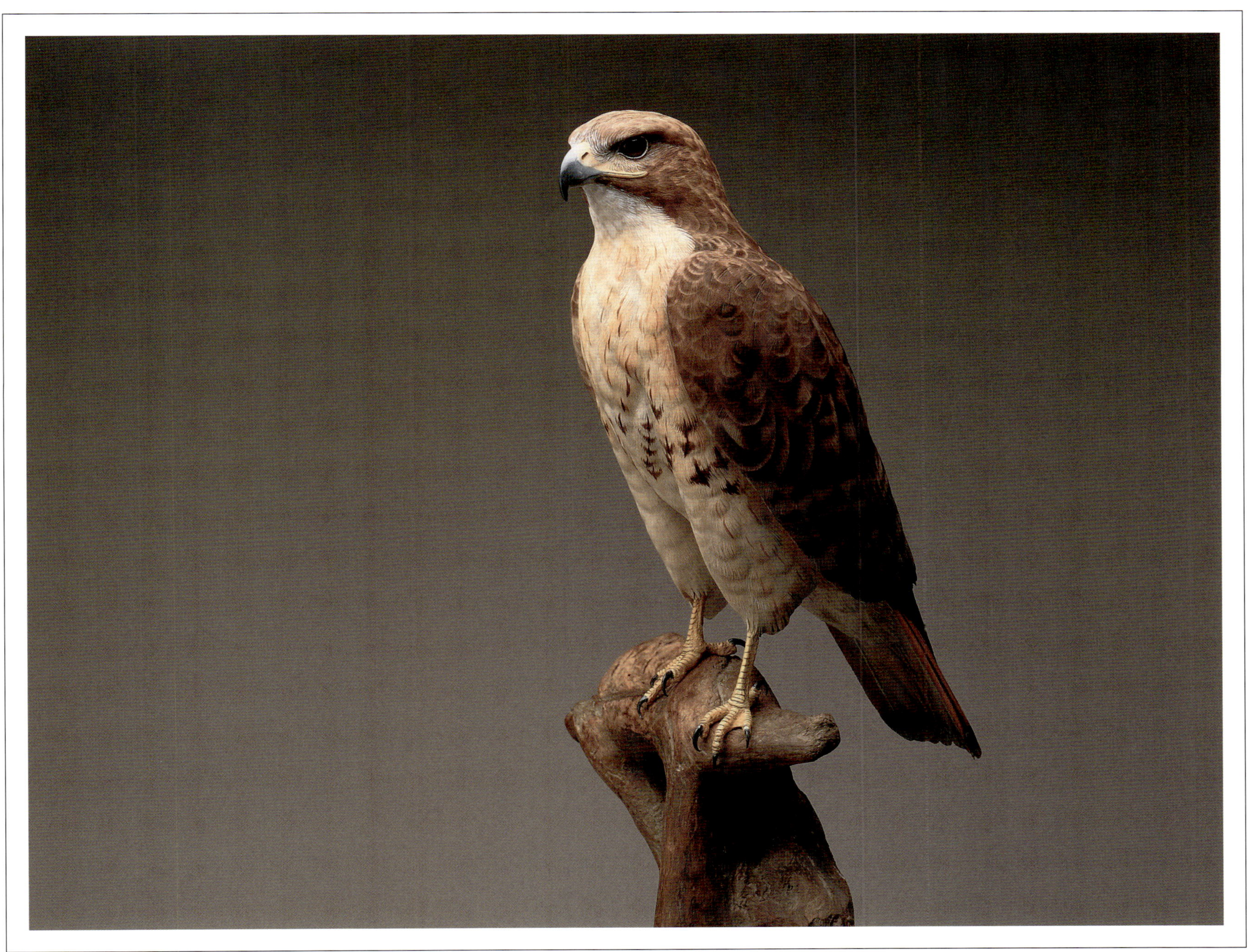

The same control and restraint that Scholz, who is a former decathlete, uses to make his brilliant tropical species convincing lend a regal air to his cryptically colored life-size birds of prey. Mixing strength and power in understated tones gives the artist's raptorial works an unrivaled grace.

Floyd Scholz
Red-Tailed Hawk
The Vigil, 1996

Jim Sprankle

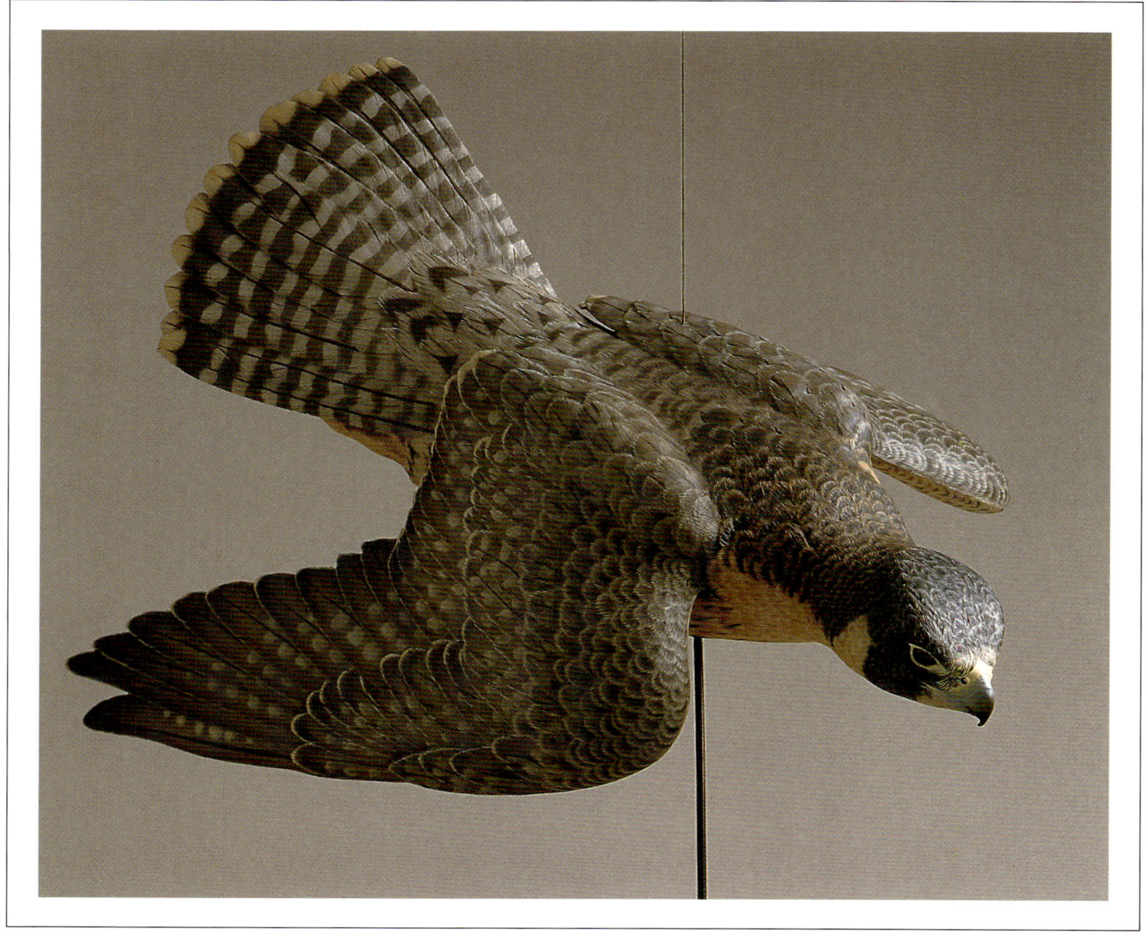

Jim Sprankle
Peregrine Falcon
Strike Two, 1995 (detail)

"I have always enjoyed birds in flight," says Jim Sprankle. "I'm not afraid of motion, and I enjoy putting some of the birds' acrobatics into my carvings." A driving force in the tradition of floating decorative decoys, Sprankle—the most recognized carver in open competition at the Ward World Championship—finally got the chance to put his birds in the air when he joined the competitive ranks of decorative life-size artists in 1990.

Though Sprankle made the move to decoratives some 30 years after becoming a serious carver, he still had his share of duck tales to tell. "I spent 16 years living on Chesapeake Bay," explains the former professional baseball player. "I was a waterfowl specialist." As a result, Sprankle featured waterfowl in his first three life-size sculptures.

In 1995, at the age of 61, Sprankle spread his artistic wings and tackled his first bird of prey. By then a permanent resident of Florida's Sanibel Island, he also began to find a world of inspiration in the subtropical wetlands, swamps and oceans around him. That Sprankle's imagination is never at rest is evident in his recent sculpture of tricolored herons. "I had no idea how beautiful these birds could be to work on," he says of his recent artistic transition. "I'm having the time of my life."

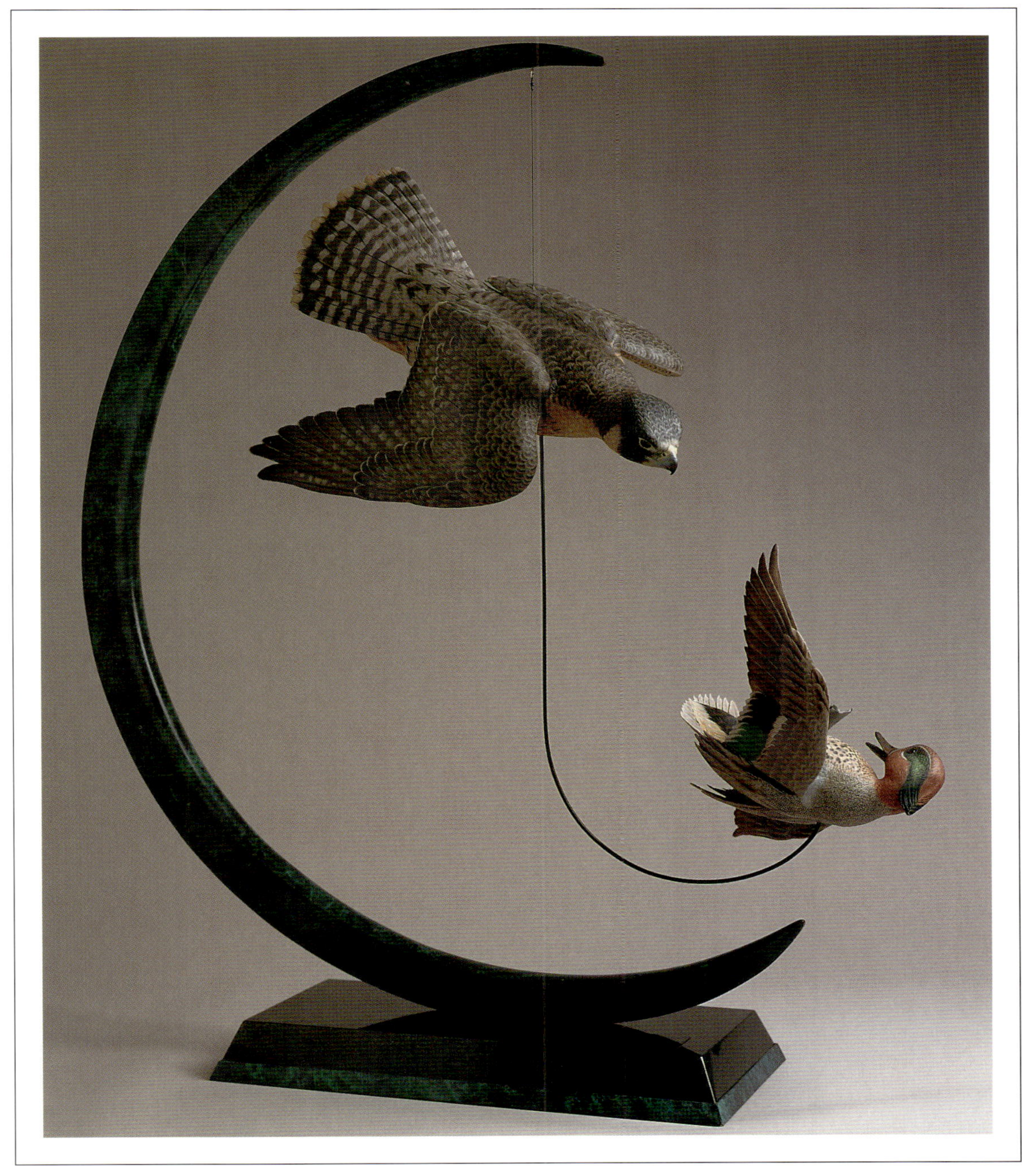

In this life-size sculpture, a peregrine falcon closes in on a vulnerable teal. While Sprankle initially designed the piece as a hanging mobile, he ultimately set the bird of prey and its quarry in a freestanding cast-bronze arc to preserve its animated mood.

Jim Sprankle
Peregrine Falcon and Green-Winged Teal
Strike Two, 1995

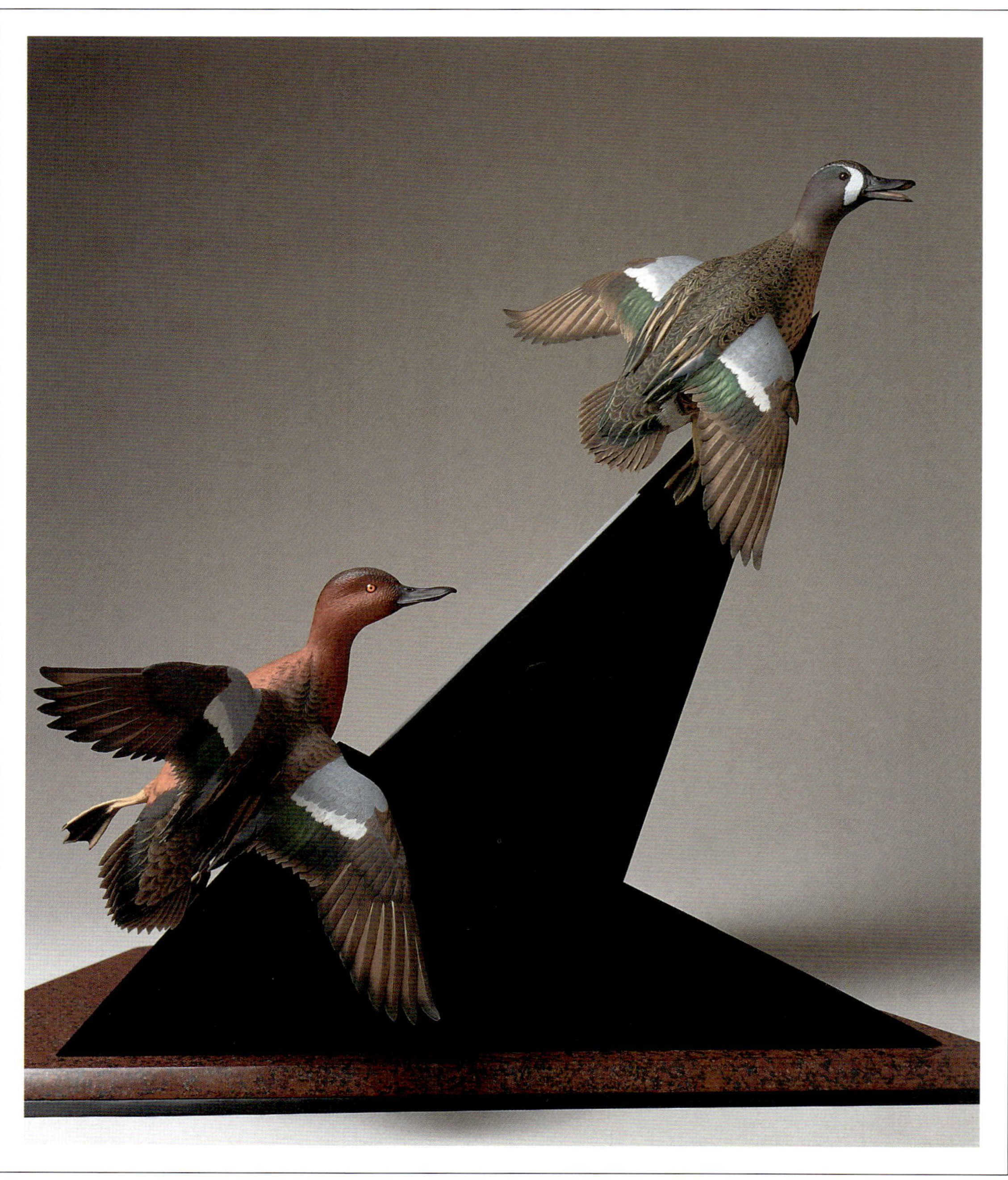

Jim Sprankle
Blue-Winged Teal and Cinnamon Teal
Mixed Flight, 1990

Black pyramids create a dramatic background for Sprankle's life-size blue-winged and cinnamon teal drakes. The artist's decision to place the teals on geometric forms rather than in a natural habitat introduces an abstract tension to the piece. Red marble and a band of black wood form the sculpture's base.

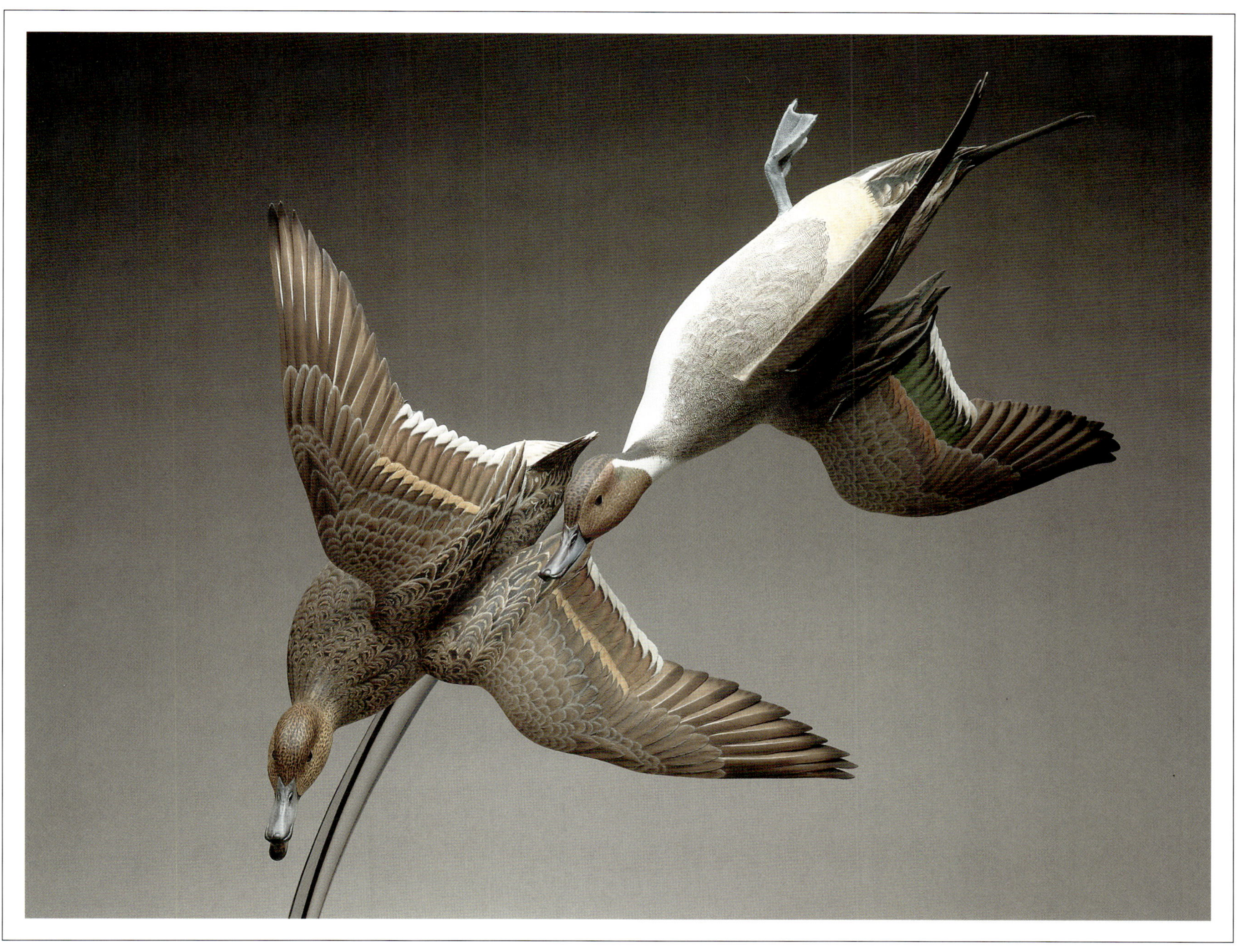

With a Plexiglas arc as their pathway, two life-size "greyhounds of the air" soar above a mighty Maryland river. The agile birds are sculpted from tupelo and basswood in a composition that Sprankle first roughed out using Styrofoam blocks. The artist worked from mounted skins to reproduce the feather groupings and anatomy. Sprankle shares his carving expertise with nearly 1,000 students whom he annually ushers through his Green Wing University.

Jim Sprankle
Pintails Over the Choptank, 1992

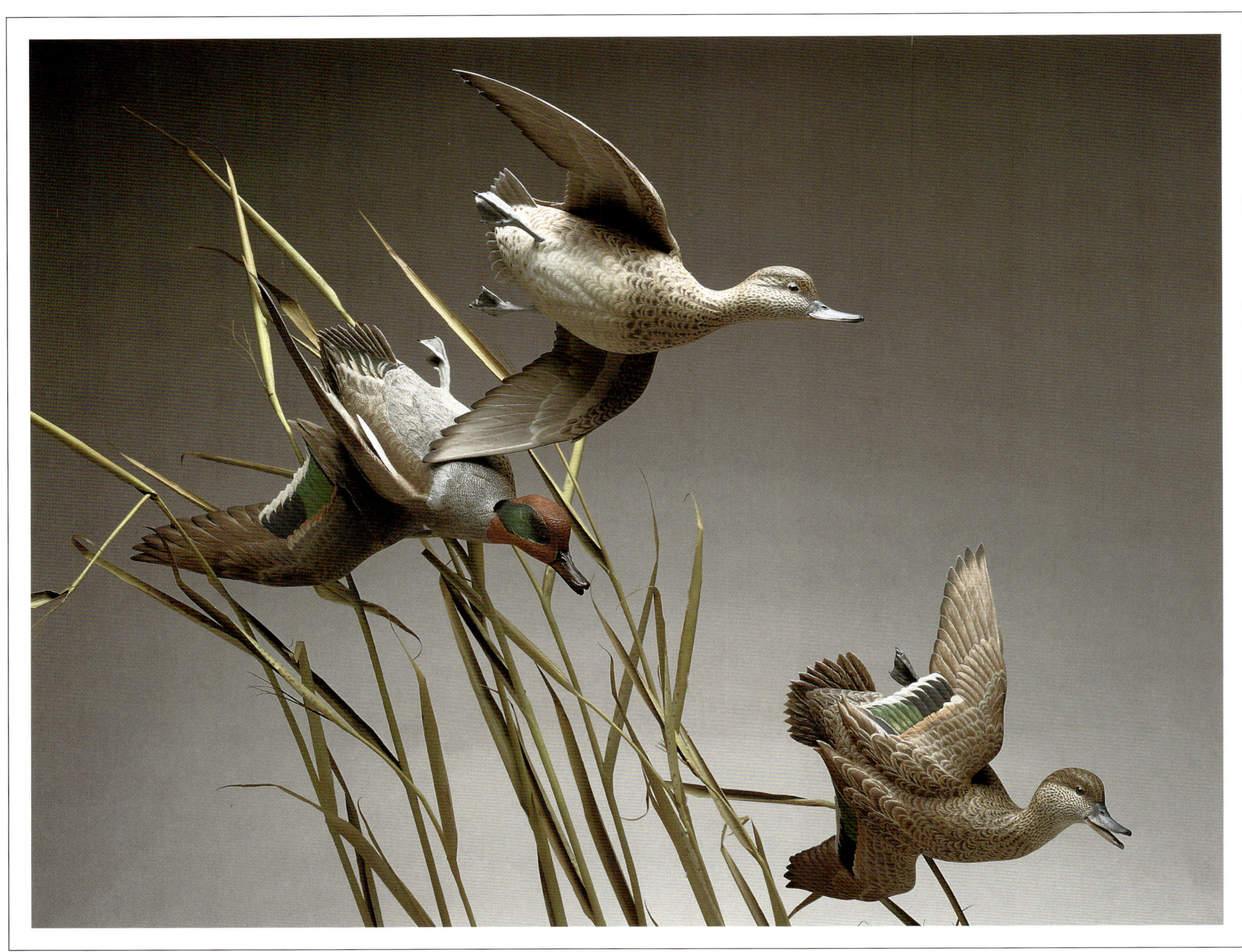

Jim Sprankle
Green-Winged Teals
Rockets in the Reeds, 1993

Sprankle's three life-size green-winged teals taking flight over a marsh of phragmites communicate the excitement and wild energy of a flock of migrating ducks. Sprankle uses his skills as a carver and painter to the fullest in this detailed rendering and complex composition of multiple subjects. Painting, in Sprankle's estimation, is 80 percent of the task, and here, he creates the depth of color in the ducks' textured plumage by applying acrylic washes.

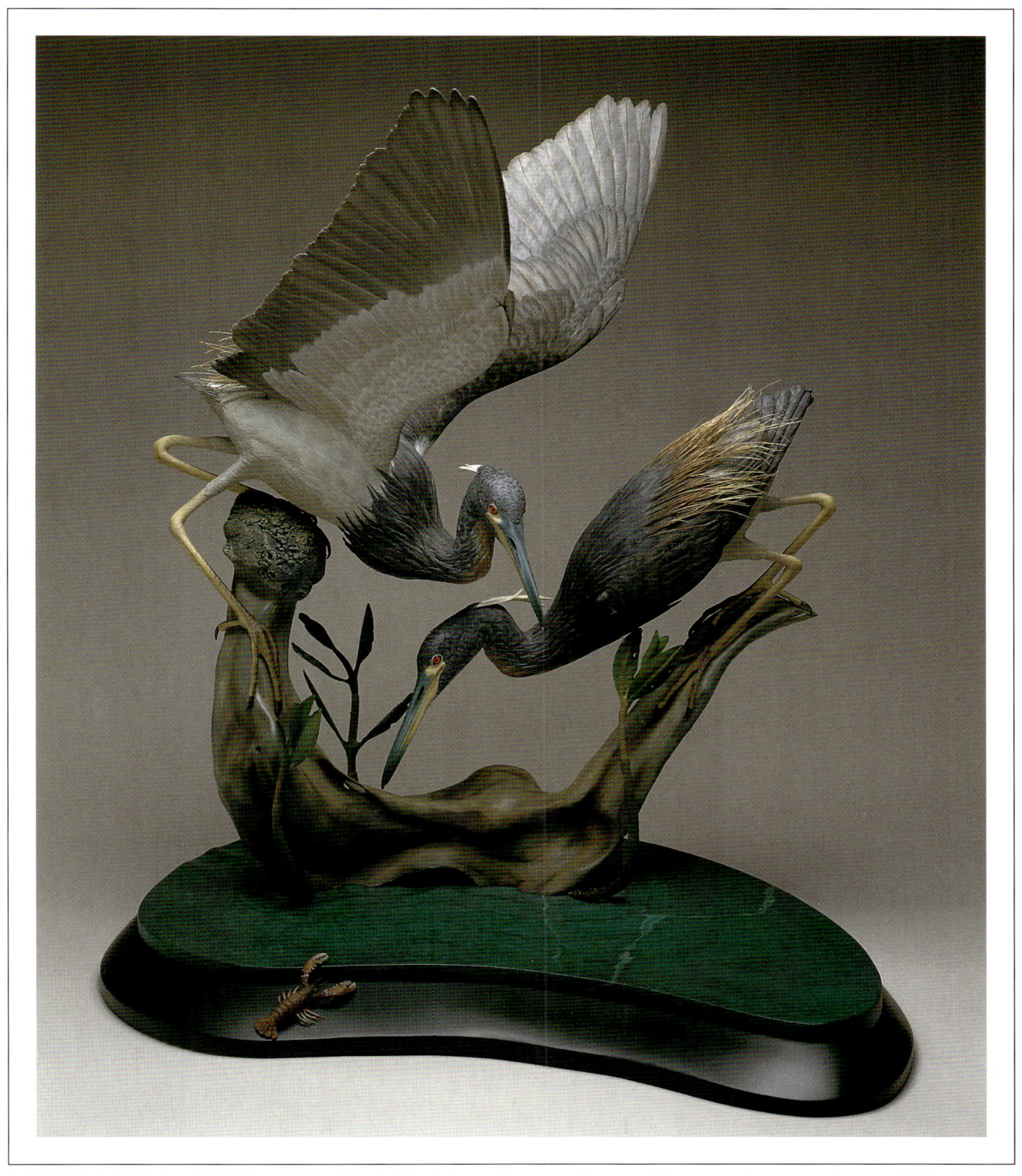

Perched on a piece of driftwood, a pair of life-size Louisiana herons sets its sights on an approaching crayfish in a standing pool. Sprankle carved the water in soapstone, then stained it to match the aquamarine waters of Florida before setting it into a basswood base. The wading birds represent the artist's second non-waterfowl subject in a career that spans three decades.

Jim Sprankle
Tricolored Herons
Ol' Fishin' Hole, 1996

Jeffrey Whiting

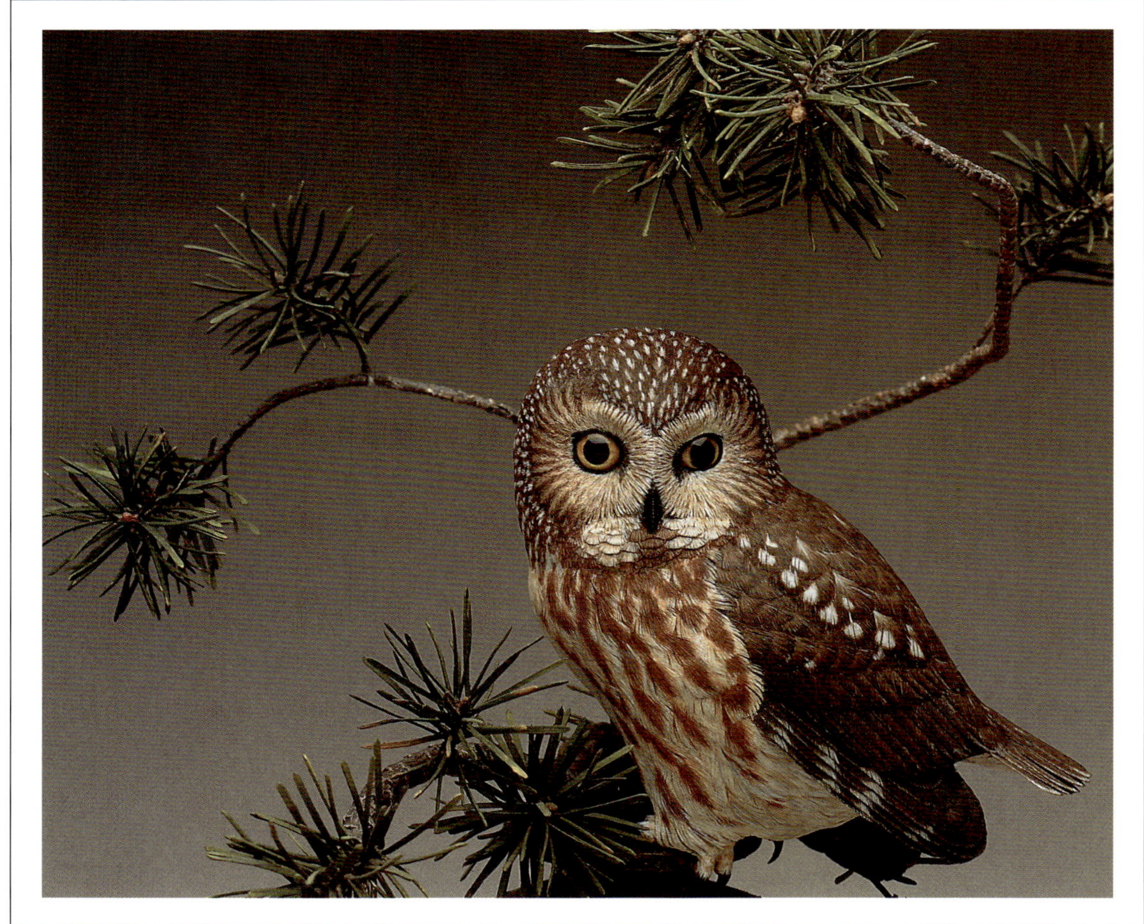

Jeffrey Whiting
Saw-Whet Owl and Jack Pine, 1996 (detail)

"My work is a bridge between art and nature," says Jeffrey Whiting. A recent graduate with an honor's degree in biology and geology, the Ottawa, Ontario, artist creates sculptures that are driven by design and influenced by the austere style and timeless composition of Oriental art. "The artistic considerations are the most important part of the work," explains the 24-year-old, a lifelong nature lover. "In the end, the bird often becomes subordinate to the entire piece." With that in mind, Whiting does not feel obliged to incorporate such elements as literally interpreted wild habitats for bases or backgrounds; many of his sculptures, in fact, begin as botanical arrangements.

Whiting is nothing if not innovative, exploiting both an encyclopedic knowledge of nature and a rich imagination to render extraordinary sculpture outside the realm of traditional wildfowl art. For his graduation-year project at Carleton University, Whiting drew on his special interest in paleontology to reconstruct a prehistoric dragonfly with a two-foot wingspan. More recently, he has worked on a dinosaur, *Styrocasaurus alberti*. "Taxonomically, birds are dinosaurs," he explains of the evolutionary connection between his interests. "It just isn't as big a leap as people might think."

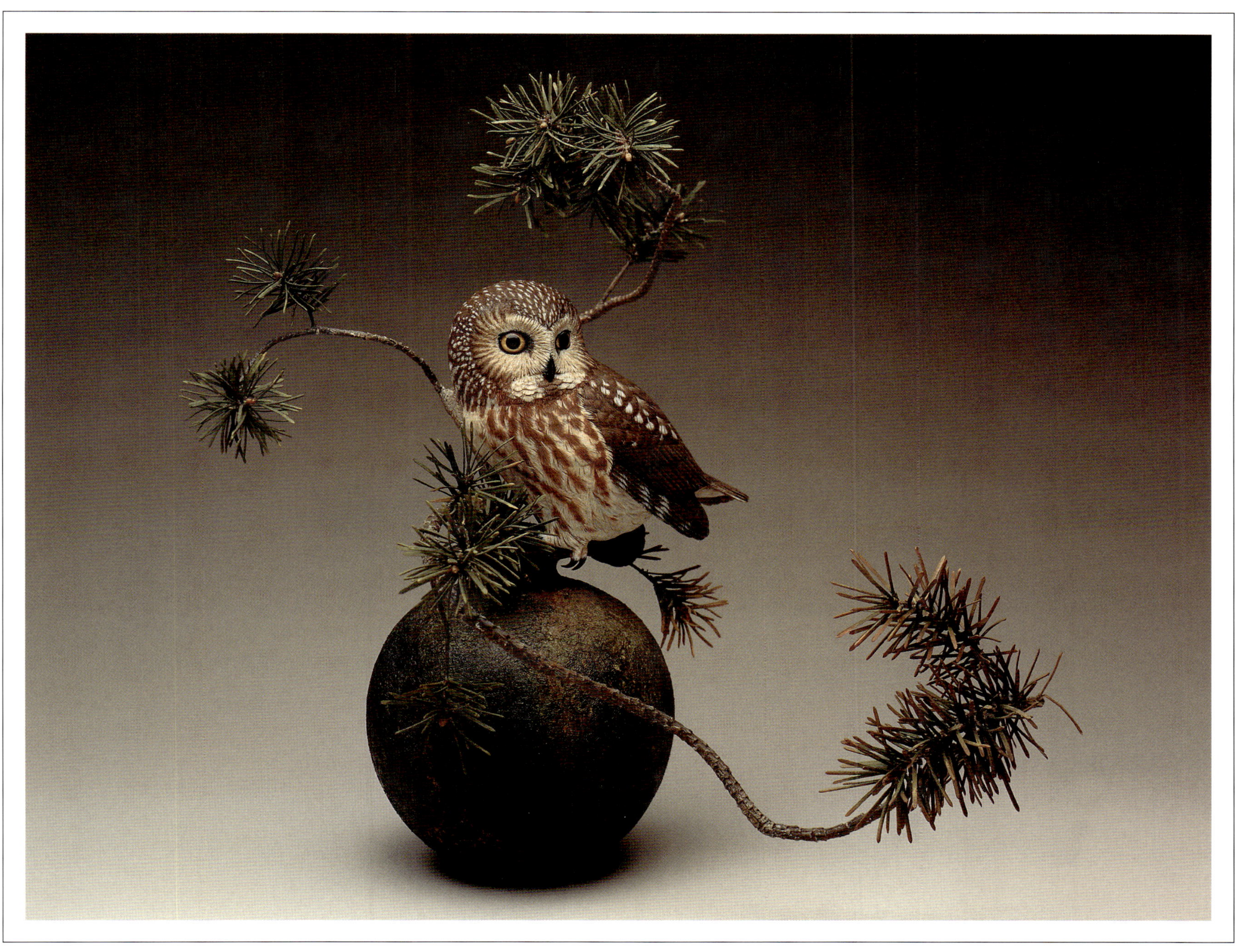

Curving boughs of prickly jack pine perfectly frame Whiting's life-size owl. Using bamboo toothpicks to create over 1,000 needles for the branches, Whiting took more than three years to perfect this dramatic piece. Carved in maple, the base was painted with the impasto technique—thick layers of paint applied with a knife to produce the look of a rusty moss-covered iron urn.

Jeffrey Whiting
Saw-Whet Owl and Jack Pine, 1996

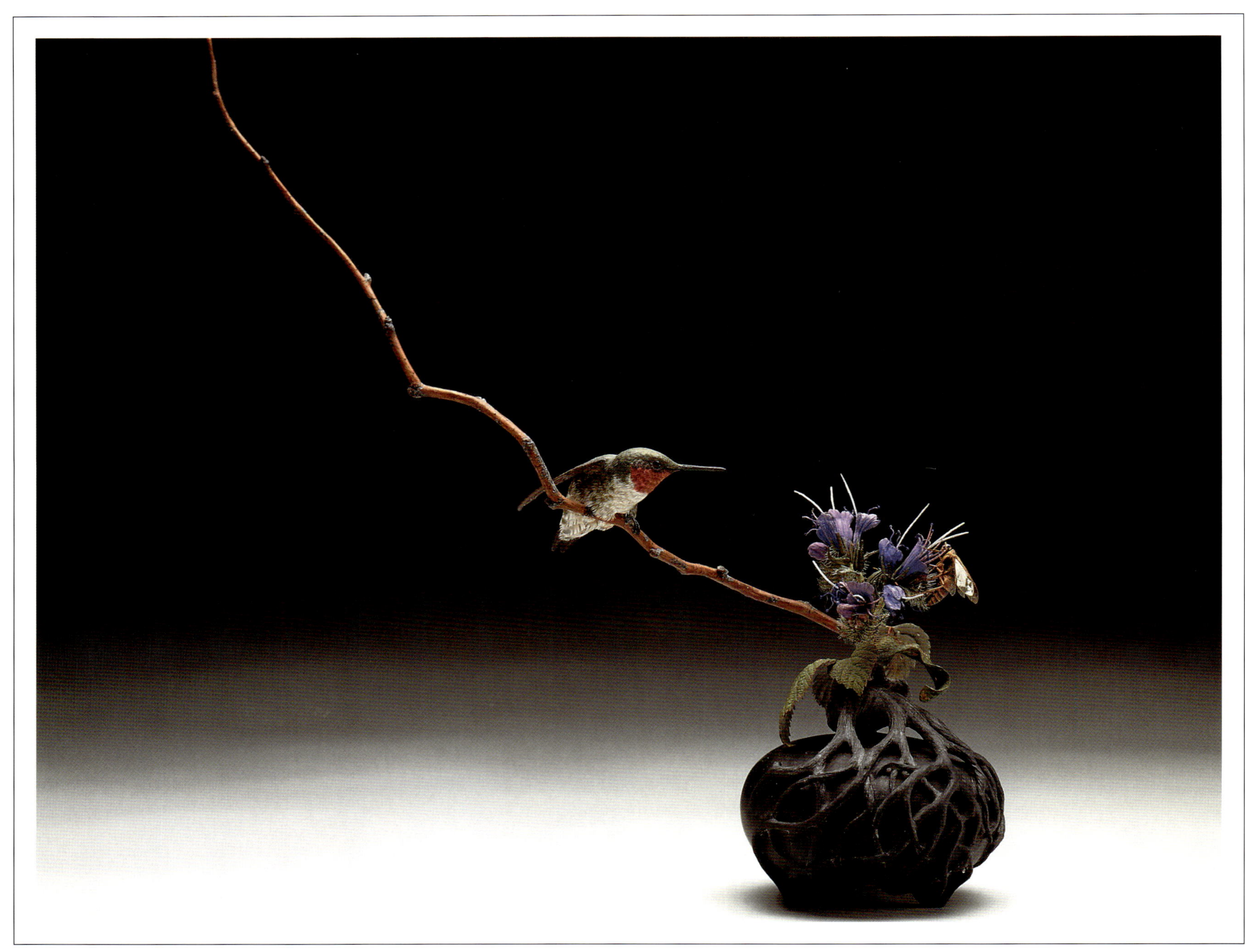

Jeffrey Whiting
Ruby-Throated Hummingbird
The Sentry, 1992

Typically aggressive when defending a food source against rival birds, a ruby-throated hummingbird confronted by a wasp patiently awaits its turn. In this piece, Whiting demonstrates his sensitivity to the natural world through a painstaking composition that required 1,500 hours of dedicated effort, using tupelo for the life-size hummer, viper's bugloss and paper wasp, metal for the wasp's appendages, acetate for its wings and wool for the plant hairs.

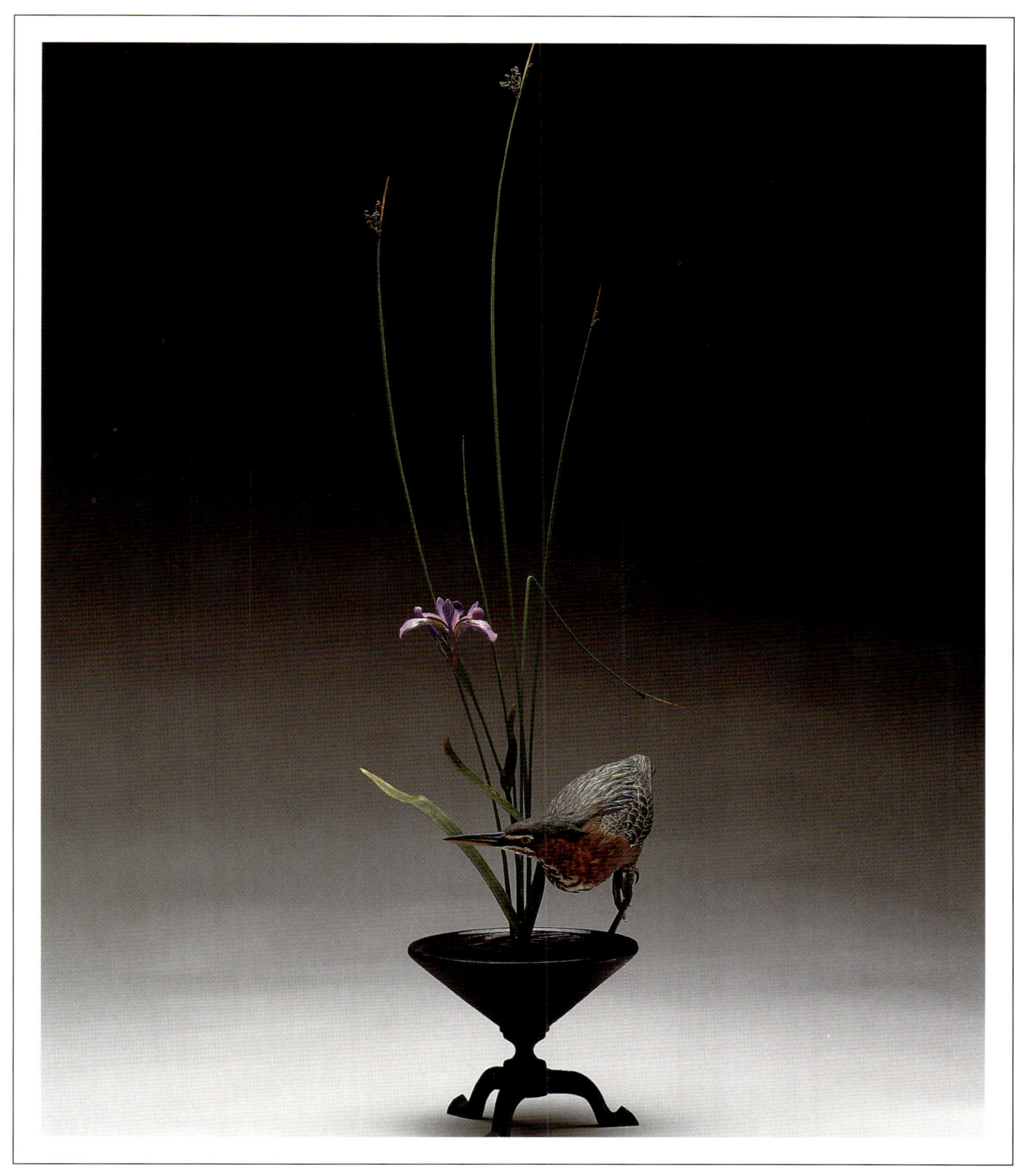

Poised on one leg in water, Whiting's miniature green-backed heron stealthily hunts around the base of a bulrush and a blue-flag iris. Whiting carved the base from maple and painted it to create a metallic finish.

Jeffrey Whiting
Green-Backed Heron
Stalker, 1992

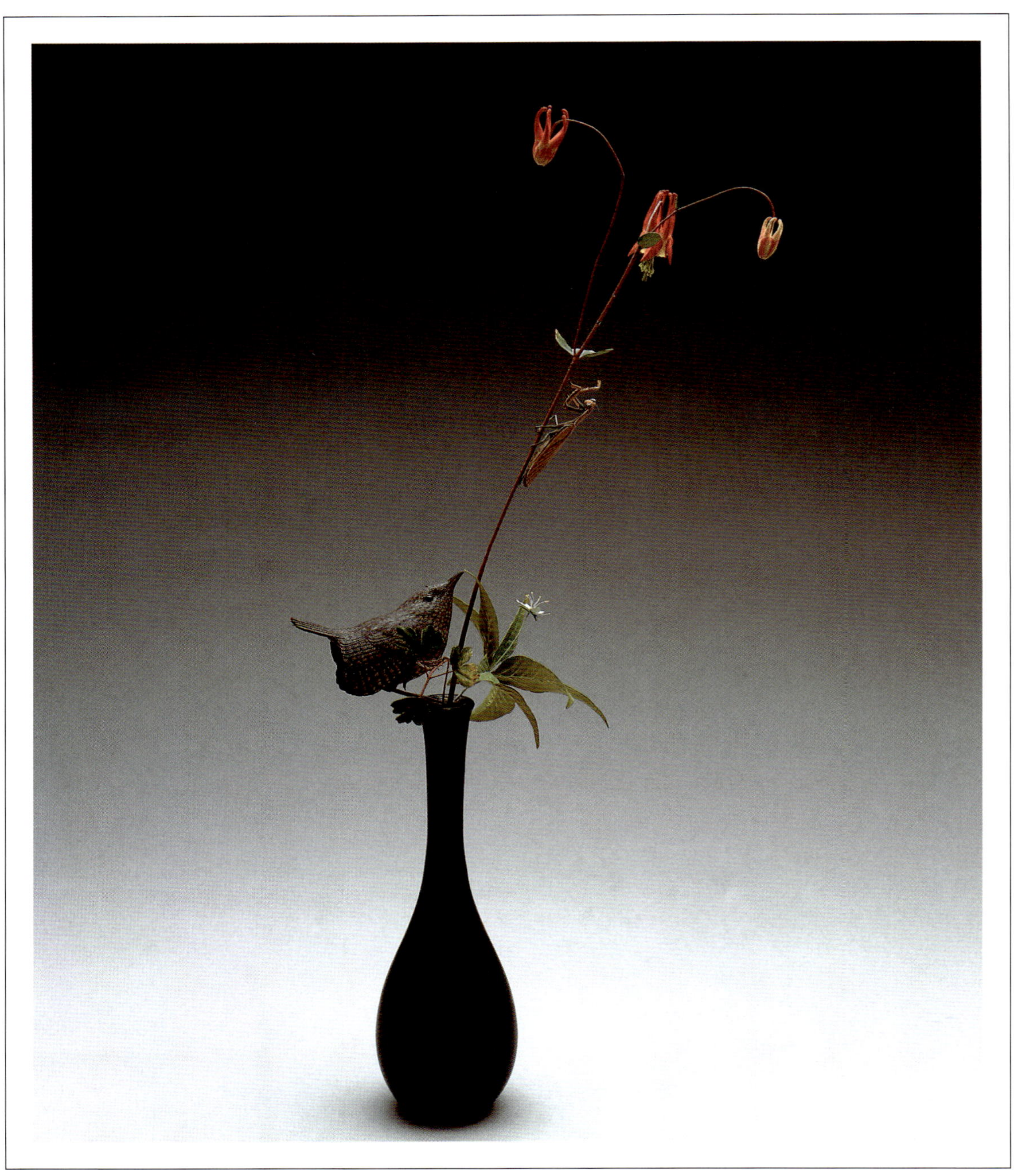

Jeffrey Whiting
Wren
Untitled #1, 1993

In what he describes as his purely artistic series on insect-eating species, Whiting used a life-size winter wren and a male praying mantis ascending a wild columbine to provide a visual twist to his creative concept.

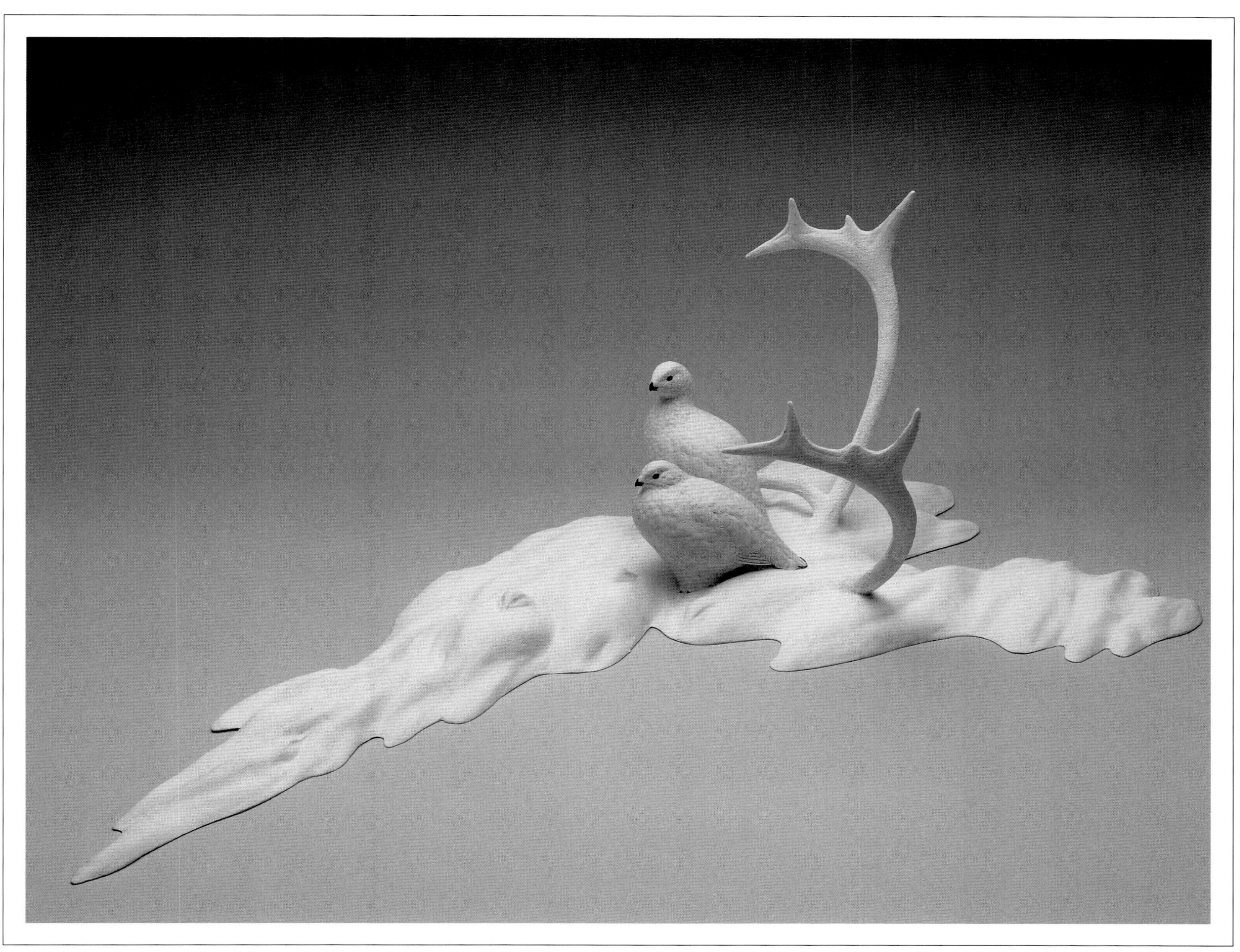

White-phase ptarmigans and a pair of caribou antlers on fresh snow capture the mood of the vast northern landscape in Whiting's miniature composition. Undulations texture the windswept powder, then rise in ghostly ptarmigan forms, reinforcing the setting's isolated atmosphere. Having carved the birds from wood, Whiting then cast the base in resin before painting the shadows and light on his sculpture.

Jeffrey Whiting
Ptarmigans
Whiteout, 1994

Todd Wohlt

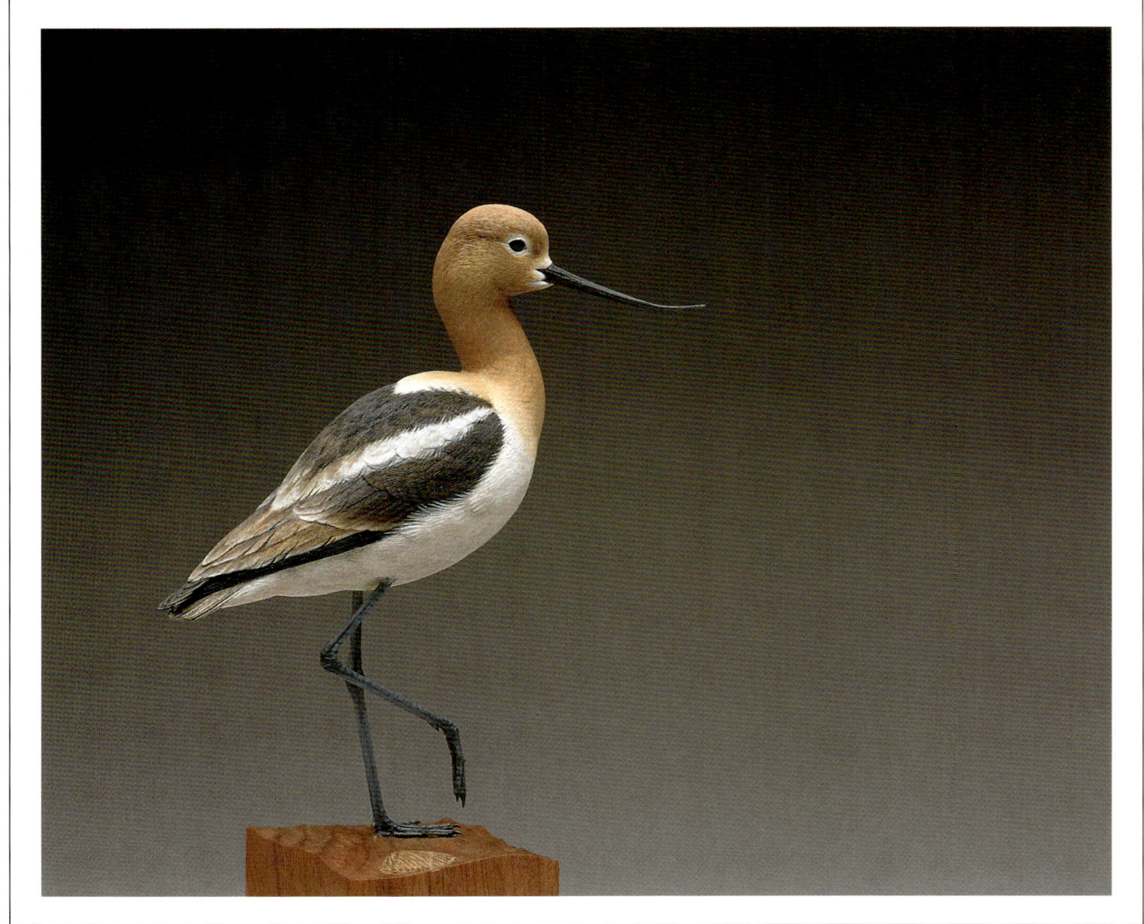

Todd Wohlt
Avocet, 1993

A high-stepper in the receding tide, this miniature American avocet reflects the artist's preference for soft-toned birds. An abalone shell carved into the base is a jewel-like adornment for the graceful avocet, which is sculpted from basswood. Working with a detailed clay model to perfect his composition, Wohlt then copied the design into wood.

"I like to think of wildfowl sculpture as my full-time hobby," says Todd Wohlt. It's a hobby that has shaped the course of Wohlt's artistic life since he first took it up at the age of 13. Even as a beginner, Wohlt immersed himself in carving books and classes in order to define his style.

Wohlt's first big break came not too long afterward. In 1986, his wood duck decoy won the A. Danner Frazer Memorial Youth Award at the Ward World Championship. Presented to the most outstanding carver under the age of 18, the award was a great motivator for Wohlt, who waited only four years before jumping into competition at the world decorative life-size level. While enrolled in fine art at the University of Wisconsin, Wohlt created his first championship piece—*Dive!*—which consumed some 1,500 hours of his precious college time.

With a second world championship under his belt, Wohlt continues to work as a full-time graphic designer for a packaging firm. Now 28, the Neenah, Wisconsin, artist is unassuming about his successes, conscious of how his applied-arts career centers him and tempers the demands for creativity in his carving. "When I carve, I don't want it to be a battle," he says. "As long as it's my hobby, I get to make the sculptures that I want."

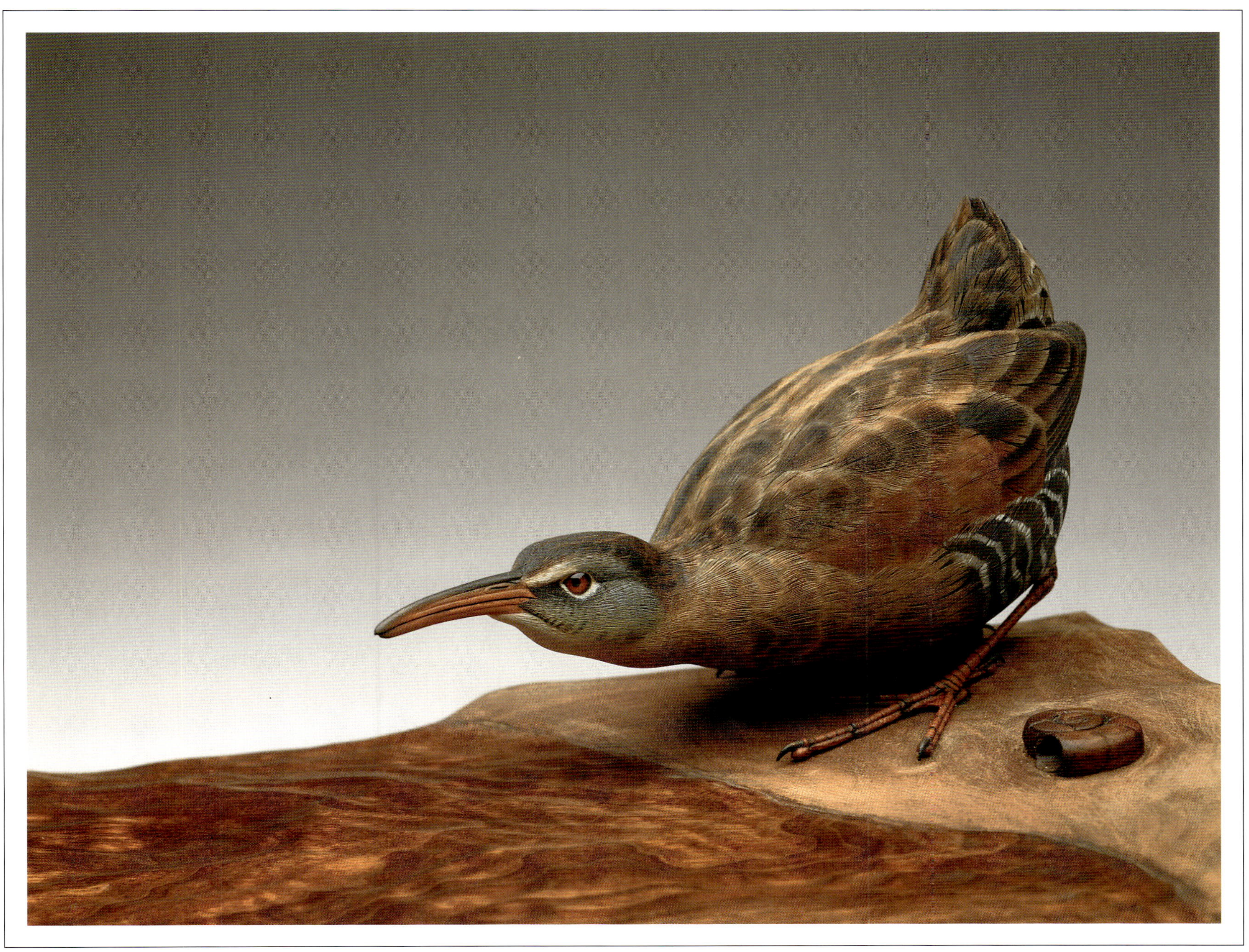

Todd Wohlt
Virginia Rail, 1995

A secretive bird that hunts close to the water's edge, Wohlt's life-size Virginia rail sports the muted earth tones which the artist likes to paint with oils. Wohlt's artistic interpretation is a reminder that less can be more: Here, he experiments with a natural-wood base treated to suggest a waterline and sandy shore. A snail shell carved into the beach is a playful motif that Wohlt sustains throughout a series of sculptures.

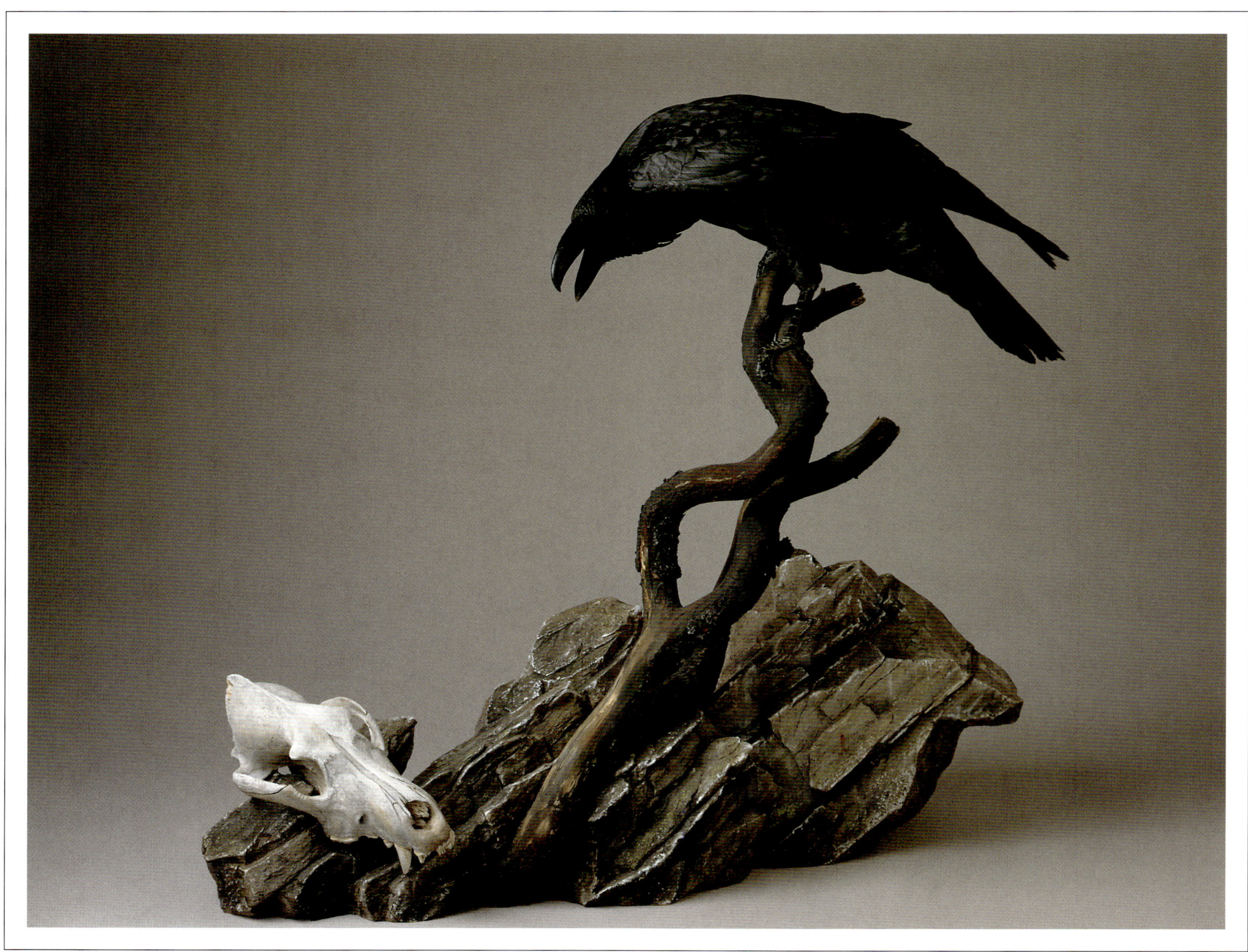

Todd Wohlt
Raven, 1991

With its dark plumage and black bill and eyes, Wohlt's raven—perched on a gnarled tree stump above a wolf kill—is a sinister depiction of a scavenger. The artist's first nonwaterfowl subject, this life-size carving represents the equivalent of 10 months' solid work and was finished during Wohlt's junior year at university.

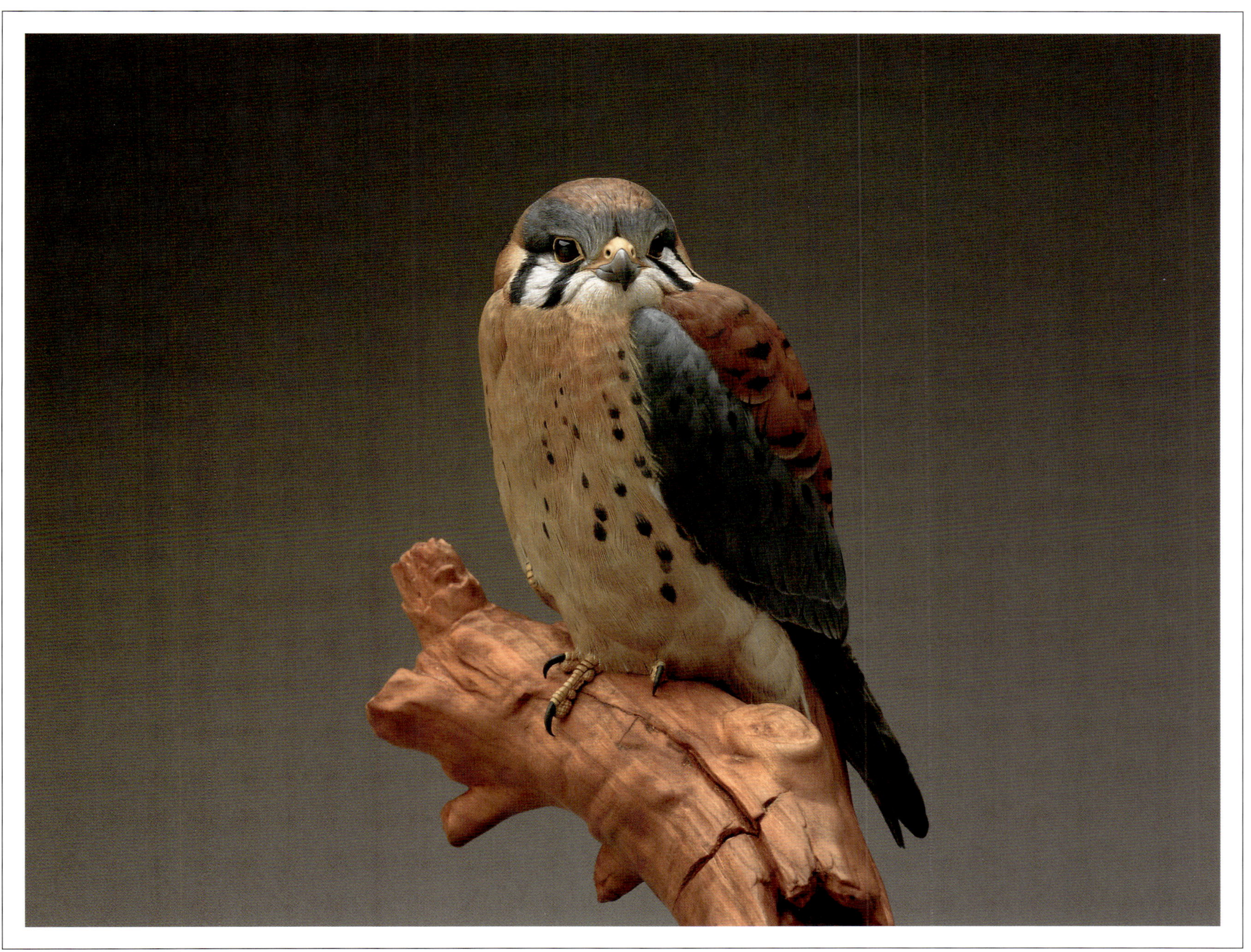

Todd Wohlt
Kestrel, 1996

With its large head and saucerlike wide-set eyes, the American kestrel is a challenging subject for the wildlife sculptor. Wohlt marshaled the disproportions of the diminutive bird in this world-championship carving, however, by communicating a momentary sweetness. To underscore a mood of tranquillity, he combined the warm tones of late-afternoon light and perched his doe-eyed life-size kestrel on a twisted old-growth branch fashioned from naturally finished cherry wood.

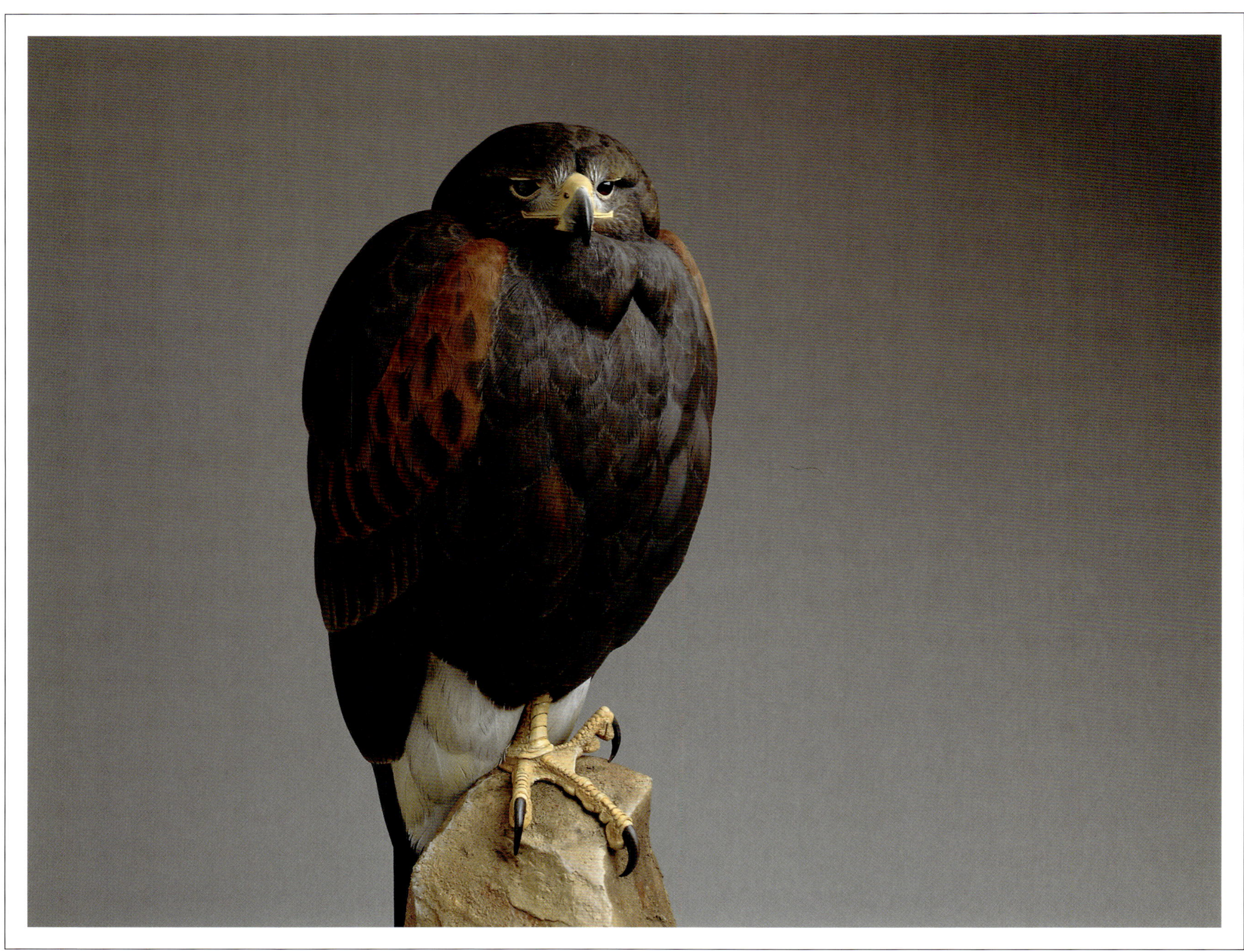

Todd Wohlt
Harris' Hawk, 1995

Hunkered down and puffed up, Wohlt's life-size raptor is the picture of predatory satisfaction. To tackle the 18-inch hawk, Wohlt employed a mix of hand and electric tools on basswood, which holds detail best, and rendered the feather detail with a wood-burning tool before using two thin glazes of oil paint to achieve the final color.

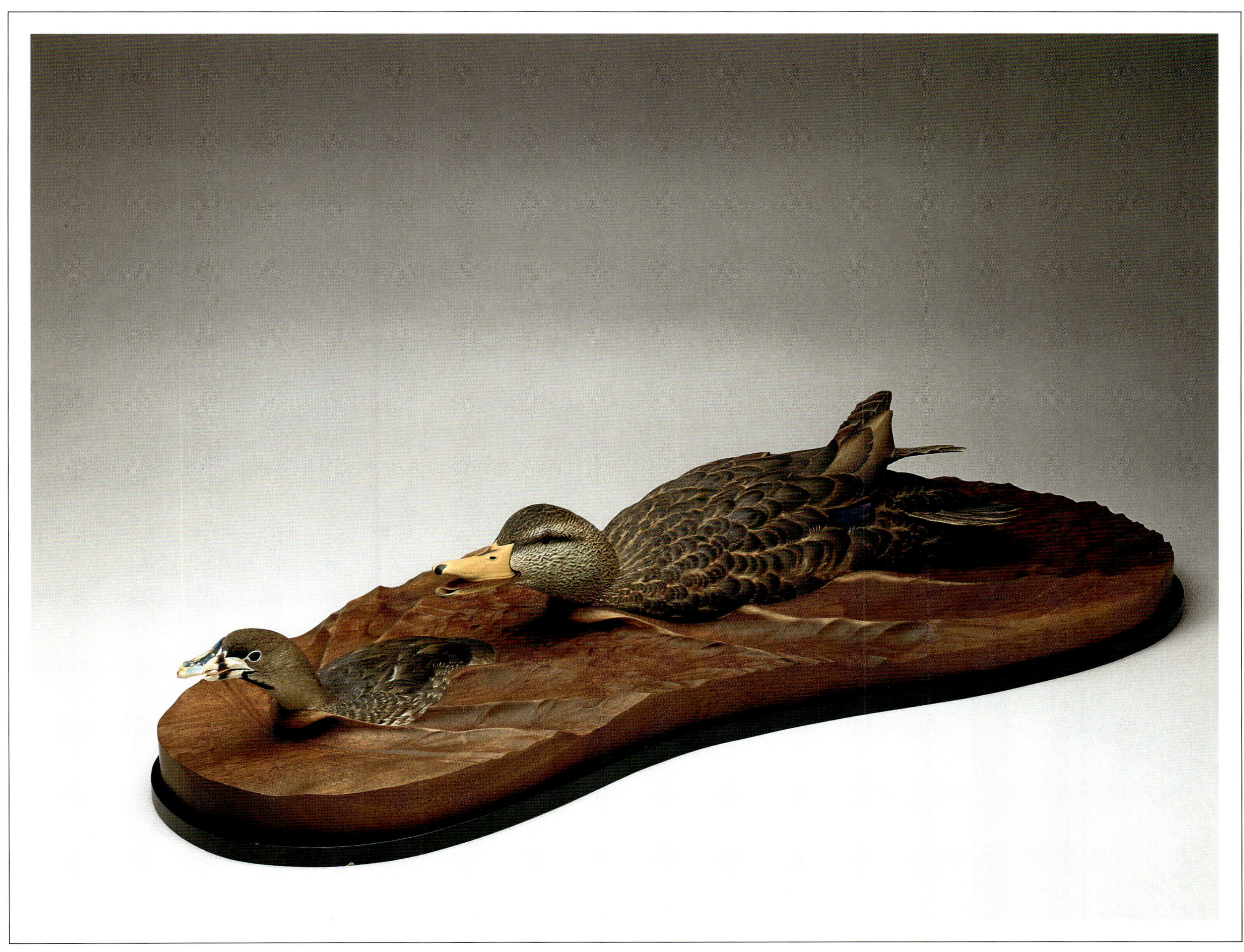

Todd Wohlt
Pied-Billed Grebe and Black Duck
Dive! 1990

Wohlt carved the undulating water in this sculpture from a three-inch-thick slab of walnut. To create the submerged birds realistically, he fashioned the lower half of the life-size black duck as part of the base, adding a basswood piece for its upper body. The grebe, however, is made entirely of walnut; only its head is added. Once Wohlt laminated the mixed woods together, he textured, burned and painted the piece.

Greg Woodard

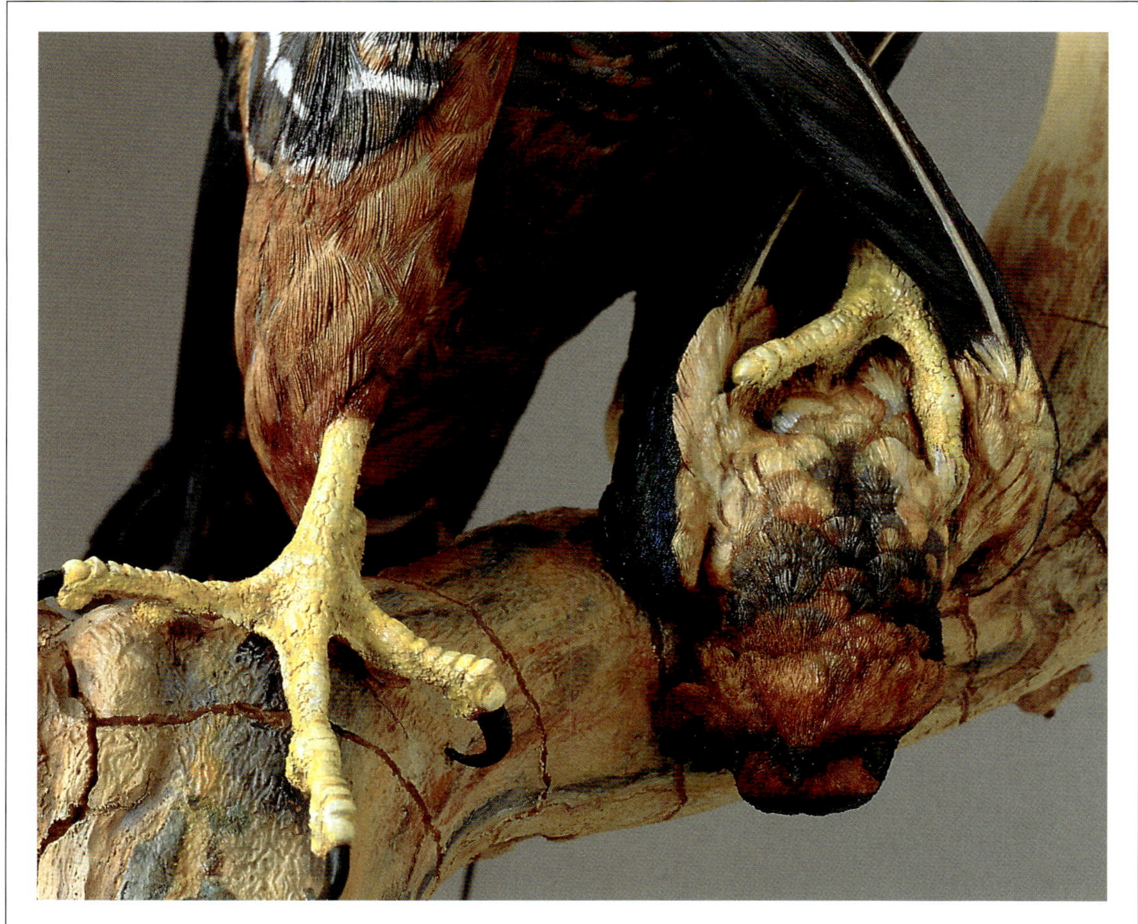

Greg Woodard
Bat Falcon With Barn Swallow, 1994 (detail)

"This area is a flyway for raptors," says Greg Woodard of the open skies above his home near Brigham City, Utah. "When I'm working, I can look up and see mountains and birds." Woodard's art is infused with a vividly untamed look that has its roots in his upbringing in the West, with the colors of the Western landscape, its vegetation and wildlife surrounding him.

Since taking up carving full time in 1983, Woodard, 38, has gone on to develop an integrated single-piece style. "My work is a tough fit. I'm breaking away from the traditional decorative looks," he explains of his choice to avoid inserts. "It borders on something more interpretive, and the artistic part comes from letting go."

The free and rustic edge to Woodard's work is closely tied to his unique method of carving almost exclusively with a chain saw. "I can get it down to within the last quarter-inch that way," he says. "I feel what I want in the wood, and then the wood comes off. The rest I do with grinders and burning."

A licensed falconer, Woodard flies his birds daily. "To know the feather layouts, their size, number and shape, it helps to know the birds," he says. "But when I work with what's in my mind, that's when magic happens."

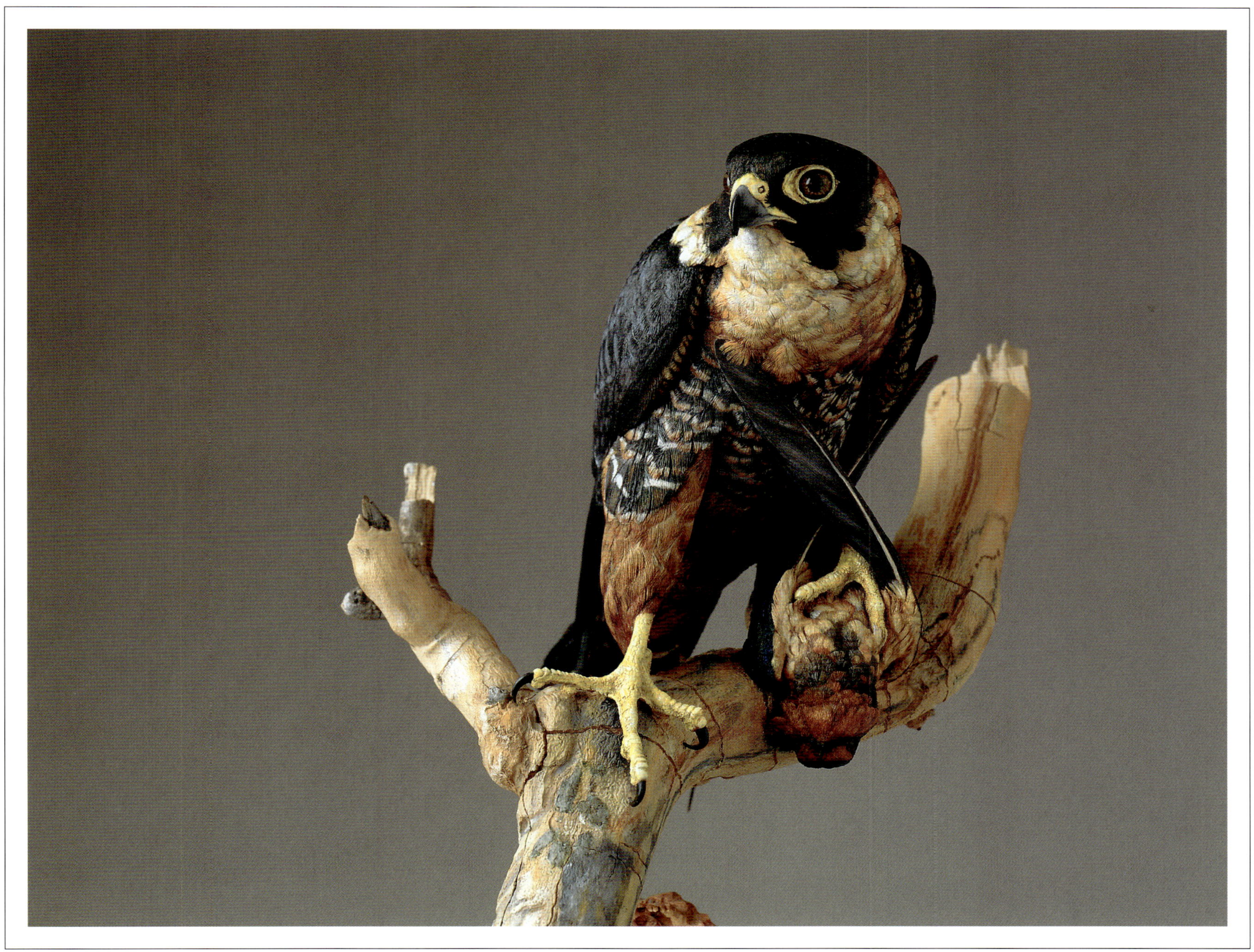

Woodard depicts the deft hunting skills of one of nature's fleet-winged predators. With its quarry clutched in a deadly grip, the life-size falcon is poised to pluck it, a composition that exploits the crossed wings of the swallow and makes the raptor's chest the focus of the piece. Using a clay model to rough out the design, Woodard then carves in tupelo; a single application of oil paint helps the artist to achieve the "loose and bold colors" of his work.

Greg Woodard
Bat Falcon With Barn Swallow, 1994

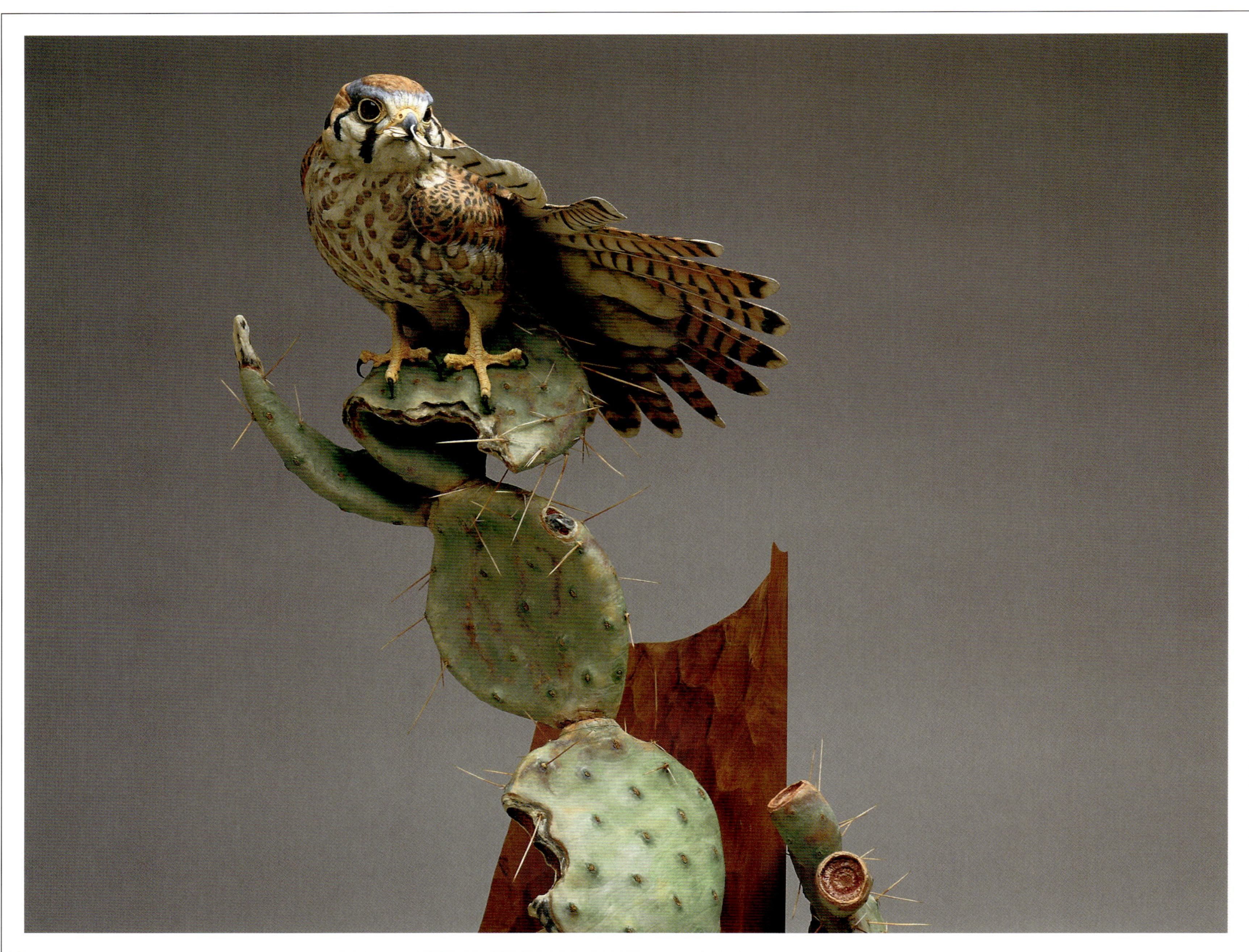

Greg Woodard
American Kestrel
Cactus Flower, 1992

A preening desert species on a prickly Western perch is the subject of Woodard's best-in-world life-size sculpture. Copying a succulent that he found on his own land, Woodard segmented the carved plant's scales in the same manner they grow in the wild. The apricot base blends naturally with the colors of the kestrel, which crowns the cactus like a flower.

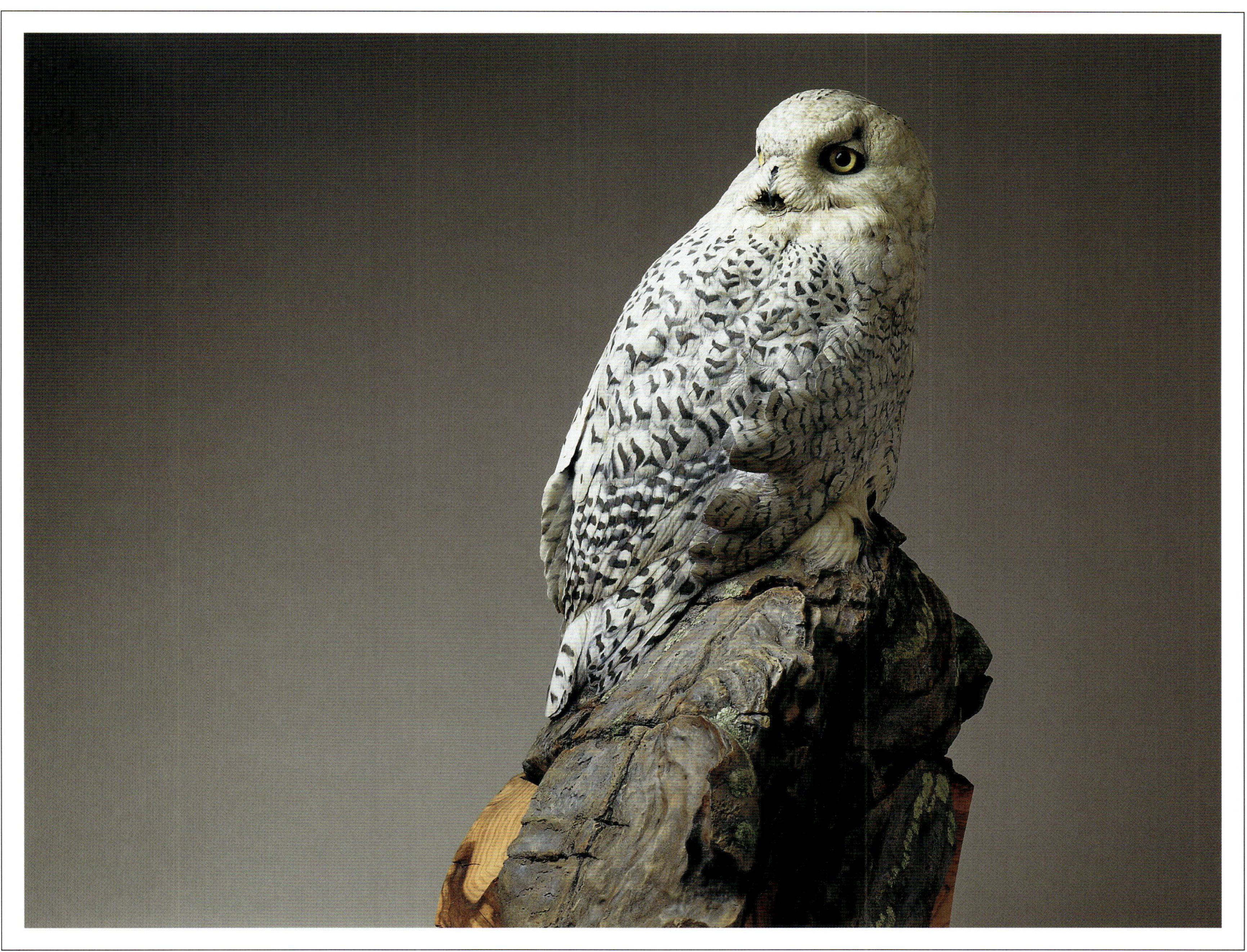

Woodard's life-size snowy owl reveals a more serene aspect of this bird of prey. A raptor's eyes constitute an important part of its look, and Woodard is among a handful of carvers who make their own bird eyes. Painting the pupil and iris on the end of a wooden dowel, he then bonds it to a slice of Plexiglas, grinds the unit into a convex lens and trims it to fit in the socket.

Greg Woodard
Snowy Owl, 1995

Gary Yoder

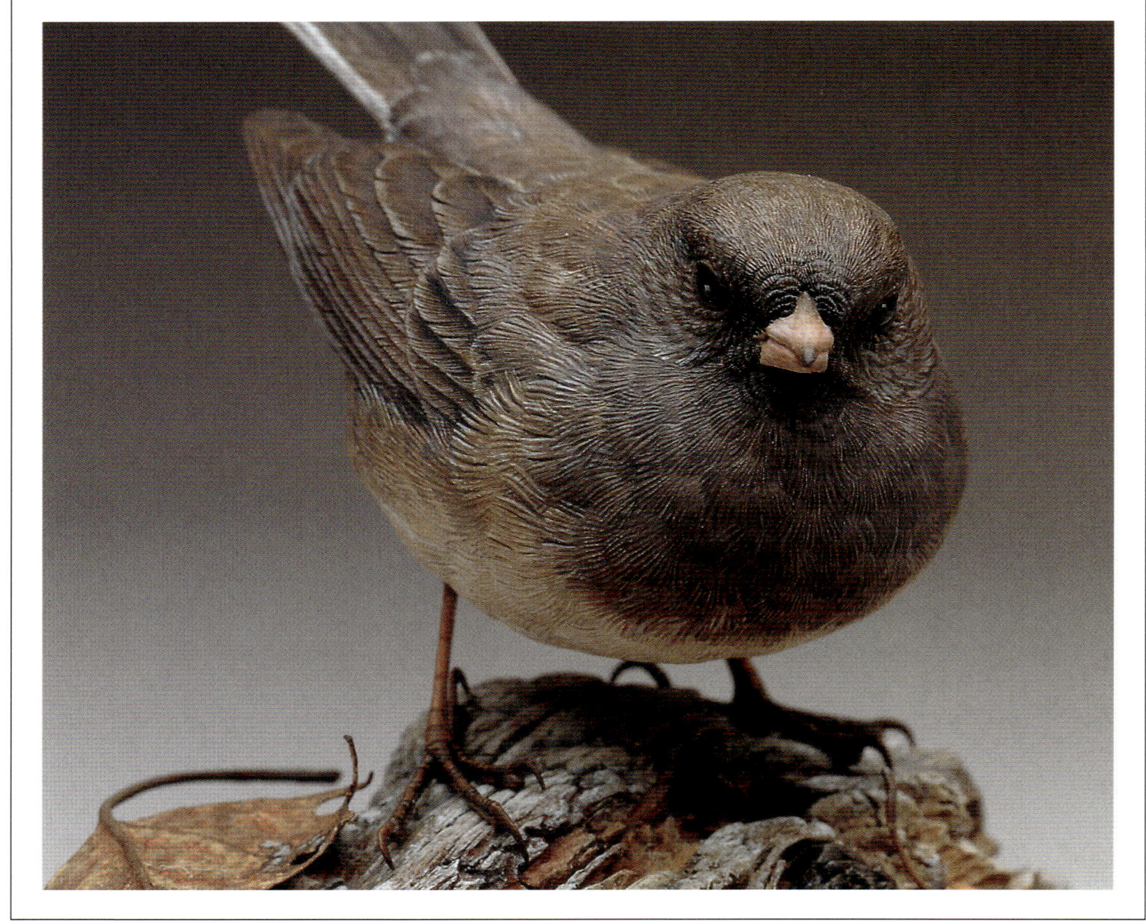

Gary Yoder
Junco, 1996 (detail)

"Lines tend to run through my carvings," explains Gary Yoder. "Even if it's in a more abstract way, a powerful line is still there." Yoder might easily be describing the trajectory of his artistic vision. Just as a visual plane runs through many of the 38-year-old carver's works, each piece is thematically connected to the last as he pushes forward, demanding greater integration between the technique and the content in his work.

Yoder's direction is common among elite carvers. It represents a trend away from a reliance on head-turning realism to works that may be less extravagant technically but stronger artistically, a transition which Yoder describes as the passage from bird carving to bird sculpture. "The medium isn't the message," he says. "Realism is a point of perspective, and it's the image that is important. Once I figure out why I want to do something, technique is just a way to get me there."

Yoder, who lives in Grantsville, Maryland, first picked up a carving knife at age 11. He continues to work on life-size songbirds but has earned a reputation as a miniature specialist, a medium that helps him find renewal in his art. "With miniatures, I can keep very focused," says Yoder, "because I'm not overwhelmed by the scale of a piece."

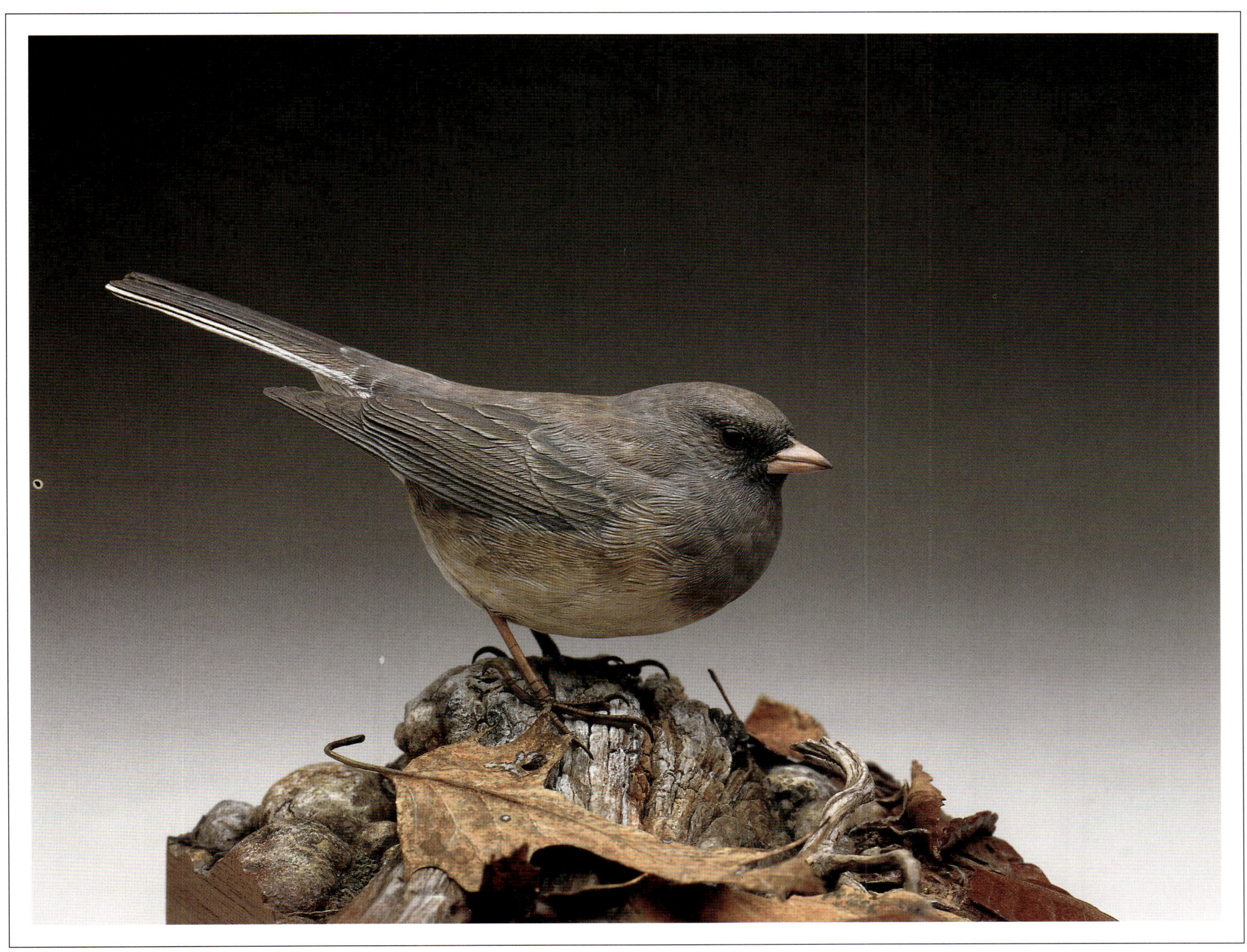

Gary Yoder
Junco, 1996

In a strategy he calls "working the corners," Yoder created a plane across the diagonals of his piece, thus establishing a strong composition for his life-size female dark-eyed junco. In addition to fixing the bird at the focal point where the diagonals intersect, Yoder developed a gentle transition from the abstract mood of the base to the realism of the bird, a shift that is reinforced by his subtle blend of colors and the hooks and sweeps on the leaf and branch stems.

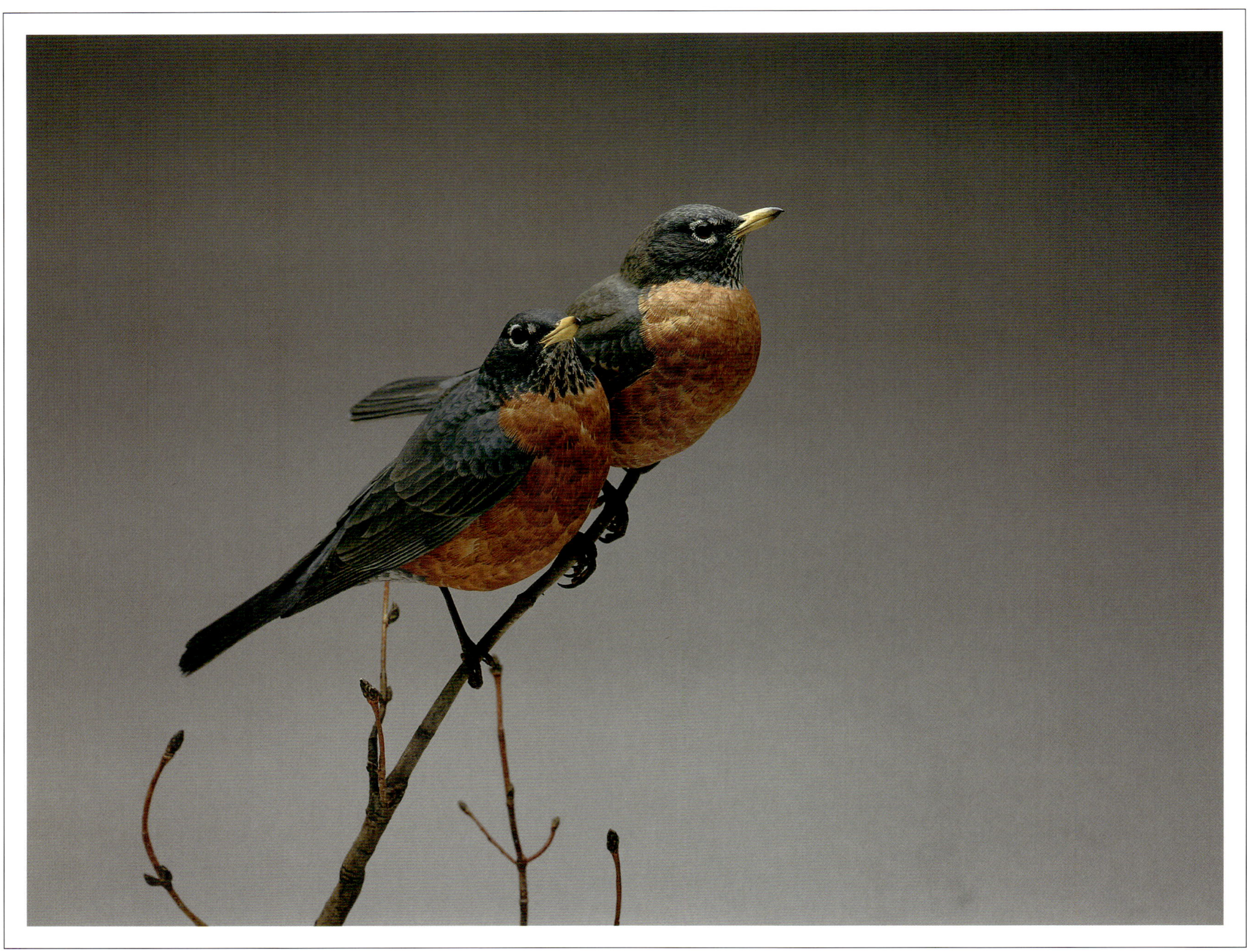

Gary Yoder
American Robins, 1989

The paradoxical relationship of Yoder's bird pairs is most strongly felt in this life-size sculpture: while the contact between the birds' bodies and their linear composition reinforce their togetherness, they cast their eyes in different directions, establishing their autonomy. Underscoring the balance, Yoder creates a mirror image of acrylic-washed color—the branches' grayish bark topped by red buds is a reflection of the birds' colorful breasts and backs.

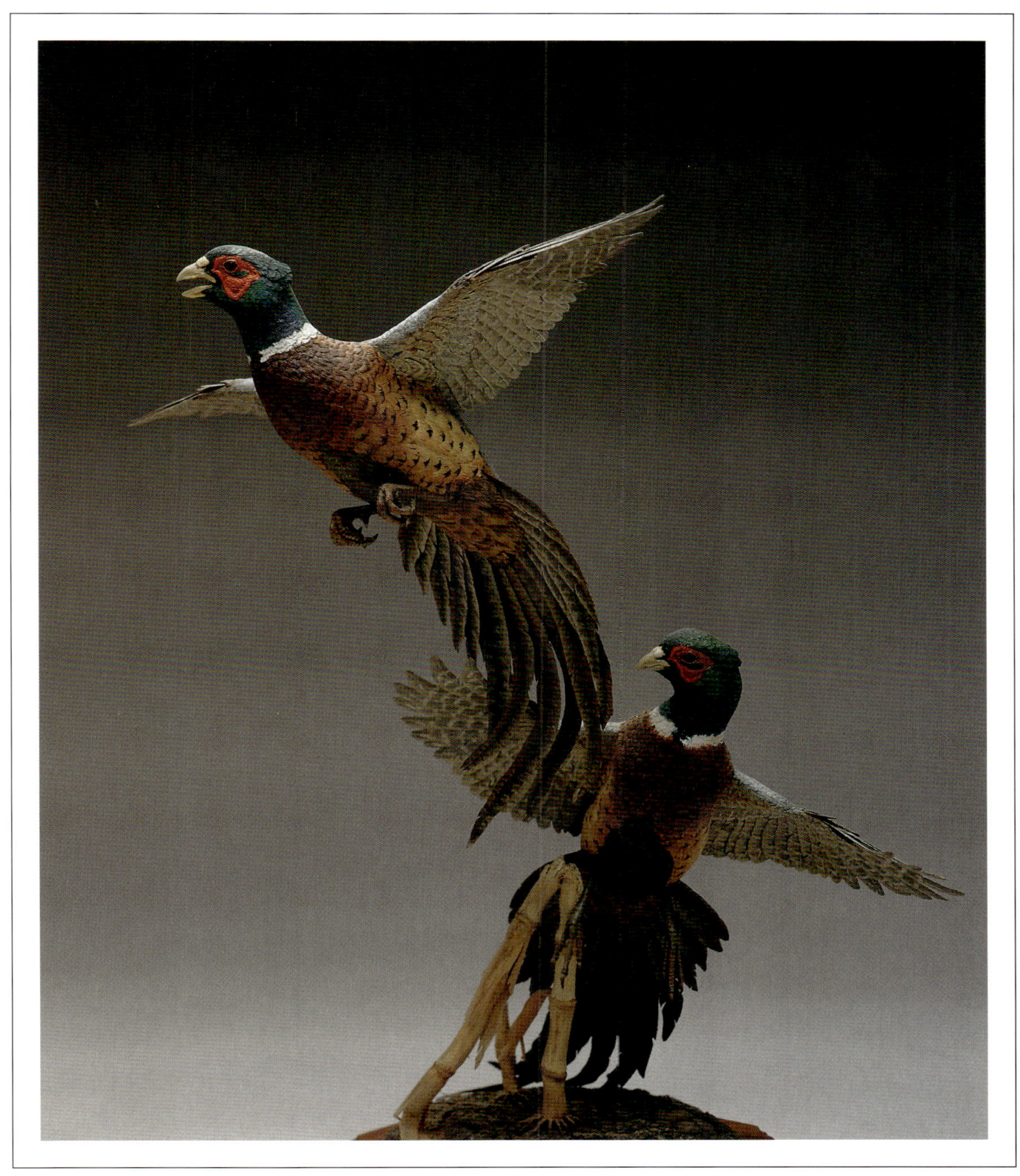

These miniature ring-necked pheasants—the first of Yoder's five world-championship winners—signaled a transition in the artist's work. Breaking away from an intricate style that gathered many elements into one setting, Yoder simplified his design and placed more emphasis on the mood and composition of the piece. While the birds still feature numerous undercuts and individualized feather groupings, the stronger message is the flow that winds through the sculpture.

Gary Yoder
Pheasants, 1980

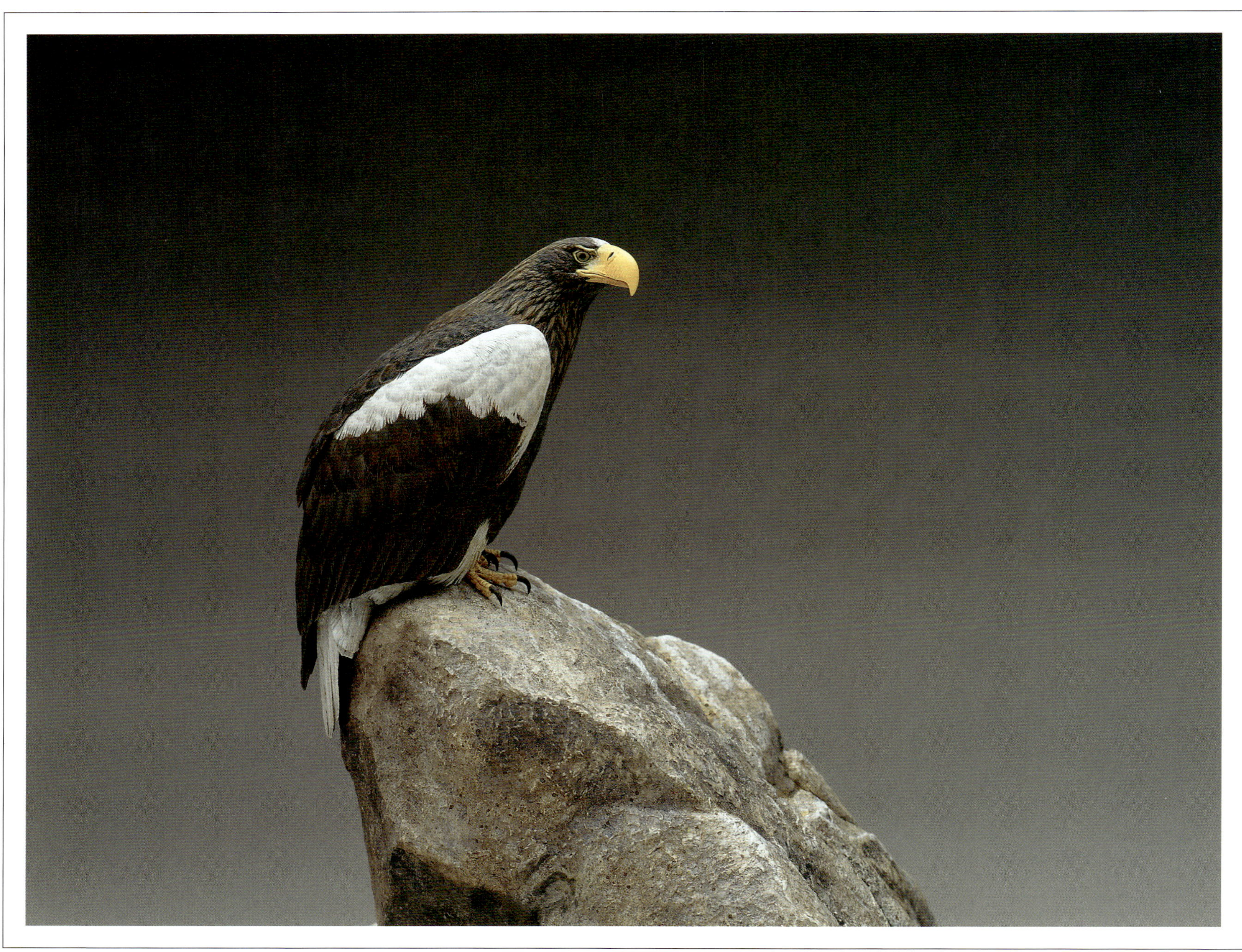

Gary Yoder
Steller's Sea Eagle, 1995

The combination of wood burning, stoning and grinding with power tools as a means of creating texture and loft in the bird's plumage reaches its full realization in the head and neck feathers of Yoder's miniature eagle. The smoother bird, showing only a few selectively undercut feathers, is a sign of a larger trend toward carving for mass and form rather than detail. Yoder made the base of his piece—a simple elevated rocky perch—as prominent in the sculpture as the bird itself.

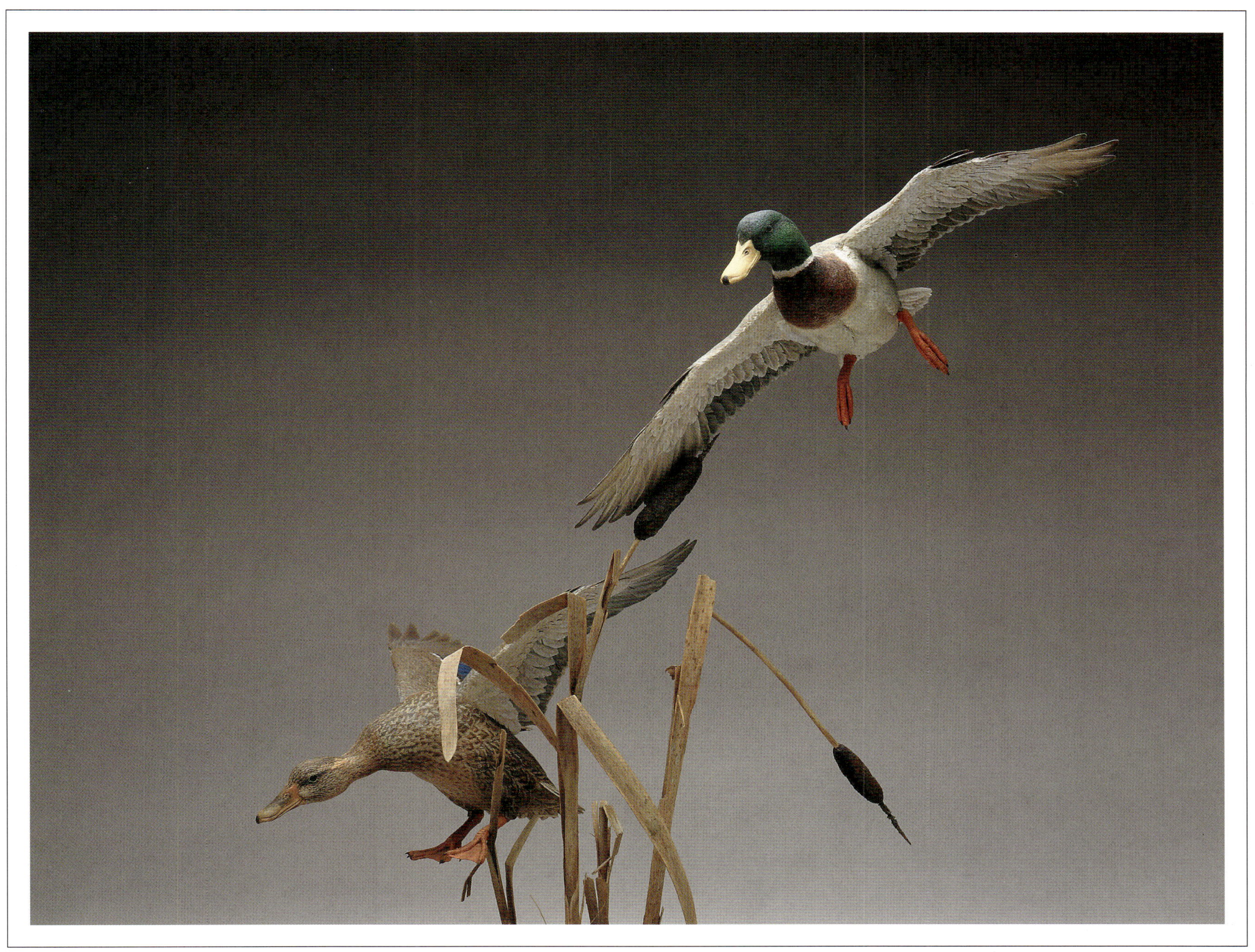

Gary Yoder
Mallards in Flight, 1982

To overcome the visual challenge inherent in composing a pair, Yoder manipulated the "line" of his miniature subjects to create a truly harmonious sculpture. By placing the birds at different heights, with their wings in complementary positions, he achieved the delicate balance he needed to depict the mallards' descent. Yoder first rehearsed the arrangement of the birds on paper, in Styrofoam and with cardboard mock-ups, creating his subtle, realistic feather renderings with wood-burning tools.

Pete Zaluzec

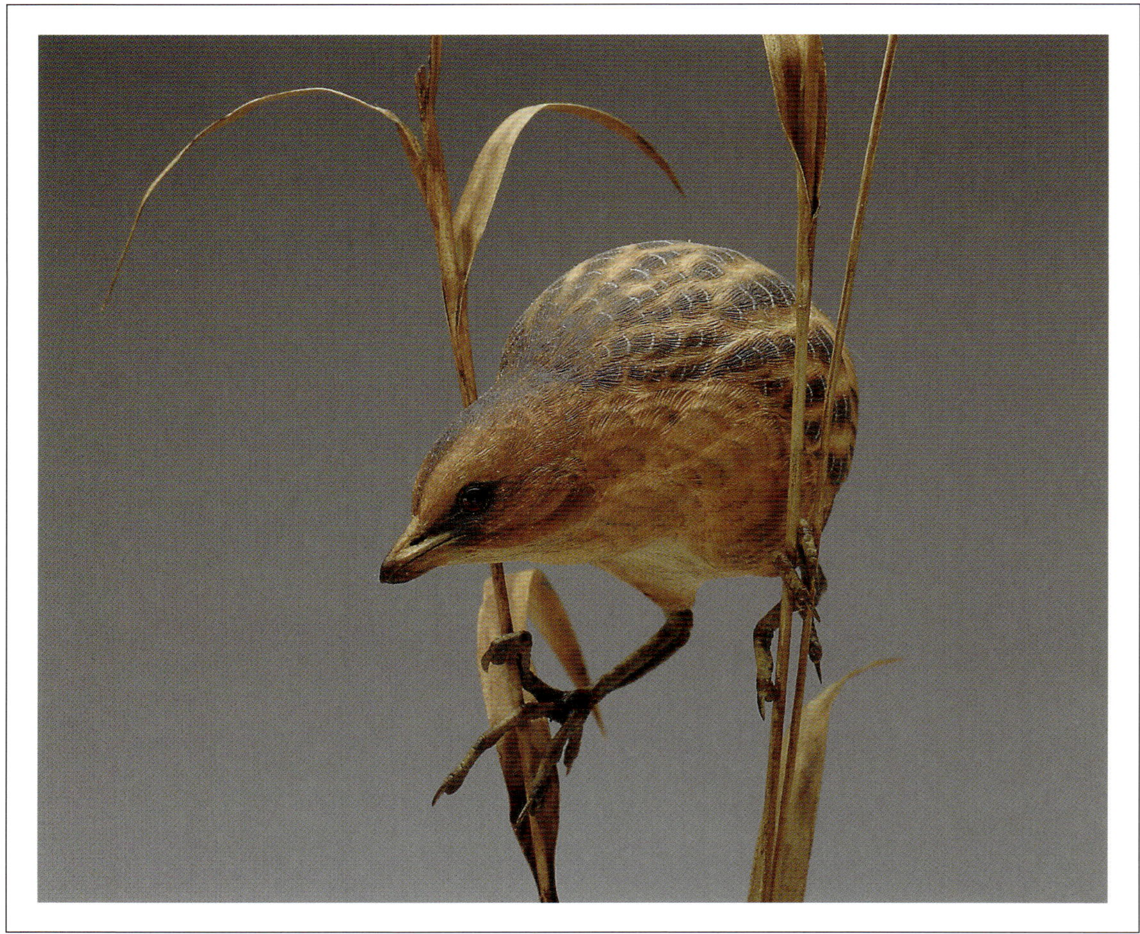

Pete Zaluzec
Yellow Rail
Water's Edge, 1992 (detail)

"Sometimes, there is more detail in the base than I put in the bird," admits Pete Zaluzec. "People may not see that at first." Since Zaluzec started to carve in 1986, his approach to wildfowl art has been consciously minimalist. Relying on his skills as a designer and an artist, he creates simpler sculptures. "It is not necessary to raise a lot of feathers," says Zaluzec. "Instead, I paint a lot and add lots of texture with wood-burning tools."

Although he began his career with life-size pieces, the Lake Villa, Illinois, artist has found his niche in miniatures, a format which allows him to focus his energy in an individual style that marries the freedom of interpretive sculpture with the precision of decorative. His highly rendered but naturally finished cherry and walnut bases provide an unadorned counterpoint to his sleek and invariably colorful birds.

The miniature format also lends itself to a more realistic timetable for Zaluzec. An architectural woodworker, the 43-year-old artist uses his skills by day to style fine-wood entrances to banks and corporate offices, stealing every other available moment for his art. "I love what I'm doing," he says. "I can work until three in the morning on a project, and even then, I don't want to stop."

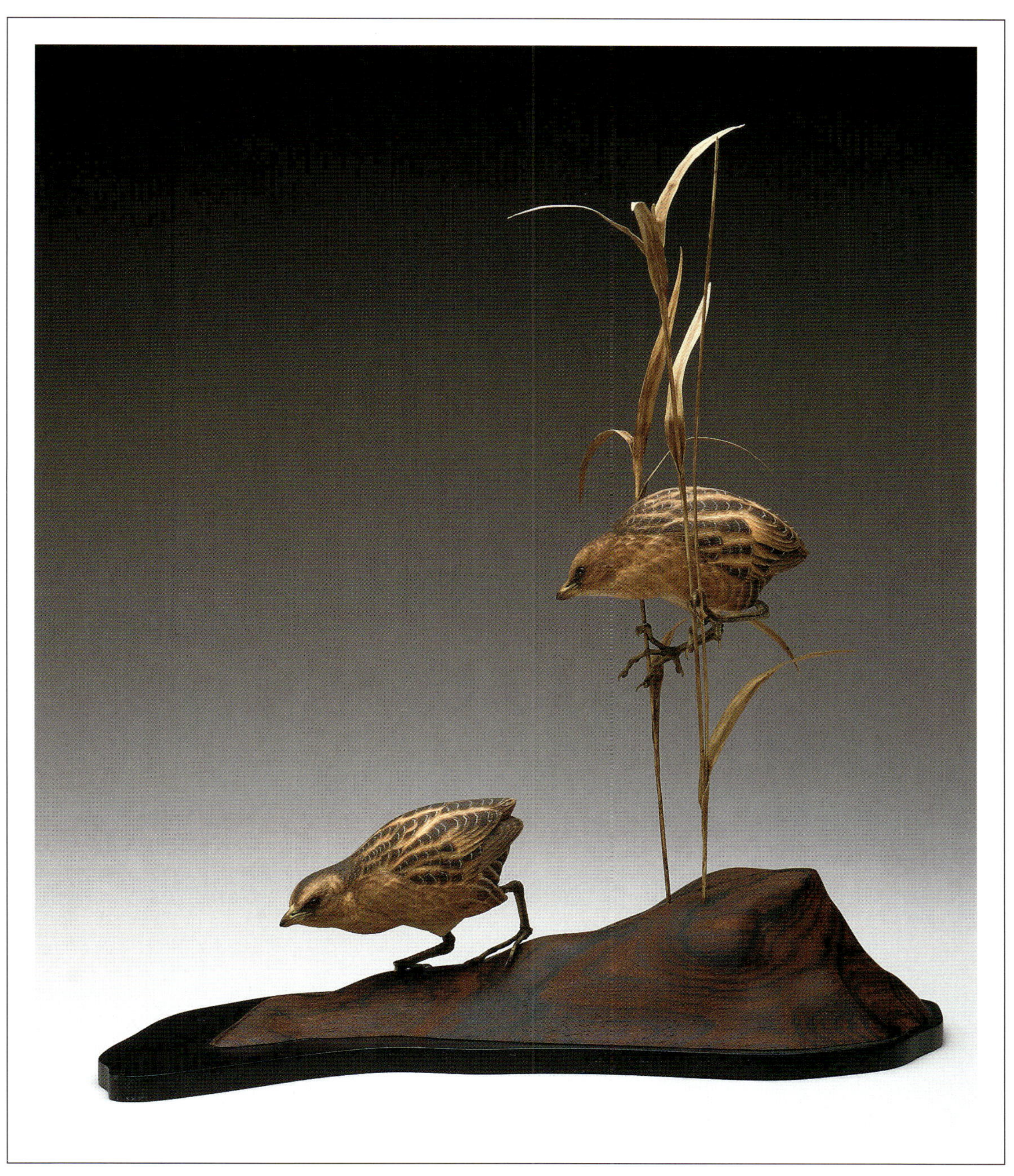

The plumage of Zaluzec's miniature yellow rails has the same "S" pattern that winds through the flow of the sculpture and is echoed in its base. The first world-class entry in the artist's decade-long career captured championship honors. Zaluzec, now a three-time world champion, created the bird from basswood, which is superior for holding detail, and painted with oils to achieve the soft colors.

Pete Zaluzec
Yellow Rails
Water's Edge, 1992

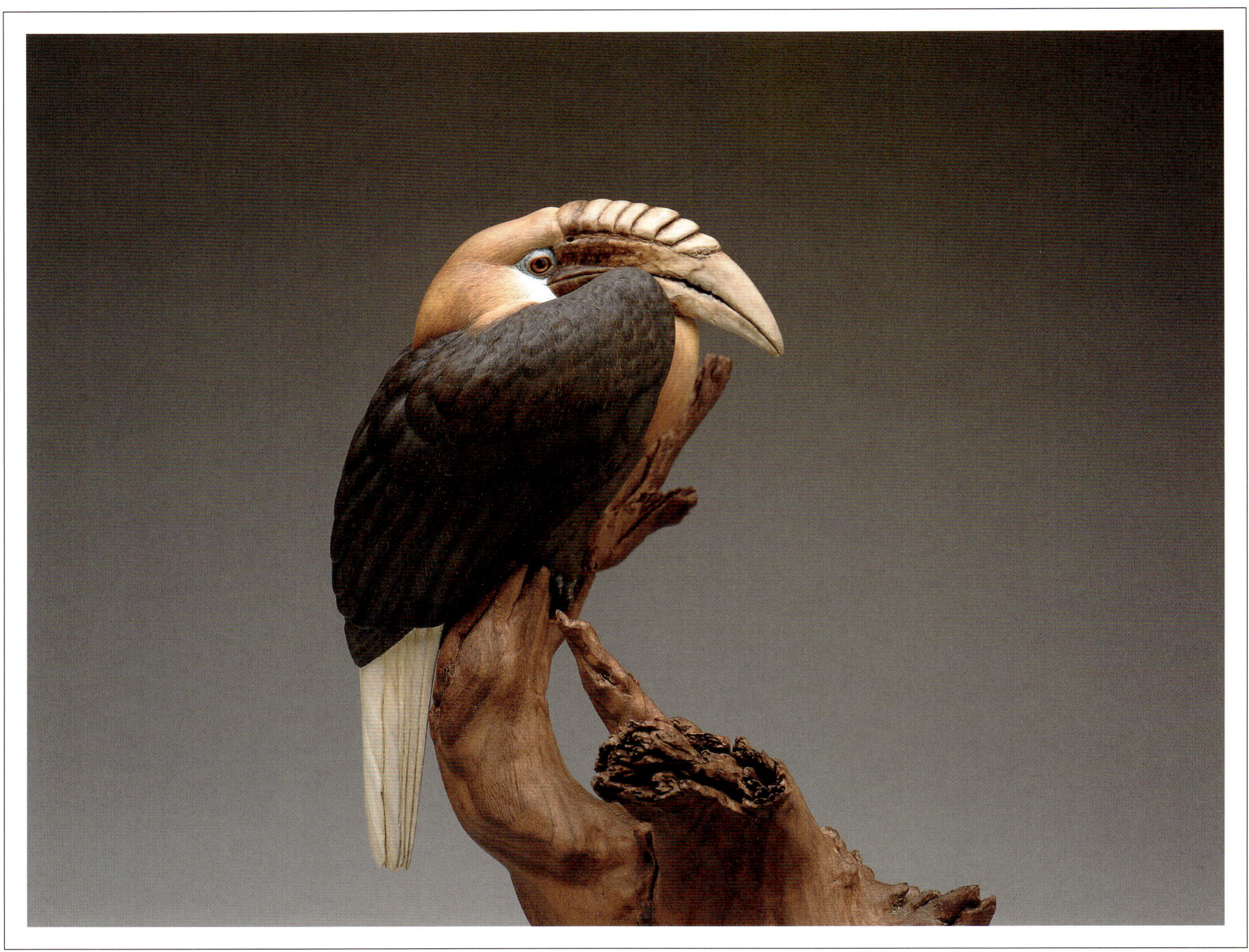

Pete Zaluzec
Blyth's Hornbill, 1996

Zaluzec's appetite for the exotic species of Asia, Africa, South America and Europe is illustrated in his miniature Blyth's hornbill. Settled in the crotch of a branch, the hornbill, with its crusty bill and three dramatically colored feather groupings, exudes an aloofness betrayed only by its alert eyes, which seem to track every movement around it.

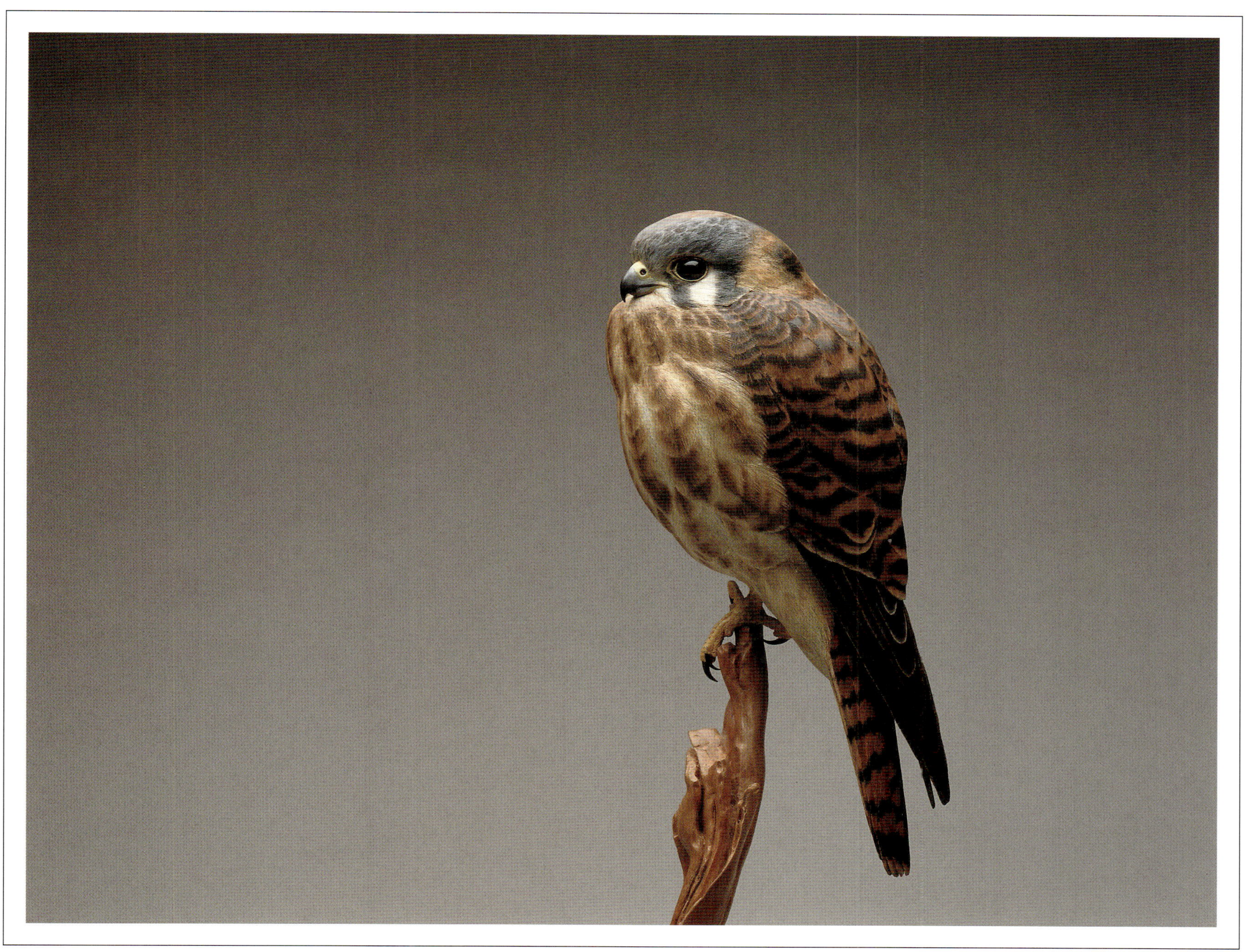

While he worked on this sculpture, Zaluzec, a licensed falconer, sought counsel from a live kestrel sitting on a perch at his workbench. With its head slightly tucked in, Zaluzec's life-size bird—delicately attached to the base by its rapierlike talons—exudes both beauty and danger.

Pete Zaluzec
American Kestrel, 1992

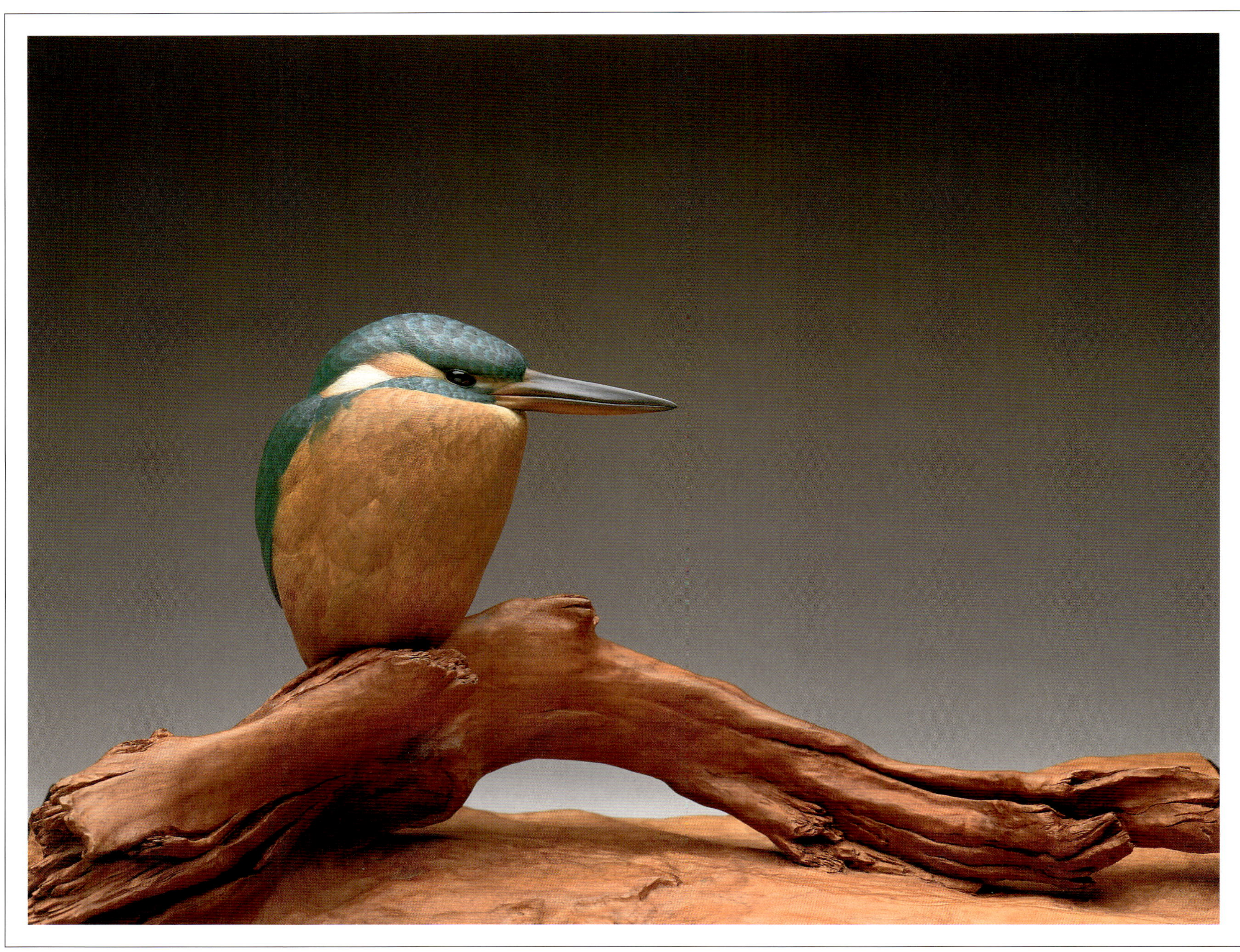

Pete Zaluzec
Eurasian Kingfisher, 1994

Zaluzec's life-size Eurasian kingfisher stands motionless at the river's edge. A testament to the artist's commitment to minimalism, the bird boasts fewer undercuts but makes its statement as a turquoise adornment offsetting the detailed base.

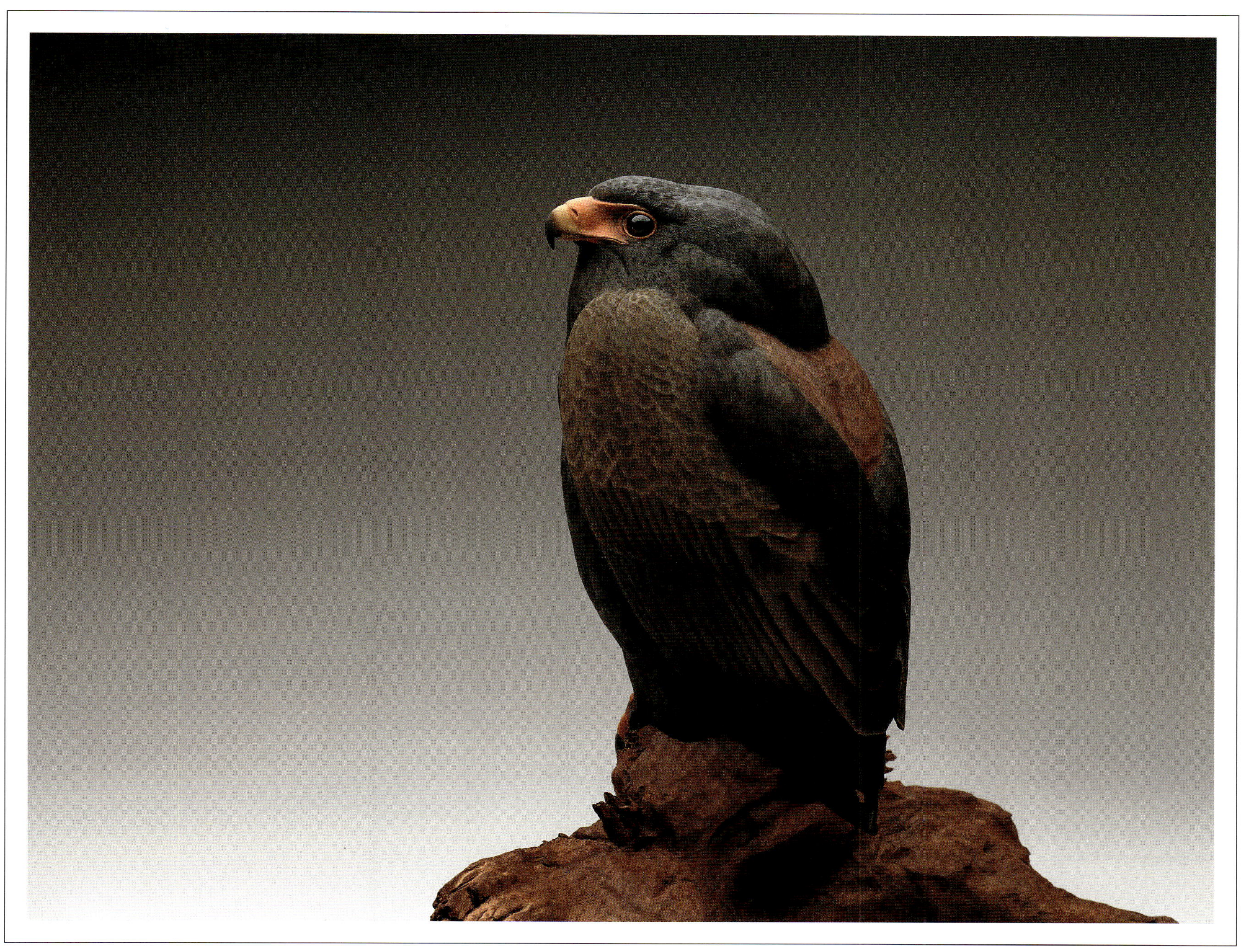

Rising like a living extension of the branch upon which it is perched, Zaluzec's richly painted miniature eagle earned best-in-world honors at the Ward World Championship. Zaluzec achieves the integrated sculptural look of his works by composing his birds in a relaxed position, which gives them a timeless appeal.

Pete Zaluzec
Bateleur Eagle, 1994

Species Index

World-Class Champions

The Ward World Championship
World Champions in Decorative Lifesize
Wildfowl and Decorative Miniature Wildfowl

Michael Arthurs
1996, Best in World, *Evening Flight* (miniature); page 15

Larry Barth
1985, Best in World, *Winter Lakeshore* (lifesize); page 25
1986, Best in World, *Terns in Flight* (lifesize); page 28
1991, Best in World, *Vantage Point* (lifesize); page 26
1993, Best in World, *In the Cattails* (lifesize); page 23

Chris Bonner
1995, Third in World, *On Silent Wings* (lifesize); page 31

Philip Galatas
1989, Best in World, *Watch On* (miniature); page 42
1990, Best in World, *Highland Defender* (miniature); page 38

Patrick Godin
1982, Best in World, *Along the Grand* (lifesize); page 44
1993, Third in World, *Birch Lake Ruffed Grouse* (lifesize); page 46
1995, Best in World, *Descent Through the Alders* (lifesize); page 47

Bob Guge
1987, Best in World, *Eastern Bluebirds* (miniature); page 53

Gordon Hare
1987, Best in World, *Hue and Cry* (lifesize); page 61
1988, Best in World, *Circles and Arrows* (lifesize); page 60

Glenn Ladenberger
1994, Best in World, *Northern Goshawk* (lifesize); page 66
1996, Third in World, *Magpie on Spruce Branch* (lifesize); page 67

Ernie Muehlmatt
1979, Best in World, *Woodcock Pair* (miniature); page 72
1981, Best in World, *Bittern Pair* (miniature); page 73
1984, Best in World, *Needle, Feather and Bone* (lifesize); page 71

Jim Sprankle
1993, Second in World, *Rockets in the Reeds* (lifesize); page 86

Todd Wohlt
1990, Best in World, *Dive!* (lifesize); page 99
1993, Third in World, *Avocet* (miniature); page 94
1996, Best in World, *Kestrel* (lifesize); page 97

Greg Woodard
1992, Best in World, *Cactus Flower* (lifesize); page 102

Gary Yoder
1980, Best in World, *Pheasants* (miniature); page 107
1982, Best in World, *Mallards in Flight* (miniature); page 109
1989, Best in World, *American Robins* (lifesize); page 106
1995, Best in World, *Steller's Sea Eagle* (miniature); page 108

Pete Zaluzec
1992, Best in World, *Water's Edge* (miniature); page 110
1994, Best in World, *Bateleur Eagle* (miniature); page 115
1996, Second in World, *Blyth's Hornbill* (miniature); page 112

The Ward Foundation

The Ward Foundation is a nonprofit member-supported art and educational organization dedicated to promoting and perpetuating wildfowl carving and art. Named for two Crisfield, Maryland, brothers, Lemuel and Stephen Ward, who are recognized as the carvers who took the craft of decoy making from function to art, the Ward Foundation was established in 1968 by a group of Salisbury-area carvers, collectors and community leaders. To foster a public appreciation for decoy making and wildfowl carving, the group began a series of annual exhibitions of work by the best traditional and contemporary artists, held each fall in Salisbury, Maryland. Collectors from around the country make the fall trip to examine and purchase the latest creations by leading artists.

In 1971, the first Ward World Championship Wildfowl Carving Competition was held. Today, it is recognized as the most prestigious wildfowl-art competition in the world—competitors come from as far away as England and Hong Kong to have their work judged against that of their peers.

There are four major categories of competition at the Ward World Championship, which takes place annually in Ocean City, Maryland, on the last weekend in April. At the top level is World Class, which is for artists of the highest level of achievement. Open Class is for carvers who are full-time professionals or have a high level of ability. Intermediate Class is for carvers who are no longer beginners but are not yet of the professional ranks. And Novice Class is for artists who are new to competitive carving. Cash awards are made in the World Class and Open Class categories; other winners receive ribbons and rosettes.

The heart of the Ward Foundation museum holdings is derived from the competition. Every year, the first place in each of the four World Class categories is added to the permanent collection, and the makers are given purchase awards. The top category is Decorative Lifesize Wildfowl Sculpture, which carries a $20,000 award.

The permanent collection—the finest and most comprehensive collection of wildfowl art in the world—is housed in the Ward Museum of Wildfowl Art, located in Chesapeake Country on Maryland's beautiful Eastern Shore. The museum's interpretive galleries guide visitors through history and heritage, from rare antique decoys to today's Best in World decorative sculptures, exploring the relationship between humans and nature that gave rise first to primitive ingenuity, then to flights of artistic genius.

The Ward Goose

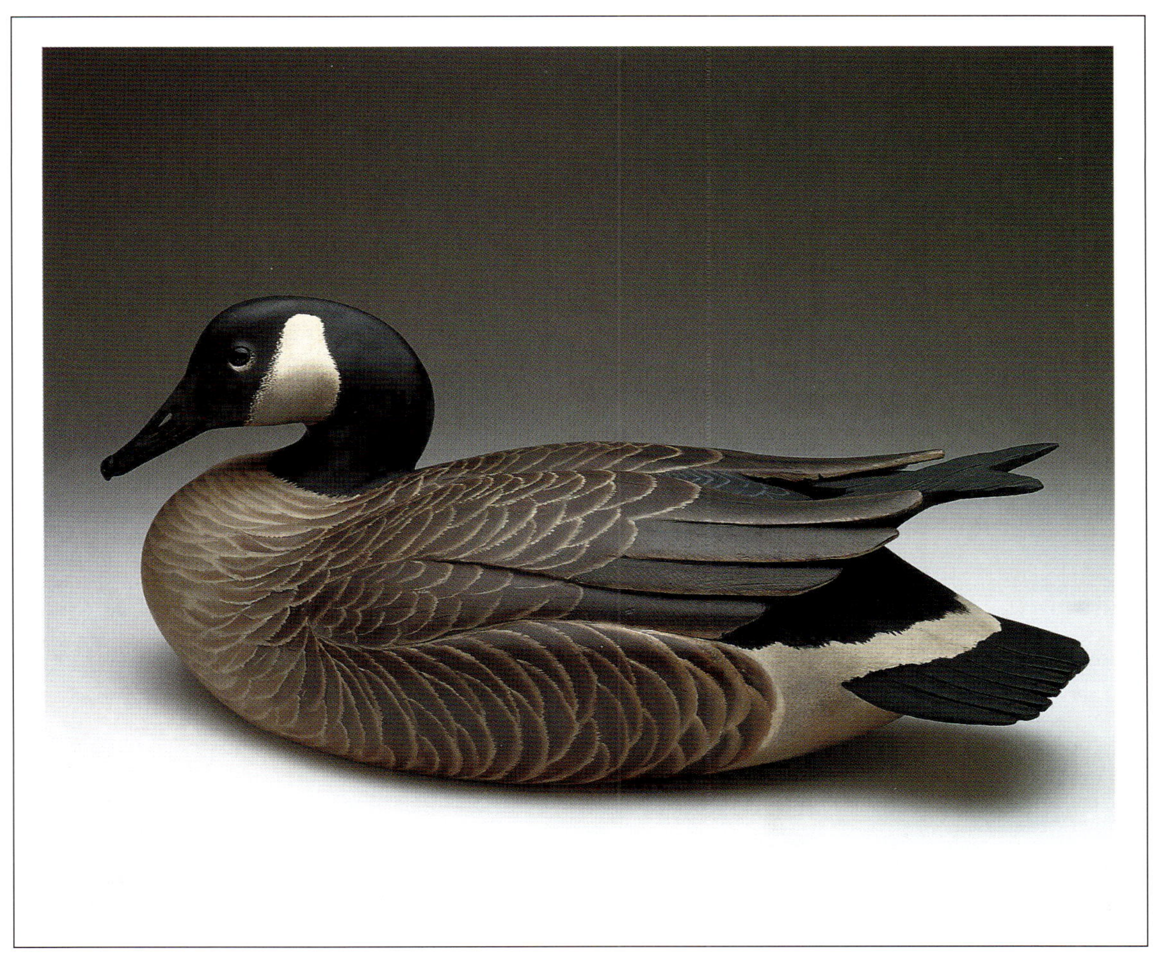

Lemuel T. Ward, Jr.
Canada Goose
The Ward Goose, 1965